142

DATE DUE			
MAY 19 '7			
MAY 27 '74			
MAY 22 '78			
OCT 23 '86			
FEB 5			
AUG 15 '88			
SEP 13 '88			

Too Many People, Too Little Love

WILMA DYKEMAN

Too Many People, Too Little Love

Edna Rankin McKinnon:
Pioneer
for Birth Control

HOLT, RINEHART AND WINSTON

New York · Chicago · San Francisco

Library of Congress Cataloging in Publication
Data

Dykeman, Wilma.
  Too many people, too little love.

    1. McKinnon, Edna Rankin,
    1893–   2. Birth control. I. Title.
HQ764.M28D9 301.32'1   [B] 73-3746
ISBN 0-03-010801-2

First Edition
Printed in the United States of America

This book is especially for Martha Ragland,
without whom it would not have been written,
and Clarence and Sarah Gamble,
the first Pathfinders.

Preface

In the late summer of 1970, while visiting in Nashville, Tennessee, I telephoned a friend, Martha Ragland, and we arranged to have lunch together. She had just returned from an extensive trip to Russia and since she had shared with me unusual experiences on other journeys to distant places, I was eager to hear about her recent travels.

As our conversation developed, however, its central subject was not the monuments and museums, the landscape and people of Moscow and Samarkand, or the many other places visited in that vast and various country two and one-half times as large as the United States. Instead, Martha's subject was a friend named Edna Rankin McKinnon, who had also made this trip.

Neither Martha nor Edna knew that the other would be among the group. Their friendship was of long standing, however, having begun thirty-five years earlier when Edna McKinnon came to Tennessee blazing her first trails for the cause of birth control. After leaving Tennessee, Kentucky, and Alabama, Edna had worked across the United States and around the world, especially in Southeast Asia and Africa. Edna's adventures in family planning in such improbable places as Bali and Fiji, Saudi Arabia and Ethiopia, intrigued Martha Ragland. Flights from Moscow to Bukhara, from Tashkent to Leningrad, that would have seemed interminable passed swiftly as Martha listened to her ebullient friend tell of sultans and princesses, midwives and villagers, who had become her friends.

Beneath the fascinating episodes of humor or pathos, however, lay the serious purpose, the critical worldwide issue Edna had faced when it was both unknown to the point of ignorance and unpopular to the point of persecution. The fact that Edna was now seventy-six years old and had retired only two years earlier, seemed incredible, to judge by her looks or by the more important criteria of her enthusiasm and energy. (Her older sister, former Congresswoman Jeannette Rankin, ninety years old, had also planned to make the trip and was furious when a broken leg intervened.)

"Someone must write about Edna's work," Martha Ragland said to me.

I resisted the suggestion, but the next thing I knew I was on the telephone to Carmel, California.

"Edna McKinnon here!" The voice was as trained and vibrant as a singer's—a young singer's. "You must come to see me."

At the end of a week—talking on her sunny patio in the Carmel Valley, driving along the spectacular precipices of the coastal highway, eating above the Pacific at Nepenthe on Big Sur, visiting friends of earlier times and places who had also come to settle in this pleasant haven—I left Carmel with some twenty tapes and a mutual agreement to write this book.

Later research took me across this country from the Countway Medical Library at Harvard University, where curators of the Dr. Clarence Gamble collection were most cooperative, and Boston, where Mrs. Clarence Gamble, her family, and officials at the Pathfinder Fund provided crucial impetus and insight, to New York; to Chicago, where Edna worked for the longest single span of time; to her native Montana; to Carmel again; and to Alabama, Tennessee, Georgia, North Carolina, and Kentucky. Numerous organizations dedicated to national and international birth control, family planning, and planned parenthood were helpful in providing necessary factual background information. Individuals in many lands, representing many backgrounds, beliefs, and ways of life, shared generously of their informal memories and their formal materials. To each one, I express my appreciation for each contribution.

There were three central reasons why I finally chose to write this book. First, Edna Rankin McKinnon's life incorporates three of the major issues of our twentieth-century life—the population explosion, the changing status of women, and the imperative for peace. Second, it is a good story. It casts complex social issues in a human framework of fallibility and humor, shows idealism sustained by common sense and incredibly hard work. Third, it demonstrates the effectiveness of the individual. In a world where the pressures of too many people and too little love often seem to diminish our human stature and to deny any belief in the power of our spirit, Edna McKinnon is an affirmation of the importance of every single human life. The implicit faith of a deeply religious person was made explicit through her daily deeds.

At eighty—still handsome, still forceful—she says, "Life is too precious to be unwanted, too short to spend on trivia. God's work wasn't meant for failure and neither are we." She speaks lightly, without grimness or self-righteousness, her faith strengthened by experience and her love tested through many conflicts.

This is an account of some of those experiences and many of those conflicts.

WILMA DYKEMAN

1

The wildest dreams of Kew
Are the facts of Khatmandhu.

—Rudyard Kipling

This birthquake —this population explosion —is the greatest problem we are facing in the world today; it is greater than the ideological threats.

—*World Health News*,
August 1960

O_N Christmas Eve, 1961, an American woman sat huddled in a Land Rover on a road some three miles outside Katmandu, the capital of the remote and exotic land of Nepal. Bitter cold transformed the shelter of the vehicle into a prison as much as a protection and gripped it no less invincibly than the loose sand and shifting gravel of the narrow roadway held the bulky van which tilted dangerously on the shoulder just ahead.

Edna McKinnon was thankful that she had worn the heavy tweed overcoat borrowed from an English friend. In Malaya and Indonesia where she had been working for a year and more, she needed only sleeveless dresses, occasional sweaters, and her faithful raincoat. But her friend in Singapore had dug out clothing suitable for this journey to the strange country snuggled between India and Tibet on the rooftop of the world. "You'll want something warm," she had predicted. Even British woolen, however, was no match for the 4,000-foot altitude of the Katmandu Valley on a December night. Hands and feet grew icier by the minute.

Edna did not want to complain to the Nepalese nurse who waited with her, a gentle woman who was already sufficiently distressed at this unfortunate conclusion to an otherwise successful evening. Edna pretended to doze while she pondered this improbable situation.

Even after a quarter-century of travel in the cause of family planning and experiencing the full range of frustration and satisfaction *that* involved, she had hardly imagined spending a Christmas Eve among strangers in this Hindu-Buddhist kingdom, stranded on a rutted, little road which seemed as if it might wind up the slopes of Mt. Everest somewhere out there among the Himalayas, rather than lead into nearby Katmandu.

Birth control in Nepal, with an American woman as its advocate! The idea was as incongruous as contraception on the legendary island of Bali, where she had been only a few weeks ago with her message of a new freedom through birth control. She could imagine the consternation of Wellington Rankin, her prominent barrister brother in Montana, the approval of Jeannette Rankin, her famous unorthodox sister in Washington, and the mingled dismay and delight of friends and coworkers across the United States if they could see her now. Even Clarence Gamble, who was supporting this pioneering venture out here in South Asia and Africa, who reveled in hardship and seemed to relish obstacles to his work, might have been momentarily nonplussed by the whole scene surrounding this evening's plight.

But after all, Dr. Gamble *did* call his organization the Pathfinder Fund. Its purpose was to blaze trails in countries where there was no birth control. This problem—this human explosion of people doubling the population on earth every thirty-five years—was the most fundamental, crucial reality stalking mankind. It distorted and diminished millions of private, individual lives. It dominated worldwide issues of war and natural resources. It was as small as the newborn whimper of an undernourished, unwanted baby. It was as large as the despairing cry of humanity doomed by its own hungry, jostling numbers. Well, she was breaking paths, all right. This one was somewhat more literal than she had anticipated.

The unwieldy van that blocked the road to Katmandu in the middle of the night had been supplied by the United States Agency for International Development. The van provided public health information and carried at this time one birth control film. Since most of the towns in the countryside surrounding Katmandu had no access to electricity, the truck was equipped with a generator for film and sound programs. These were effective—indeed, essential—in reaching a population that was 90 percent illiterate.

Three years before, another of Pathfinder's roving ambassadors, Margaret Roots, had come to Nepal, where she found a

4

country of more than eight and a half million people with one of the highest infant death rates in the world. She had helped form a family planning board, which opened a weekly clinic in Katmandu and sent a team of doctors into outlying parts of the country. Subsequently, some small assistance had come from the International Planned Parenthood Federation. But, like the stalled van on the rough road ahead, birth control was still floundering, here as in most of the world, seeking a firm hold on national consciousness and personal consciences.

Now Edna had come on a follow-up mission. She agreed wholeheartedly with Dr. Gamble's belief that local groups should plan and carry out their own programs to fit their own needs and traditions; but occasional prodding, suggesting, and support from the outside could provide necessary transfusions of enthusiasm and know-how. No one could provide those two essentials more abundantly than Edna McKinnon.

Even the chill of the winter wind sweeping down from the glacier-crusted heights of the Himalayas could not totally check her enthusiasm. She considered the hundred or so men who had congregated out there on the road after the accident had occurred. They seemed to have materialized from nowhere, eager to help, trying again and again to get the spinning wheels of the awkward vehicle back onto the roadbed, to right the toppling loaded van before it fell and crushed someone or destroyed its unique, precious cargo. The machine looked like a beetle half-capsized onto its hard shell, one set of feet uselessly clawing the air, while small ants scurried around helplessly.

Edna understood why these courteous rural people were not adept with machines. As others had pointed out, despite their reliance on the prayer wheel in their religion, they were late in making use of the wheel as a tool of transportation. The terrain of Nepal did not encourage use of even bullock carts or yak carts, much less automobiles. Most of the trade between Nepal and the outside world—especially adjoining Tibet—was carried on by human backpack until the arrival of the airplane.

Everyone who had visited Nepal—and as recently as 1950 that had consisted only of some two hundred Europeans and perhaps thirty Americans—had afterward observed that roads were the key to Nepal's history and to its future. Ornitholo-

5

gists, geologists, educators, economists, and family planning workers—everyone agreed that the isolation of the people must be overcome by creating some kind of highway system. Earlier this evening it had taken almost three hours to drive the nine miles from Katmandu to the village where the Department of Public Health program was to be presented.

It was young Dr. Poudayl, whose home had become one of the family planning clinics where he advised patients late each afternoon, who had invited Edna to visit the countryside. She had pounced on the invitation. After all, this was one of the reasons why she had come—to discover what was behind the paperwork of reports and forms; to know the people, to let them know her if they wished, and by the knowing demonstrate that they shared a common threat which was not insurmountable; and to implement by any practical suggestions the efficiency and influence of the program.

Others had come here to meet the challenge of the forbidding mountains' rarefied altitudes. She was here to cope with the challenge of humble humanity's common attitudes—habits of reproduction which could turn the earth into a crowded zoo. She wished that the patient, persistent Dr. Poudayl had half a chance of someday becoming one-tenth as well known as the world-famous Sherpa, Tenzing Norkey, who had stood with Sir Edmund Hillary atop Everest in 1953.

Dr. Poudayl and Edna had been accompanied tonight by the country's only trained nurse, and they had followed the van in their rented Land Rover. Entering the village, they had seen that the massive equipment truck was arranged in such a way that pictures could be projected on both sides of the screen, for men and women would have to view the program separately. They did not mingle in public. (In view of the nature of the film, there seemed some irony in this formal separation of the sexes!)

Almost everyone in the gathered crowd was barefoot. The men, wearing their cloth caps and blousy white trousers and shirts, and the women, with their jet braids falling down their backs and with odd, thick sashes wound around their waists, watched intently a film on flies, the danger of filth and infection they carried, and the film on birth control. Its message was simple and basic. In a family (or a world) where there are too many children, there is too little food or space or love for survival. There are ways to be sure that *you* do not bring too many children into *your* family. It was a new concept; those listening would have to ponder both it and the help offered by these visiting officials from the capital—and from far away.

Following the program, Dr. Poudayl advised Edna and the nurse that an invitation had been extended to dine at the home of the village's chief citizen. Edna never refused an invitation, be it to a palace, a hut, a forum, or a tent, for there were always ways the conversation could be turned to family planning.

The home of the village leader appeared to be built of mud bricks and dirt. Its ground floor was a store and the visitors climbed an almost perpendicular ladder to reach the upper-story living quarters. There were two small windows in the room. A large bamboo chair was brought for Edna. Everyone else sat on mats around the table which stood only a few inches off the floor. With grace and good humor Edna accepted her exalted if self-conscious position.

Supper was served from a brass tray. It consisted of crisp kernels of rice roasted and salted, sprays of cooked cauliflower, and a banana apiece. For Edna, with her hearty appetite, the delicious crunchy rice and bit of vegetable and fruit would have made fine hors d'oeuvres. But they were the entire meal, and they took a long time to eat because there were numerous intermittent courtesies to be observed. In Nepal, man obviously did not live by bread alone. In fact, judging by the multitude of shrines that dotted the towns and countryside (nearly 3,000 in the great Katmandu Valley alone) and the scarcity of grazing land and meat, it seemed that here the spirit might often be better fed than the body.

After supper and farewell amenities, the trip back to the city was begun. About halfway along, they had found the Public Health Department's proud and valuable possession, the sound and film van, dangerously balanced on the embankment. Dr. Poudayl and the gathering crowd of villagers worked in vain to bring traction to the spinning tires. There was no wood, no rocks in the vicinity, to put beneath the wheels.

"Couldn't we send into town for some sort of derrick?" Edna

finally asked Dr. Poudayl in her most resonant, helpful voice.

He shook his head. It mustn't become known in town that there had been this trouble with the van or it might not be permitted to go out into the country again.

The cold bit more sharply. Edna wondered at the sound judgment of introducing such expensive mechanized equipment as this van into a land more compatible with simple tools and means.

After a while she tendered another suggestion. "I believe, if we drove carefully, that the Land Rover might squeeze around the van and we could go on into Katmandu."

Dr. Poudayl only shook his head again, regretfully. He could not leave. It would not be appropriate for the head of the country's Department of Health to desert the scene of an accident.

"Of course," Edna agreed. "I understand." She huddled down again in the thick British coat inside the Land Rover.

Suddenly a head appeared in one of the windows. "Mrs. McKinnon!" a deep voice called. "We have been worried about you."

As she tried to unbend her stiff limbs, an armful of heavy quilts was tumbled into her lap. The head clerk from the hotel in Katmandu had come out searching for her. After she and her nurse friend were bundled up in the thickly padded quilts, the newcomer turned his attention to the stalled truck. Some suggestion, or mechanical know-how he had picked up in his advanced education, solved the problem. Within a short while the two vehicles were jostling their way back into the fold of the capital metropolis.

At the hotel, hot stones had been tucked into Edna's bed and an electric heater placed nearby. The warmth of the personal thought and care evidenced by those baked stones thawed her even more quickly than the heated room and bed. At three o'clock on Christmas morning she settled down to enjoy a cozy sleep. Wherever she traveled in the world she had the knack of making that place her home. It was a good kind of security.

Christmas Day did not allow for any extra rest, however. There were three social events. They were typical of Edna's variety of friends and interests.

First, there was Christmas dinner at an American official's in Katmandu. Edna was the only other American present at the meal. She felt that she had been allowed to enter an inner circle and participate, somewhat as she had at the village chief's the night before.

Then, in the afternoon, there was a meeting of the Katmandu Family Planning Association board of directors, at which Edna spoke. The gathering was at a centrally located building in the tiny dark room which was used as the clinic. It allowed little privacy for patients and less inspiration for the over-worked public health nurse or the doctors. Before she left Nepal, Edna had made arrangements for the birth control clinic to be held in a hospital in the city.

The president of the Association's board was a fascinating woman. Her husband's family story documented the radical but peaceful change possible in this country. Mrs. Kamal Rana was a member of the leading family of Nepal. For more than a century, from 1846 until 1951, the Rana family held undisputed right to the position of hereditary prime minister. Since all power was vested in this office—the prime minister was also called Maharaja, Supreme Commander in Chief, and Marshall—he was in reality above the King. Palaces of the Rana family, while not as stupendous as the Emperor's thousand-room mansion, created an ornate elegance in certain sections of Katmandu.

In 1951 the Nepal Congress Party and the King had entered into an alliance. The result was a revised constitution, a new cabinet, and another prime minister. So the power of the Ranas was broken, part of it invested once more in the monarch. When the progressive young Hindu King Mahendra ascended the throne after his father's death in 1956, one of the first women elected to the Parliament was Mrs. Kamal Rana.

Without this woman's support, the purpose and program of family planning work in Nepal would have been severely hindered. It was just such leadership—at the highest level, effective, concerned, and dedicated—that Edna sought out, inspired, and trained in every country she visited. She knew that in tackling the immense and emotionally charged problem of family planning, anything she did would be only a drop in the

9

surging ocean of humanity. But if she could help marshal the right forces, gather strong enough influences, it might be possible to keep that ocean from swelling into a destructive tidal wave. Until the world's leaders became enlightened and fulfilled their role of leadership on this crucial front, how could the beleaguered, apprehensive, searching hosts be alerted to the tragedy of unwanted children everywhere in the world, and to the disaster implicit in the reckless multiplication of people? In America in the thirties, forties, and fifties—and in her present work abroad—Edna had found that the approval and energy of leaders had to be marshaled even as the slow steps in birth control education and research were going forward.

Also on the Katmandu board with Mrs. Kamal Rana and Dr. Poudayl were two women doctors, Dilli Rana and Dibya Shree, who performed much of the diligent volunteer work necessary in every clinic. Three of the board members were not present at the meeting: one was in the United States at Johns Hopkins in Baltimore; the other two were in London. And Edna was interested to learn that Nepal's public health nurse, also on the board, had done her training at Chapel Hill, North Carolina, and Albuquerque, New Mexico. Family planning was indeed international in its reach.

Edna also learned that the King's strong statement approving of the family planning program had been printed and widely distributed throughout the kingdom. Here, again, the low literacy rate nullified much of the effort, however.

In discussion with the board, Edna discovered that other government leaders were also informed and favorable to the program, but there existed a general attitude that the work should be soundly established on a voluntary basis before being taken over by the government. Only through government effort, however, would two of the chief obstacles be overcome: bad roads which did not permit easy communication throughout the country and lack of trained personnel. Meanwhile, ways had to be found to improve the existing situation wherever possible.

Later, she suggested to Dr. Poudayl that he prepare three tentative budgets and submit them to the International Planned Parenthood Federation and to the Pathfinder Fund.

The three would range from an estimate of the minimum funds required for the program's survival and distribution of contraceptive materials, to a larger plan designed to help relieve the two basic needs of transportation and training. She hoped that Dr. Gamble and others would grasp the urgent need for major investment in this magnificent, terrifying country where unparalleled scenic splendor and treasures in princely crowns and jewels coexisted with a labor force ninety-four percent engaged in agriculture and a per capita gross national product of less than seventy-five dollars a year.

When Edna met King Mahendra's sister at a luncheon given by Mrs. Kamal Rana later in the week, Edna expressed her appreciation for the King's support of family planning. The Princess, limited in her knowledge of English, was nonetheless pleased and charmed. Edna's friendship toward the Nepalese people, so tolerant in their several religions that Buddhists and Hindus could share harmoniously the same temple on occasions, was not difficult to comprehend.

That friendship was underscored by the third social encounter she had on Christmas Day. This one did not take place at the royal palace. It occurred at the Hotel Royal, where Edna had two callers. The boys were perhaps ten and eleven years old. They brought gifts: two small strands of hand-strung beads and two richly colored pictures they had painted. The pictures were of a lady in a vivid dress wearing beads, a lady resembling, in fact, Edna herself except for the halo just above her dark blond hair!

Edna had made these friends during her first days in Katmandu. Exploring along the broad paved avenues and the tortuous narrow alleys of this city of some one hundred and fifty thousand people, she had felt a tug at her hand. There stood the youngsters—solemn, barefooted, bright-eyed. These grave, courteous children of Asia reminded Edna in many ways of the proud, sweet children she had found in eastern Kentucky and other pockets of Appalachia when she first began her family planning work. One of the Nepalese boys asked, "You American?"

"Yes," Edna nodded. "American."

"You like temples? We will guide."

With pomp and ceremony they escorted her to a number of the shrines that gave the city its distinctly Oriental flavor. The early inhabitants of this valley, the Newars, are believed by many historians to have originated the pagoda style which today characterizes the architecture of the Orient.

Edna found Katmandu an intriguing city, with its white stucco palaces, spacious central plaza, earth-colored houses, giant stone gods and goddesses, and temples that might boast walls or corridors plated with gleaming brass. For contrast, in the midst of these riches, a woodsman down from the hills might be peddling bundles of firewood from the basket on his back while vendors arranged small pyramids of colorful fruits on bamboo mats and baskets along the street. Although they could not understand each other's words, Edna and her guides shared sober awe before the more fearsome statues and delighted approval at the colorful shrines and temples. After a while her guides announced, "We will take you back to Missus' hotel."

When the manager caught sight of the unkempt boys he made ready to throw them out, until Edna rushed to assure him that they were her friends. She paid and thanked the boys and they departed triumphantly. Now these gifts on Christmas cemented the friendship. For years, Edna and two Nepalese street boys would keep up a correspondence; their English gradually grew decipherable and they became able to read her letters without an interpreter.

A few years before Edna arrived in Nepal, a naturalist studying the uplands between the great valley of Katmandu and the frozen waves of the distant Himalayan ranges where carefully tended terraces marched like green stairways down the hills observed that he had come "expecting to see Nepal underpopulated and underexploited, but had found exactly the reverse. To feed themselves, the people cultivated every slanting acre to the point where soil erosion threatened their future."

And only the year before Edna's visit, a Swiss geologist had written of observations gleaned during some of his hikes over the country. "Beyond a few miles of paved highway in Katmandu's valley there are—with one exception—no roads worthy of the name. The single exception is the recently completed motor road from Katmandu to India. During monsoon, even this thin link with the world is frequently blocked by land- and rockslides. The slides often result from severe soil erosion, which in turn is the product of uncontrolled deforestation."

And, "Too often I saw the consequences of this overintensive cultivation of every inch of arable land, coupled with uncontrolled deforestation. Great earth- and rockslides wipe out villages and engulf fields. For the inhabitants, there is the grim choice of abandoning their homes or villages and seeking new land elsewhere, or building all over again."

Forests = land = water = people.

Everywhere around the globe natural and human resources coexist in delicate equilibrium, or destroy each other in a reckless capsizing of the symmetry, the balance, of life.

Even if they labored unaware of the ultimate implications of their work, even if their resolute, unswerving dedication to birth control wrought changes measurable only in inches where strides covering leagues were necessary, Edna McKinnon and all the others striving at home or on distant frontiers for recognition of the value of life were blazing paths that would soon come to be regarded as the roads to human survival.

2

Everyone should have a sense of responsibility that the community is working and functioning well.

—John Rankin, Edna's father

It is estimated that the population of the world totaled around a quarter of a billion persons at the time of Christ and that it took over sixteen centuries for that number to double. It doubled again within the next two hundred years and the one billion mark was reached early in the nineteenth century. In hardly more than one hundred years the number doubled again to two billion by around 1925. A third billion was added in about thirty years. The world total in 1970 is 3.6 billion; at the present rate of growth an increase of one billion in population takes place in about fifteen years. It took a million years to generate the first billion human beings, but only fifteen years for the fourth billion to appear.

—*Human Fertility and National Development*,
United Nations publication, 1971

IN THE BEGINNING Edna gave little enough thought to birth control as the central factor of world hunger, aggression, conservation, economics—all the problems which seemed to be boiling to a head as the twentieth century progressed. In the beginning birth control was, for her, a highly personal cause: saving women, couples, and children from the tragedy of unwanted, unloved lives. The issue of birth control as human survival had not yet clearly emerged. And yet—right from the start she pursued this work as if she realized its largest dimensions and implications. She persisted in spite of public apathy and suspicion, in defiance of the biting scorn and commanding advice of a brother she idolized.

A prophetic item appeared in one of Washington columnist Drew Pearson's articles in the mid-thirties, when his brother noted seeing, in one of the Capitol corridors, a pair of ladies walking toward him. One was Jeannette Rankin, the first woman ever elected to the U.S. Congress, dressed in blue, lobbying for peace. The other was her younger sister, Edna Rankin McKinnon, dressed in green, lobbying for birth control. At least no one could say the girls from Montana had chosen trivial goals for their lives! No more important issues than these would face mankind for the rest of the century. It was no accident that these two sisters should choose to be pioneers in basic and controversial fields.

They had been born in Montana and their family reflected the size, energy, and free-wheeling diversity that was part of the character of their state. It was a frontier demanding courage, imagination, and self-reliance to sustain not only physical survival but spiritual and intellectual health as well.

It was also a society seeking the refinements of civilization—education, social amenities, and awareness of the arts. The tandem influences of Montana remained with Edna throughout her life, endowing her with the blunt strength of a pioneer in situations fraught with danger and discouragement, and the innate grace of a well-bred lady in situations which yielded less to force than to courtesy and to the small civilities which make life pleasant.

When Jeannette, oldest of the family, was born in 1880, Montana was still a territory. When Edna, youngest of the seven children, was born in 1893, Montana had been a state for four years. It was a land "high, wide, and lonesome," a land of "the big sky," rich with the treasures of the earth: forests, minerals, scenery piled up in glacier-covered mountains, snow-fed lakes, and rushing rivers. Larger than Japan or Italy, everything came out-size except the population. By the 1970s there would still be fewer than three-quarters of a million people within its boundaries.

Missoula, in the western part of the state, was little more than a village and a fort when John Rankin arrived in 1869. A Scotchman born in Canada, one of twelve children, he left home at fourteen. When he heard that the town of Helena had suffered a devastating fire and needed carpenters he decided to help rebuild.

A short while later he traveled farther west and came to Missoula. The prospect pleased him and he promptly turned his tremendous physical energy to examining and developing each natural advantage of the area. He bought ranch land and established one of the first sawmills in Montana. Cattle and lumber became his mainstays, but he remained a builder, constructing the first sawed-lumber buildings at nearby Fort Missoula, thrusting the first bridge across the river, erecting the town's first Presbyterian church and its first hotel, making the first large residences in town—including his own gabled mansion. Eventually, he helped establish the state university in Missoula.

Nine years after John Rankin, Olive Pickering came to Missoula from Portsmouth, New Hampshire, and from a family of nine children to teach in the only school in all of western Montana. Her journey west had been all that a carefully protected young New England schoolmarm could have anticipated. From Ogden, Utah, she had traveled by covered wagon. When the road passed through Indian country the women were advised to be very quiet and lie down on the floor. The endless stretches of land and sky, the strange animals and birds that abounded everywhere along the way, and the raw, little settlements and government posts that broke the vast spaces were in sharp contrast to the villages and cities of the East that she had left.

A year after she began her teaching career she married the most eligible bachelor in town, thirty-nine-year-old John Rankin who drove a spanking fine team. They settled six miles out of Missoula on a ranch which also boasted a sawmill, and here the young wife cooked for both the ranch and sawmill hands, ran her house, and bore four babies in four years: Jeannette, Philena, Harriet, and Wellington. It was sixteen years before she returned to visit her family in New Hampshire, but she never lost her New England accent.

Three more children—Mary, Grace, and Edna—were born after the family moved into town, in the mansion on the Rattlesnake River, which became one of Missoula's landmarks. That house was also a symbol and influence in the lives of those who grew up there.

John Rankin had planned it in his mind when he was twelve years old: a huge house built in the style of a Maltese cross. Two rooms at the front were parlors, chilly, orderly, slightly musty because they were almost never used. Since Mrs. Rankin often sat in the large hall, which also offered the presence of a piano, this was the center of much family activity. The other two key rooms downstairs were the kitchen and the dining room. The kitchen, with its wood stove, also boasted a large water tank, for this was the first house in town to enjoy hot and cold running water. The innovation that caused most comment in the local newspaper, however, was the pantry. It was reported that "Johnny has built Olive a flour bin on a pivot!" This storage space for flour and sugar, with a stationary dough board on top, was an enviable luxury.

Up a flight of stairs were the bedrooms and the only

bathroom in Missoula with a zinc tub, surrounded by a wooden railing. In front of the toilet was a big square register that conducted much of the heat from the kitchen below to the upstairs quarters. It also carried the voices of those who might be talking on the lower floor. Understandably, this became a favorite meditation perch for all the children.

The most memorable room in the house was the dining room, not so much for its long table, massive furniture, and hearty meals as for the spirit that reached its climax there. It was a spirit of hospitality and passionate discussion.

With their father at one end of the table and Grace and Edna in youth chairs at the opposite end, with their mother seated in the middle along one side and the other children ranged on either side, the Rankins seldom sat down to a meal where there were no guests present. Girls who wished to come to school in town from the ranches scattered out in the countryside found board and companionship in this household. Travelers enjoyed the comfort of a spacious frontier dwelling with rare central heating and a family of wide-ranging interests. Politicians, educators, and other leaders in the region sought the support of a public-spirited citizen who wanted to make Missoula a "proper" as well as a prosperous place in which to live.

Here was a household that appeared to be a bastion of security and satisfaction for its children. School friends who came in the afternoons for snacks of the delicious cookies and brownies that Mrs. Rankin always seemed to have in ready supply looked with envy upon the lively family and its constant flow of friends, merriment, and talk. And yet—there were currents and crosscurrents not always apparent to casual visitors.

Throughout Edna's childhood she harbored the suspicion, the fear, that she was not really wanted, that she had arrived on this brilliant, turbulent scene either as an accident or an afterthought to Jeannette and Wellington, the stars of the family. Sometimes it seemed that here, as she would later discover elsewhere in the world, there were too many people with too little love.

It was in the dining room that their individuality and energy exercised fullest sway. There was endless conversation. It often developed into debate and sometimes flared into hot dissension. The memorable differences were between Jeannette and Wellington.

The second child, Philena, had died from appendicitis when she was twelve years old, and Wellington, the only son, grew up with two older and three younger sisters, each adoring him and following his advice. To their mother he remained, throughout his life, The Boy. After the death of their father, when Edna was only ten years old, Wellington's leadership of the family was undisputed. Almost undisputed.

This was the frontier, and women assumed responsibilities and rights. Jeannette differed with her brother on many fundamental principles, and she would not compromise them for an instant. On occasion, when their arguments reached an impasse where words seemed inadequate, a plate or tumbler of water might sail through the air. Their mother tolerated almost any behavior from Jeannette and Wellington, for they were her special children. Or so it seemed to the others.

Jeannette had been a mainstay of her father's. The oldest child in any family in that place and time had to bear unusual burdens, not because of anyone's special calculation but because of the demands of daily existence in a harsh and arbitrary environment. When her father came in from the ranch one day and said that Prince had torn an ugly gash in his side, Jeannette seized darning needle and thread and hurried to patch up the suffering horse. When Shep dug into a gopher hole and injured his paw in a hidden trap set there, Jeannette fashioned a little boot for the wounded dog so that eventually he walked as well as ever. She could also run her father's sawmill.

And she was always for peace, against killing. While still a child, she heard talk about the hanging of four Indians on a hill behind the Rankin home. Such talk was engraved in her memory; she knew violence to be wrong.

Many such stories circulated as the Rankin children grew up. There were accounts of rumors that had exploded in the past: Indians were riding against Fort Missoula! All able-bodied men rushed to seize their arms and meet the invaders. At a pass in the Bitterroot Mountains they confronted Chief Joseph and a small band of his followers who refused to yield their guns. The Indians were hunting and could not survive without weapons to bring down the game. The white men could see this logic and reluctantly withdrew, but back at the camp some of the soldiers decided to return and attack the Indian encampments at four o'clock the next morning. When they arrived, Joseph and his men were gone. Some of the wags in Missoula nicknamed that place Fort Fizzle. And later, when several of the soldiers went to a nearby town and massacred a number of the Indians one by one, that was called Camp Scalawag.

Thus, along with schools, churches, and small social clubs formed among various groups of girls in town, there persisted an atmosphere of violence, a pervasive undercurrent of force and death. Jeannette Rankin rejected it at every level. In school she was chosen to recite "The Charge of the Light Brigade," because of its high drama, but when she understood its contents she handed the poem back to her teacher and refused to declaim. Hers *was* to "reason why"!

After graduating from the University of Montana, Jeannette spent six years at home helping her mother assume the responsibility for the younger children's education. During this time, she read of the work of Jane Addams. The experience was electrifying. Jeannette had discovered a woman who believed that women could seek fulfillment outside their homes, perhaps in helping secure happier, more permanent homes for others. In 1908 Jeannette entered the New York School of Philanthropy, which later became the Columbia School of Social Work.

She returned to Montana with a fresh perspective on her home town. She looked at the condition of the Missoula jail and was shocked. Action was called for, and she set about arousing public opinion and launching a move for immediate improvement. A judge who did not put her aside with outright discouragement became the mainstay of her effort, and she called upon him frequently. Famous for being slightly hard of hearing and talking to himself, the elderly man was seated at his desk one day when he looked up and saw Jeannette Rankin once more standing in his office.

"Oh God, that woman again!" he muttered, perhaps only the

first in a long line of indifferent people who would wish to escape this insistent woman's conscience.

Her project for the Missoula jail delayed only briefly her departure for Washington state, where she continued her social work with orphan children. Two realities soon became apparent to her, however. One was the universal discrimination against women. The other was the political basis of many of the problems with which she was trying to cope. She left social work and turned to woman's suffrage. She would spend the rest of her life working for the vote, through the vote, and with the vote for people and for causes that seemed just and humane.

In 1916, four years before passage of the Woman's Suffrage amendment to the Constitution, Jeannette Rankin, after a history-making campaign, was elected to Congress and became the first woman in history elected to a major legislative body in a free country. Again in 1940 she was sent to Congress from Montana. By a strange irony, each time she held office she had the opportunity to vote against the United States' involvement in world war. Each time she was in the minority, the second time a minority of one! And each time, her vote acutely embarrassed her brother Wellington.

A graduate of Harvard Law School at the age of eighteen, Wellington Rankin traveled to England for further study at Oxford University, then returned to Helena, Montana, where he opened a law firm, became a power in the Republican party, and accumulated one of the most extensive private land holdings in the United States.

The influence of these two stimulating individualists converged on their youngest sister. The "middle girls," Harriet, Mary, and Grace, were attractive and popular; their husbands and homes marked the circumference of their world. It was Edna whom Wellington directed to study law, Edna who helped Jeannette in her earliest political campaigning.

Edna lived up to her parents' standards of securing a good education: she attended Wellesley, the University of Wisconsin, and the University of Montana, where she dutifully followed her brother's decree and studied law. But in many ways she was a more "social" creature than either of her older mentors. Possessed of no less energy or determination than Jeannette or Wellington, she nevertheless discovered that there were genial pleasures which could soften the grim thrust of purpose. She enjoyed attractive clothes, travel, banter, and parties; and, although she was the first to admit that these were not the most important features of citizenship, she also had to admit that they helped give life zest and variety.

She hated study of the law. But Wellington had said that it would be useful, and so she slaved away at the legal volumes. "How can you possibly read eight, ten hours a day?" her brother would demand. "Why is it necessary?"

"I can do it because I have to," Edna would reply. "I've always had trouble reading. I have to re-read to get the sense of it. And I'd really rather be out with people, doing things—" But she persisted.

Law school was very much a man's world. One year she was slated to receive an award, a scholarship. Then it was discovered that a man in the class would have to give up his studies unless he received the scholarship. It was awarded to him. No honor, no mention was made of Edna. The award committee did not wish the young man to know that he had not really been first.

The hostility of one of the professors was particularly evident. In studies of criminal law he pointedly assigned Edna the rape cases. At a time when "nice" girls did not publicly acknowledge the existence of such a word as rape, much less the reality behind it, Edna learned to accept these assignments and discuss them openly, objectively. If the professor intended to embarrass or discourage his sole female student, he accomplished just the opposite goal, because these classes helped condition Edna for later work in a field whose subtlest handicap was false modesty and public silence on the part of those who should have been the most outspoken: the women. She learned some necessary skills in discussing before men a taboo subject with logic, force, and consummate objectivity. She became the first native-born Montana woman to receive a law degree and be admitted to the bar in that state.

While Edna was still in college, Wellington also insisted that she study public speaking. He and Jeannette were excellent speakers. Edna, too, learned the art of articulation, projection, and confidence on the platform. This was an asset she would always appreciate, especially after she entered work for birth control, where the need for clear, convincing communication was especially acute.

For she did not go into practice of law. She helped Jeannette campaign for Congress in the race of 1916. They traveled throughout the state, from the ranches to the mines, from the capital city to lonely little schoolhouses. Edna learned to speak in uncomfortable, sometimes hostile, surroundings. She also learned to listen. And perhaps most important of all, she became aware of the necessity to adapt. Success in public discussion or private persuasion often lay in shaping a message to the specific needs that were stirring people's emotions, the dreams that were arousing their hopes.

Jeannette's victory, which attracted national fame and world-wide attention, gave Edna the taste of success, too. She was triumphant when Jeannette, after arrival in Congress, introduced the first bill to grant women citizenship independent of their husbands, and the first bill recommending subsidy for health care and teaching women hygiene during pregnancy and early maternity.

Edna was also finding a personal life of her own. She married Jack McKinnon, a handsome young Harvard graduate, scion of a prominent and wealthy Boston family, who had come to the Bitterroot Valley to manage a fruit-growing venture sponsored by a group of eastern businessmen. The project failed. Jack's family hoped he might become a bond salesman. His talent and enthusiasm leaned more to inventing, however. Bond salesman or inventor—each found equally hard going during the financial crisis of 1929 and the Depression years which followed. The McKinnons, who now had two children, Dorothy and John (there had been one miscarriage), lived on the thin edge of hope. Inventing was not a lucrative pastime, but it kindled constant expectations. They were always going to be rich next Tuesday. Meanwhile, Edna found work at Best and Company in New York.

At Best's she threw herself into salesmanship with her usual

25

heartiness, and her innate regard for each individual contact. She didn't wish to sell dresses that were expensive only, she also wanted them to look good on the wearer. But it was hard, discouraging work of a kind she had never undertaken before, and after several weeks she decided she was a failure. She went to the manager and with Montana candor offered to resign. He looked up her record, found several letters that had been received from customers who were appreciative of this clerk's special attention and helpfulness, and Edna, instead of being dismissed, was promoted.

After a while, she was designated to help open two of the first branch stores established by Best's. Just before the second opening, tragedy struck. John, seven years old, in boys' summer camp up in Dutchess County, was seized with a mysterious malady and died suddenly. Meningitis? Complications of some other infection? The diagnosis remained vague. But the reality of grief was painfully concrete.

As chief saleswoman in the boys' department at Best's, there were reminders of her child at every turn. Yet her family had no other income at this time. Edna had to hold this job. She clung to it desperately, and progressed to appointment as a buyer. This promotion marked one of the few failures of her life. Inexperienced in the details of this specialized field, often distraught by the sorrow that she tried to conceal, Edna did not make a success as a buyer in the merchandising jungles of New York.

The marriage was not a success, either. Jack McKinnon was a bright, well-educated, personable aristocrat who abruptly found himself without either employment or special skills. A genteel introvert, he could spend an evening reading or playing bridge with friends and never say a word. He was willing to accept life as it came—he would agree to a truce of mutual coexistence with the world if it would just leave him alone without too many demands or threats. Edna felt that she was forced to assume responsibilities which should have been shared. Her zest for experience was continually blunted by his quest for peace. Her energy offended his inertia. His solitude disparaged her gaiety and gregariousness.

By mutual consent, the McKinnons parted ways, exchanging

native regions: he went to Idaho to take an office job in a lumber camp, while she remained in the East and kept their daughter, Dorothy. In later years, Edna would reply to inquiries about her marital status with the brief explanation, "I lost my husband during the Depression." Indeed, she had.

Jeannette, who had stayed on in Washington as a lobbyist for the peace movement after her Congressional term expired, found Edna a job in the Resettlement Administration. The morning Edna arrived for her interview, after having spent hours refurbishing an old suit and adding the most stylish touches she could invent to her appearance, Jeannette gave her one glance and announced, "You don't look as if you need a job!" Somewhat subdued, Edna went ahead with her interview and was successful.

Edna's training as a lawyer secured her the post. The fact that she was without practical experience in the field caused many of the bright young men with whom she worked to look upon her as a dilettante. They also considered her a feminist— which frightened, amused, and interested them.

A young colleague said to Edna one day, "There's a big birth control luncheon. Are you going?"

"Of course," she retorted airily. "Why not?"

Then she had to scurry around and find out about this cause she had so readily adopted. A secretary in the office invited her as a guest to the meeting.

An attorney named Mordecai Ezekiel, working in the agriculture department, delivered the after-luncheon speech. It was on a subject Edna had scarcely heard mentioned in all her life, much less discussed in any depth. But Mordecai Ezekiel spoke publicly and brilliantly about birth control. His words electrified Edna. She had gone into marriage uninformed about her own body or the process of birth, unaware that there was such a thing as birth control. Multiply her own confusion and ignorance millions of times—and the needs of the United States, the world, appeared staggering.

Following the talk, Edna's questions tumbled out faster than the speaker—or, later, the secretary-friend on the way back to the office—could answer. She learned of a law which made it a criminal offense for any doctor to give or receive through the mail anything pertaining to contraception. A pamphlet on birth control was treated as pornography in many quarters.

The next day Edna received a telephone call. Someone in New York had heard of Edna's enthusiastic response to the luncheon speech. Would she be interested in working with a small legislative committee which was a branch of the Margaret Sanger Research Bureau? Edna was surprised and intrigued. Her curiosity, her faith in justice, her instincts as a mother and a woman, and her belief in freedom and the possibility of a more humane world, had been aroused by this subject of birth control. She agreed to ponder the offer.

"In that case, while you're considering, will you come up to New York and talk with Margaret Sanger?"

Edna agreed to come.

3

Wifehood is the crowning glory of a woman. In it
she is bound for all time. To her husband she owes
the duty of unqualified obedience. There is no crime
which a man can commit which justifies his wife in
leaving him or applying for that monstrous thing,
divorce. It is her duty to subject herself to him
always, and no crime that he can commit can justify
her lack of obedience. . . . Think of the blessedness
of having children. I am the father of many children
and there have been those who have ventured to pity
me. "Keep your pity for yourself," I have replied,
"they never cost me a single pang." In this matter let
women exercise that endurance and loving
submission which, with intricacy of thought, are
their only characteristics.

—The Rev. William John Knox Little, 1880

Alexander the Great changed a few boundaries and
killed a few men. Both he and Napoleon were forced
into fame by circumstances outside of themselves
and by the currents of the time, but Margaret
Sanger made currents and circumstances. When the
history of our civilization is written, it will be a
biological history and Margaret Sanger will be its
heroine.

—H. G. Wells

WHEN EDNA, on a summer morning in 1936, walked into the sitting room of the apartment on the top floor of the Margaret Sanger Research Bureau in New York, she was greeted by the person who at that moment was perhaps the most enchanting and controversial woman on the world scene.

The name of Margaret Sanger was whispered in some quarters with the dark awe and consternation reserved for the devil's allies, while in other localities it was proclaimed with the ardor accorded only the greatest benefactors of mankind. Many who thought of her as a forbidding Amazon of a female could not have been more mistaken. Her petite grace and Irish charm were the essence of the romantic ideals of femininity. But they belied the iron will which had already made headlines and changed attitudes around the globe. Margaret Sanger, now married to a wealthy industrialist named Noah Slee, had long since learned the uses of wile and will in furthering her cause of birth control.

Writing in her monthly magazine, "The Woman Rebel," in 1914–15, it was Margaret Sanger who coined the term, "birth control." Birth control would eventually become known as "planned parenthood" and, especially abroad, as "family planning," with other titles such as "maternal health" or "child spacing" along the way. The various emphases in names only underscored the constant need to use every means possible in describing, explaining, and winning people to the basic premise. That premise held simply that birth is humanity's closest approach to the mystery of all creation, and is also humanity's likeliest potential for ultimate destruction, either as individuals or as a species. A baby can be the source of immeasurable happiness—or tragedy. Margaret Sanger had seen, Edna McKinnon would see, countless instances of both the joy and the agony.

As a young trained nurse working on New York's East Side, Margaret Sanger had experienced at firsthand the misery of families with too many children born too close together. A turning point in her life had come in October 1912, when she helplessly watched Sadie Sachs, a young mother in her fifth pregnancy, die. The woman had begged for medical advice and help to prevent that pregnancy, but neither the doctor who had warned her against another baby, nor Margaret Sanger the nurse, could tell her what to do—except for the doctor's bantering prescription concerning her husband: "Tell Jake to sleep on the roof!"

Even when Edna McKinnon met her nearly a quarter-century later, Margaret Sanger was still haunted by Sadie Sachs and that sad October night, for in 1936 she wrote of returning to her rooms after Sadie's death and looking out over the city at three o'clock in the morning. She recalled seeing

> with photographic clearness women writhing in travail to bring forth little babies; the babies themselves naked and hungry, wrapped in newspapers to keep them from the cold; six-year-old children with pinched, pale, wrinkled faces, old in concentrated wretchedness, pushed into gray and fetid cellars, crouching on stone floors, their small scrawny hands scuttling through rags, making lamp shades, artificial flowers; white coffins, black coffins, coffins interminably passing in never-ending procession.

Anger generated by that vision sustained her through a long lifetime of struggle and conquest. Eight times she went to prison, beginning in 1916 when she opened the first birth control clinic in the United States in Brooklyn. That initial injustice impressed her with the helplessness of the poor and the ignorant, especially when they were mothers. She wrote, "The women of leisure must listen, the women of wealth must give, the women of influence must protest."

By the time Edna met Margaret Sanger, she had overcome some of the excoriation by doctors, politicians, editors, and religious and reform leaders which at first had seemed unanimous and impenetrable. Across America and around the world she had traveled on grueling lecture tours, shaking villages and nations out of their ignorance and indifference to the perils of uncontrolled birth. Everywhere, great men had been impressed by her intelligence, wit, and charm. Havelock Ellis and H. G. Wells were two of the most eminent. One of them had described her as a "delicious blend of the great queen and little girl," which probably summarized as well as any statement could the paradox of her public and private appeal.

Her work embraced the poverty-stricken and the world's leaders. She had walked with Mahatma Gandhi along the dusty streets and roads of his Indian village. The poet Tagore had written her, "I am of the opinion that the Birth Control Movement is a great movement not only because it will save women from enforced and undesirable maternity, but because it will help the cause of peace by lessening the number of surplus population of a country, scrambling for food and space outside its own rightful limits."

Desperate people turned to her, such as the wife who had given birth to eight children, endured two abortions, and numerous miscarriages: "If you don't help me, I'm going to chop up glass and swallow it tonight." Exaggerated messages came, such as the telegram from an illustrious professor at England's Cambridge University, who addressed her simply as "Saint Margaret, New York."

During her day with this extraordinary woman, Edna was captivated as so many others had been, but not in any shallow, transitory way. She was captured by an idea, an insight into the realities of life all around her—and the possibilities of how it might be made better. The small slender woman with chestnut-colored hair (some called it titian, others bronze) framing her heart-shaped face, with green eyes that looked directly, clearly into one's own, communicated her ideas and insights with passionate conviction. A judge had once said of Margaret Sanger that when she set her mind, you couldn't dynamite it. Now she had set her will to overcome the Comstock law, and that was what she wanted to discuss with Edna.

For more than sixty years the tyranny of Anthony Comstock's personal prejudice and public inquisition had held the subject of birth control in a prison of silence and ignorance. Comstock was one of those self-appointed purifiers of public morals who perennially afflict the American scene. From his actions and their consequences it would have been difficult to say whether he was more eager for purity or persecution. While he was in the tradition of those later political zealots who would dominate the 1950s with their witch hunts, Comstock ruled the latter decades of the nineteenth century and the early decades of the twentieth. And unfortunately, despite his platitudes to the contrary, he seemed to suspect that every person would choose vice over virture (vice and virtue according to his own narrow definition) unless protected and held in check by rigid laws and harsh enforcement. His personal neuroses coincided with the country's latent Puritanism to create one of the more destructive convulsions of public suppression and private repression.

Anthony Comstock was never elected to any government office, nor was he chosen by the people for any role of leadership. His education consisted of a high school diploma, and his experience in world or national affairs consisted of service in the Civil War from his native Connecticut. Yet for almost half a century he shaped much of America's cultural and medical history.

He achieved this by organizing in 1873 the New York Society for the Suppression of Vice and by being appointed the society's chief special agent. Later in that same year, his lobbying ramrodded through Congress a bill barring all "obscene, lewd, lascivious, filthy, and indecent" materials from the mails. When President Grant signed the bill into law, it was not generally understood that the description of lewd and lascivious applied not only to the French picture post cards that so infuriated Mr. Comstock, but also to information concerning the "prevention of conception." Even when that information was of a strictly scientific nature and dispensed by a qualified physician, it was considered filthy and indecent.

Comstock then succeeded in having himself appointed a special agent for the postmaster general, which meant that he could make inspections and authorize arrests. With zeal and relish the self-appointed censor with the leonine head and bull neck launched an era of persecution which would memorialize his name and his activity with the term, "Comstockery."

In Anthony Comstock's mind there was no difference between pornography and science, obscenity and medicine, indecency and birth control—if the taboo subject of sex were involved. He hunted, not for the cause of syphilis and prostitution, but for the citizens who dared admit such realities existed. He persecuted those doctors who sent out contraceptive materials or advice necessary to save a life, and he ignored the reasons behind that need.

Indulging in outright trickery to trap many of his victims, Comstock boasted of convicting 3,760 persons under his law, and of driving 15 to suicide. As a result of his fanatic labors, sex in the United States was not annihilated, it was merely made to seem dirty in all its manifestations. Disease, prostitution, and pornography were not abolished but were simply driven deeper underground, while the wholesome need for forthrightly confronting birth control was summarily denied.

It was Comstock's law that brought Margaret Sanger to court when she tried to write openly and constructively about birth control, that put her in jail when she tried to establish a reliable birth control clinic to forestall the need for the brutal illegal abortions which abounded everywhere. It was Comstock's law that kept doctors from joining her crusade. She was determined to render that law impotent.

When she had fled arrest in 1914 for publishing the pamphlet *Family Limitations* she looked up Dr. George Drysdale in London. More than a half-century earlier his book, *Elements of Social Science,* had proclaimed the need for birth control, and while this young woman told him about her fight he walked around the room, rubbing his hands together, until he finally exclaimed: "Would to God we had a Comstock law! There's nothing that stirs the British like a bad law."

It also stirred Margaret Sanger. For this reason she had asked Edna McKinnon to come and talk with her. Margaret Sanger wanted Edna to know the sordid, savage history of the legalities forbidding knowledge of birth control, and she wanted to enlist Edna's help as a trained lawyer in fighting that law. Edna would not be working for the Margaret Sanger

Research Bureau or the American Birth Control League, but for a small separate committee which functioned on its own. A bright young lawyer named Morris L. Ernst had been enlisted to break the hold of Comstockery.

Ernst stated the strategy he and Margaret Sanger were following when he observed, "In the United States we almost never repeal outmoded legislation in the field of morals. We either allow it to fall into disuse by ignoring it . . . or we bring persuasive cases to the courts and get the obsolete laws modified by judicial interpretation."

Fired with enthusiasm, Edna returned to Washington. Within two weeks she was employed by Margaret Sanger for a year. In addition to having a law degree, Edna had Jeannette Rankin for a sister. During her years as a congresswoman and subsequently as a lobbyist for peace, Jeannette had become acquainted with many of the influential congressmen and senators who could be useful to Edna and her new-found cause.

In September, however, Congress was not in session. Edna devoured all the material she could gather about birth control, especially about previous campaigns to change the law, all of which had failed. Under the title of Executive Director of the National Committee for Federal Legislation on Birth Control, she established contact with several key senators and occasionally made speeches to groups in or near Washington. One of the first audiences was a group of naval wives at the Academy in Annapolis who wanted to form a clinic. After she had carefully written and rehearsed her talk, she tested it on her mother, who was then in her eighties and visiting Edna and Jeannette in their Washington apartment. When Edna had finished, Mrs. Rankin asked, "Well, what are you going to do about it?" The question lodged in Edna's mind like a cockleburr.

In the course of her research Edna discovered that although they rendered almost every other kind of medical service, the U.S. Public Health Department offered no help in the field of birth control. A recent breakthrough on discussion and control of venereal disease gave Edna the idea of making an appointment with the surgeon general of the United States. She found Dr. Parran a courteous, cautious man who was horrified at the suggestion of undertaking something so controversial. He admitted surprise that acceptance of the venereal disease program was affirmative. But if he undertook birth control, he might be excommunicated. For the first time, Edna realized that his religion was also involved, and so she did not pursue the conversation.

As she left, however, Dr. Parran told her, "In the Public Health Department we don't initiate programs. We let various states demand a program, and then we work out ways in which the U.S. Public Health Service can assist them." It was a useful hint. Edna felt that her ingenuous approach had not been entirely fruitless. In fact, her work would soon be following just the path Dr. Parran described.

For Margaret Sanger had failed to tell Edna one important fact: that a crucial legal case, under direction of Morris Ernst, was already pending in the courts. Known as the *One Package* case, it challenged interference with the free flow of information to the medical profession. Dr. Hannah Stone, a dedicated pioneer in birth control work and in improving understanding of the marriage experience, had agreed to receive a package containing contraceptive materials sent from Japan by a Japanese doctor. When the package was seized by customs officials, Dr. Stone took her claim to court. Arguments of Ernst, her lawyer, were buttressed by testimony from a group of impressive medical authorities who described "the many conditions under which contraception should safeguard the life and health of mothers and children."

On November 30, 1936, the *One Package* case reached its final decision. Judge Augustus N. Hand pointed out that this and similar statutes had common origin in the Comstock law, and ruled: "Its design, in our opinion, was not to prevent the importation, sale, or carriage by mail of things which might intelligently be employed by conscientious and competent physicians for the purpose of saving life or promoting the well-being of their patients. . . ." It was a landmark decision.

Edna learned of "the greatest victory in birth control history" with mixed emotions. She celebrated the assurance of a long overdue freedom, but she sensed that this would bring her an undesirable personal freedom from work. Her talents were no longer needed. When Margaret Sanger came down from New York to break the year's contract she had signed, Edna encountered the inexorable single-mindedness, bordering on ruthlessness, which drove the petite charmer with a will of iron. Knowing, however, that Margaret Sanger's budget watchfulness and willingness to use people or bypass them grew from dedication to a cause which had often seemed lonely and hopeless, Edna did not harbor any ill will over her abrupt severance.

On the other hand, Edna could not avoid a feeling of unaccustomed despondency. Just as she had discovered work in a movement of paramount importance, a purpose which would provide her with an opportunity not only for a livelihood but also for personal contribution to the betterment of the world, she was no longer needed.

While she was preparing to close her office, a colleague casually asked one day if she had ever heard of Dr. Clarence J. Gamble. Edna shook her head. The friend explained that he was a wealthy man, heir to part of the Proctor and Gamble soap fortune. He was vigorously interested in every phase of birth control. Dr. Gamble's work consisted, in part, of employing field representatives who set up organizations or clinics in different areas of the country. "Why don't you talk with him and see if he doesn't have something you could do?" the colleague suggested.

"I don't know what it would be," Edna replied.

It was a long shot, but she asked for an interview.

When Edna went into the office where Dr. Gamble waited, she found a man of rather slight build peering out from behind glasses with intense blue eyes that had a disconcerting expression blending puckish humor with high seriousness. Standing at a filing cabinet, riffling through a folder of papers, he launched a swift interrogation into Edna's background—her family, home, education, and work. There was a directness, almost abruptness, about his questions that would have been annoying if it had not been tempered by another quality which was also evident—innate kindliness. That day Edna experienced what she would watch many others accept during years to come: Clarence Gamble's ability to draw other people into conversation about themselves, so that in a short while he knew more than they often were aware of telling. Insatiable in his desire to know the smallest detail about others, he managed to keep his own life and thoughts remarkably private.

A graduate of Harvard Medical School, he had undertaken teaching and research at the University of Pennsylvania Medical School until his attention became more and more focused on the field of family planning. Inspired by two of the pioneers, Margaret Sanger and Dr. Robert L. Dickinson, Clarence Gamble himself became a pioneer in 1929 when he sent a social worker to Cincinnati to organize the Maternal Health Association. It took two years to launch this early, modest birth control service. From that time forward, Dr. Gamble's influence in this important field had a dual thrust: the research involved in seeking better contraceptive methods, materials, and education, and the promotion of healthy attitudes and universal awareness of the urgent need for family planning. To this cause—he readily admitted it was his monomania—he dedicated his life's effort and the fortune of which he was a steward.

Perhaps the only real inconsistency in his career was the fact that he did not practice what he preached. He and his wife, Sarah, a slender, refined woman, naturally aristocratic in the best sense of that term, who shared his population concerns and supported his birth control commitments, had five children. But this contradiction was partly eliminated when each of the five became a strong supporter of their parents' family planning work.

After a few minutes of conversation in 1936, Dr. Clarence Gamble knew a great deal about Edna McKinnon while she knew practically nothing about him. When he turned to a discussion of birth control work, his face grew animated. "Are you interested in this program?" he asked Edna.

She answered that she was and told him why. It seemed to her a basic program, influencing not only the personal happiness—or misery—of millions of individuals but the social health of a country as well. Her explanation was somewhat lengthy, but Edna had the fire of a new convert.

"Do you have an automobile?" Dr. Gamble asked.

She did.

"Are you free to travel?"

She was.

"Would you like to do field work, organize clinics for birth control?"

"Yes, I think I would like to do that very much."

"It's the worst season in the year to start such work." But he thanked her, and she left him standing beside the filing cabinet, where she had found him.

A few days later Dr. Gamble telephoned. He would like to take Edna on his payroll. She would receive a salary of one hundred and fifty dollars a month and five cents a mile travel allowance for her car, plus hotel expenses. There was no pension fund or retirement plan. Her work would begin on the first of May in Montana, since she had some knowledge of that state and influential acquaintances there.

Objectives, in order of desirability, were: first, persuasion of the state board of health to include birth control in a public health program; should this prove impossible, the second aim would be to secure installation of birth control programs in the health activities of as many counties as possible; if this failed, the third goal would be to organize charitable birth control groups including representative medical and community leaders who could win attention and then support for the birth control effort. There was also the stipulation that before her departure Edna should spend a week of concentrated work at the New York clinic to become well informed about the medical part of the program. She agreed to all of these conditions.

Later, Edna learned that in Dr. Gamble's discussion with Margaret Sanger about the advisability of hiring Edna, Margaret Sanger had restated her lifelong belief that only nurses should be employed in establishing clinics. But Clarence Gamble felt that people with organizational skills could be as effective as nurses, sometimes more so. Medical aspects of birth control could be learned. In fact, this was the next step in Edna's education.

When Edna went to the Margaret Sanger Clinic for her crash course of study and observation, she had never even seen a contraceptive. She quickly learned that the basic impediment to birth control efforts was lack of an effective and inexpensive means which could be widely distributed and easily used. One of the oldest methods, the condom, was often imperfectly manufactured and unreliable, and the widespread attitude both in the United States and abroad was that a man should not be asked to use a sheath except for illicit relations which might involve venereal disease. The douche was totally undependable. A device called the Graffenberg ring had been manufactured in Germany and used to some extent in Europe with very bad results. Inserted in the uterus, the ring had reputedly caused many serious complications.

At the clinic Edna learned of the diaphragm and spermicidal jelly, which was the birth control method most widely accepted. Made of soft rubber with a flexible metal rim, its dome shape was fitted over the mouth of the uterus to prevent entrance of the sperm and fertilization of the egg. In addition, a spermicidal jelly was used to coat the diaphragm. The diaphragm had to be initially fitted by a doctor, which meant that its use was severely limited; many women did not have a doctor on whom they could call for this help, while others lacked the initiative (sometimes the courage) required to seek such help. The other method encouraged at this time by the clinic was the use of foam powder and sponge. This was a spermicidal chemical powder sprinkled on a sponge and inserted into the vagina. It was a simpler device than the diaphragm and did not require a doctor for distribution, but it was also much less reliable.

The general state of birth control methods was incredibly primitive and would remain so for a long time to come. Margaret Sanger had expended much of her anguish and energy in trying to encourage research for other means of birth control. Dr. Gamble spent considerable time and money in efforts to discover the most effective methods. Other leaders in the field devoted attention to the lagging technology that hampered even the best, and most sustained, commitment. But the paradox of the nation's and society's values remained. While well-financed and socially acclaimed research in methods of death control made impressive strides and brought an increasingly lengthened life expectancy, the niggling funds and harassed efforts expended in birth control brought only minimal progress. Lavish care in postponing death would seem at least partially selfish and hypocritical until there was some equal concern and remedy for carelessness in breeding life.

And women everywhere were the guinea pigs. It was they who tried all the scientific and unscientific concoctions; it was they on whom experiments in the rhythm method (abstinence during certain days of the month when the woman could conceive), douches, suppositories, and creams were tested; it was they whose bodies became a proving ground for new discoveries or techniques in birth control. The years Edna worked in this field would see two breakthroughs: discovery of "the Pill" and of the IUD (intrauterine device), both of which had drawbacks even as they permitted the first real widespread freedom to choose and regulate conception and birth.

At this beginning, however, Edna learned of the diaphragm and of the foam and sponge. In addition to this knowledge, which Dr. Gamble knew she could quickly assimilate at the clinic, there was her varied educational background in both the East and the West, which could prove useful. Dr. Gamble was also attracted by her practical political experiences during her sister's campaigns, by the thorough study she had already tried to make of the whole birth control movement, and by her excitement, her enthusiasm.

Enthusiasm—that was the key. Years later, when Edna was looking for a clinic director in a country halfway around the globe, Dr. Gamble urged her to be sure that the person was enthusiastic. He knew that this was the inner fuel which could generate courage and skill to overcome long odds and keep on working. Dr. Gamble told Margaret Sanger that he would pay Edna's initial salary, and that after a while, if her work proved successful, she could be transferred to the payroll of the Margaret Sanger Research Bureau.

Thus, it was not so much Margaret Sanger's influence as Clarence Gamble's intuition and investment of money that finally assured Edna McKinnon a place in the field of family planning in the spring of 1937. She would devote the rest of her life to this work, much of it with the unique, artful, and indomitable doctor who had seen so promptly and clearly that she possessed skills which should not be lost to the cause.

4

It is, of course, socially very acceptable to reduce the
death rate. . . . All our biological urges are for more
reproduction, and they are all too often reinforced
by our culture. In brief, death control goes with the
grain, birth control against it.

—Dr. Paul R. Ehrlich

Back to Montana!

Edna remembered the evening, during her early campaign trips for Jeannette, when she had spoken at a high school in the northwestern corner of the state and afterward a lady said to her: "You must be a Rankin. You look like the others, and talk like them. But I always thought there were only Jeannette and her brother, Wellington, in the Rankin family." It often seemed that her mother and sisters and many friends shared this view.

But now she, Edna, had found vital and significant work which she could claim as her own. After the period of utter bafflement and despair when she was carrying out routine office chores in the Washington bureaucracy, and after the alarm that had shaken her when Margaret Sanger's legal assignments proved unnecessary, this new undertaking filled her with hope and energy.

The pendulum swings in Edna's own life were reflected in the world tumult around her. People everywhere were in upheaval. At home, labor conflicts brought 4,740 strikes in 1937 alone, many of which erupted into bloody violence. In Washington, President Roosevelt was trying to figure out the strength and vulnerability of the German leader named Adolf Hitler. Throughout that spring and summer newspapers and radio carried warnings of the dictator's plan to attack the little country of Czechoslovakia. It seemed that war, that oldest of birth control agents, would forever move more rapidly than the efforts of birth control workers to take center stage in human affairs.

During these years, movies and radio provided the central

entertainment of daily life, particularly in the small towns and countryside where much of the nation lived. Effects of the Depression still lingered: an average factory worker's wages were twenty dollars a week, for a foreman perhaps forty. The nation's health left much to be desired, especially in the care of infants. The death rate was fifty-seven for every thousand live births. Never had the need of birth control seemed more urgent in America than during the troubled years of the thirties.

That spring of 1937, Edna's daughter, a student at the University of Wisconsin in Madison, was out of school in mid-May. She and Edna spent the rest of the month together until Dorothy was to visit her father. Therefore, it was not until the beginning of June that the "Montana Expeditionary Force," as Dr. Gamble designated Edna's trailblazing, set forth.

Bouncing along in her new black Ford, she crisscrossed the state from the blue-gray-green spaces of sagebrush country to the evergreen slopes and snow-capped heights of mountain ranges, from Billings on the Yellowstone River to Great Falls on the Missouri, from the ranch and farm country of Bozeman to the capital of Helena and to the Anaconda Copper Company city of Butte, "the richest hill on earth."

The pitfalls and rewards, rejections and problems she encountered were forerunners of those she would meet in distant countries among strange people in later pathfinding efforts. Strengths and techniques she began to develop during this period would meet their ultimate test at an international level.

Each adversity brought fresh recognition of the wall of silence which stifled the whole subject of birth control and prevented an enlightened discussion. Catholic doctrine and Protestant prudery combined with traditional frontier values (masculine virility and large families—as a necessary work force and for old age security) to keep birth control a taboo subject. Those few giants who preceded Edna had met many kinds of resistance and she began to understand that the unspoken, unseen forms might be the most insidious and difficult to combat.

One of the most frustrating sources of opposition was the attitude of many of the women themselves. They found it shocking that a lady of Edna's background, a member of one of the state's leading families, would discuss diaphragms and jellies and foam powders in public meetings. Head high (reddish-blond hair always elegantly styled), she carried her subject into social gatherings as well as public forums. When a few women began to ask questions she felt that the wall was at least breached. In her home town of Missoula she succeeded in making birth control the topic of the day—at least in private conversations.

After examining the Montana law, she concluded that it would not be wise for her to distribute the foam powder Dr. Gamble had furnished, although—she assured him—it wouldn't bother her too much if she were arrested. Would it be helpful to the cause, however? She decided her most effective course would be to cultivate doctors and nurses. One of her first contacts was a woman doctor who was director of a state advisory committee on child welfare. The doctor was in total accord with birth control. After a year's work in Montana, how-ever, she had decided that in terms of establishing a health pro-gram of any sort it was probably the most difficult state in the Union because, she tersely explained, "of the religious situa-tion."

Gradually Edna began to become familiar with the litany of defeatism. An official in the child protection agency wished Edna power but hastened to add that her bureau couldn't touch the subject. After a long conversation she agreed that her nurses might be permitted to tell patients they could get medical aid—somewhere—in limiting the number of their children, if they chose. A director of orthopedic work insisted that her field was the care of crippled children—in which there was no place for consideration of birth control. This was specialization grown brutally shortsighted—an affliction Edna would encounter many times in the future. Another woman doctor informed Edna that she made it a practice to take no part in the meetings of her county medical society because she was the only female member of the society. Yet this seemed to Edna precisely the opposite approach that a person placed in such a position should have taken. Why attain prominence if one then abdicated responsibility?

Even among the nurses, doctors, and civic leaders who announced strong opposition to birth control, there was an urgent, if implicit, admission of its need. An influential Catholic nurse who publicly vowed no support for such a program, a doctor at the state tuberculosis sanitarium, a psychiatrist at the state asylum for the insane—each of these related case after case where birth control seemed essential. The psychiatrist assured Edna that the doctors themselves stood in critical need of education on the subject.

The doctors differed in the intensity of their attitudes. An earnest young physician in one of Montana's larger towns informed Edna that during the years he was in medical school only one lecture had been offered on birth control methods, and the invitation to that lecture emphasized it was optional. In addition, it had contained little information. He quizzed Edna about the latest birth control devices, requested samples of the foaming powder with which Dr. Gamble had been working, and rushed off to a waiting patient. As a departing thought, he reassured Edna about the worth of what she was doing. She must not give up!

Another doctor, an official of the state board of health, virtually quaked at the thought of controversy over contraception and warned Edna that he suspected more harm had been done by the advocates of birth control than by any other group he knew. What kind of harm and to whom, he could not specify.

A Norwegian doctor she approached informed Edna that he believed birth control was an economic necessity, while another physician tentatively agreed that family planning had come to stay but that its progress should be delayed all along the way so that it would not get out of hand. He seemed to fear rampaging nonfertility!

In one of Montana's largest cities she discovered that the doctors had entered into a gentleman's agreement opposing any sort of free clinic, although the heavy relief rolls which had built up during the Depression years were worrying many of the industrialists and city fathers. In another county, citizens voiced concern over the large and growing Spanish-American colony in their midst and accepted birth control as a topic of discussion.

The wide range of reasons for accepting or rejecting birth control left Edna both dismayed and exhilarated. She saw her work as bringing benefit to everyone, and she would never demean it by using it as a weapon against anyone. She fought for true reverence for life, all life. Neither the practice nor the benefits were to be the exclusive rights of any group.

There was one source of rejection with which she could not cope. That was her brother Wellington. Fifty-three years old, unmarried, an acknowledged political power in Republican circles, well known throughout the state, Wellington Rankin was a conservative, proper man. His youngest sister's work shocked him profoundly. In his opinion it was iniquitous, particularly since it could give rise to that most demeaning of all weapons, laughter. Such ridicule could wreck his prestige and would certainly undermine Edna's good reputation.

Edna was surprised by the vehemence of his views and hoped that after she had been at work for a little while, after she had had a chance to talk with him further, he would begin to modify his objections. Such a tempering did not come, however. Wellington's full contempt for her work was finally brought home to her after she had spent an entire conversation with him trying to point out the humane need for birth control and its importance to people everywhere around the world.

"That may be," Wellington finally replied, "but it's not going to be your life work."

"And why shouldn't it be?" Edna asked. "It's important."

"Sewers are important. But *you* don't have to dig them!"

There was no further need for words between them.

In September she wrote to Dr. Gamble and asked to be relieved of her job. She said that she could not work in Montana against her brother's opposition. That letter was a sacrifice that cost her dearly. Dr. Gamble replied that there were other places besides Montana. One of them was Tennessee. He had recently become interested in the possibilities at Knoxville, a city in east Tennessee. If she would like to continue in her work, she could go down to the southern mountains.

Plagued by a gnawing sense of guilt (had she failed her family in some way?) and failure (the first field she entered for Dr.

Gamble had been abandoned), she agreed to go to a city, a state, and a region she knew absolutely nothing about—except through the statistics and myths by which the South and Appalachia had been explained and sometimes exploited for generations.

5

We could use a dozen of you.

—Clarence Gamble to Edna

The development of a socially constructive *attitude*
toward birth control is as important as the provision
of adequate birth control *technology*.

—Richard A. Falk,
This Endangered Planet

Edna arrived in Tennessee in September 1937. The trunk of her car held suitcases containing all of her clothes. In a small gesture of protest and commitment she had brought everything she owned of a personal nature from Montana. Along with these belongings, she hauled a large square box which contained the several kinds of contraceptives Dr. Gamble had provided for distribution through her official employer, the Birth Control Clinical Research Bureau in New York.

Knoxville was a city of some 105,000 people, not a one of whom was known to Edna at that moment. The Great Smoky Mountains National Park nearby was attracting ever-increasing numbers of visitors to the area, and the lakes and conservation activities of the Tennessee Valley Authority, whose headquarters were in Knoxville, were changing the face of the region. And this was the home of the University of Tennessee, where it was still against the law to teach the theory of evolution. Contentedly provincial in many ways, the city and surrounding areas also displayed a willingness to adapt to meet selected problems exposed by the Depression and the "Second Reconstruction" which had followed. Low incomes and high birth rates were central to those problems. In fact, the South as a whole had only recently been recognized as the cradle of the nation: the poorest of the regions, it was also the most fertile. Its greatest resource and export was its people.

In fact, the situation in Tennessee, Kentucky, Alabama, Georgia, and several of the other states in which Edna initially worked was similar in many ways to aspects of the situation she would eventually confront in distant countries of Asia and Africa. She could not have known it at the time, but the experience she was to have here would find triumphant culmination in her later achievement.

During the next nine years, from 1937 to 1946, Edna threw all her reserves of buoyancy, resilience, and imagination into the work that would take her into thirty-two states across the country. In that time she learned several important principles and techniques which were to set her accomplishment apart from that of any other of the paid professionals or dedicated volunteers in the birth control movement. Among these simple essentials, three were paramount—and permanent.

First, unwavering faith. She believed completely in her work and its importance. To communicate that belief, she must start on the positive and refuse to accept no for an answer.

Second, maximum effectiveness. She must seek out top echelon people for fundamental support. There was no need, for instance, to go to nurses to initiate a birth control program; she would talk to the doctors who controlled the decision. But the doctors needed public support. And the public would not move without leadership. Therefore, in Edna's plan, the success of birth control work had to rely on two groups functioning together: committees of lay people who could arouse and sustain effective public approval; and trained professionals—the doctors and nurses—who could carry on the work, reassured and sometimes nudged a bit by the laymen.

Third, basic motivation. She must approach leaders and public with an acceptable idea in acceptable form. This meant an idea so demonstrably true, fulfilling so obvious a common family and community need, that it could not be rejected. Theoretical discussions of population control, abstract predictions of future doom were fruitless. Explanations of what birth control could mean to the fulfillment and happiness of an individual family and to the economy of a specific city or county, won attention and endorsement.

Edna began putting these precepts into practice in Knoxville. She bought a map of the city and became familiar with its topography. Through discreet inquiry and observation, she became acquainted with the general social landscape as well. One of the first persons she called upon was a prominent director of the hospital where she hoped to secure a birth control clinic. He was also a physician, a member of the House of Delegates of the powerful American Medical Association. Just before leaving the Research Bureau, Edna had learned that the AMA—taking into account the court decision in the *One Package* case—had approved for the first time a resolution saying in effect that doctors should be made aware of their legal freedom to give contraceptive information and that birth control should be taught in medical schools. On this first visit, however, she knew that she must not appear too well-informed in the doctor's field.

After exchanging pleasantries, Edna explained the purpose of her presence in Knoxville. Her enthusiasm was not shared by the doctor.

"And I understand that a resolution favorable to birth control was passed by the delegates at the last AMA meeting," she added tentatively.

"I should say not," he retorted. "We've never had anything in favor of birth control."

"Well, I may have been mistaken—" Edna offered. "I thought it had been approved."

"No!"

Edna paused. "Could we glance through your AMA journal?" she asked. A copy was tucked in her car parked just outside—she had practically memorized the resolution reprinted therein—but she knew better than to reveal that she carried such ammunition.

Somewhat brusquely, the doctor searched out his copy of the journal and turned the pages. When he discovered the resolution he paused, read it, then glanced at Edna. "By gosh, I voted for that. Didn't quite realize what I was voting for. Well, since it's already passed I guess we ought to do something for it."

"Good!" Edna said. "I'm here simply to help any way I can."

"Well, I don't know of anything—" he demurred.

"The very best thing possible would be to open a birth control clinic at the hospital."

The director was silent.

"I might be of help to you in establishing one," Edna suggested.

55

"Now, I don't know about that," he said, then added in a flush of inspiration, "look here, our hospital board is having a dinner meeting next week. Why don't you come and talk to us?"

Edna left his office alarmed by her success. She had had no experience at all in establishing a clinic; she scarcely knew how to appeal to a group of doctors; she was unacquainted with Knoxville facts and figures. She plunged into the effort to learn all she could and prepare an effective appeal to meet this unexpected opportunity.

A windfall came when she visited the office of the city manager. An imposing-looking extrovert, outspoken and cordial, with a reputation for honesty and progressive change as well as great success in his own business, George Dempster welcomed Edna with an eagerness that buoyed her spirit. As soon as she had introduced her purpose he replied, "We've got to put this over. Your program is absolutely essential. Our city is going broke paying for free deliveries of babies to welfare patients." He handed Edna a sheet with the statistics confirming his statement. She realized this was another kind of ammunition for her cause. She memorized those statistics.

Then a friendly doctor she had met through his past correspondence with the Margaret Sanger Research Bureau invited her to visit a local hospital. As they paused in one ward, the physician told Edna that with one exception none of the women there had borne fewer than six children. Most of them had had more. The doctor nodded toward an envelope of curtains surrounding the excepted patient. "She's dying," he said quietly. "She had two children and developed tuberculosis. When she left the sanitorium, they told her that she had an arrested case of TB and she'd have to be very careful. Almost immediately she became pregnant again. Now she's just had this third baby. We hope it will live."

"They should have given her birth control information at the sanitorium!" Edna protested.

But there was no such information available. When the woman died a few days later, Edna learned that the cause of death was listed as tuberculosis. No mention was made of the fact that the immediate cause was an unnecessary, debilitating pregnancy. How many such deaths were there across the country each year, buried under erroneous "facts" and incomplete diagnoses?

Armed with the logic of the city manager's statistics and the emotion charged by her visit to the hospital, Edna labored over her after-dinner speech to the board of the hospital. When the doctor who had invited her to attend made her acquainted with the dozen or so men present, she flashed them her most winning smile. Their response was restrained. As she ate dinner in almost complete silence, she remembered one doctor who had said to her, in his office, shortly after she had arrived in Knoxville: "Why aren't you at home? Do you have any children? Why aren't you home taking care of them?"

She had flinched before his rudeness, then stiffened her backbone. In her resonant, modulated voice she had answered him: "Yes, I've had three pregnancies. I miscarried the last one because it came too soon after my second child was born. My little boy died. I lost my husband during the Depression. Now I earn a living for myself and my daughter. And I work for something in which I believe with every ounce of my being."

"I beg your pardon," he had replied, obviously moved by her history. She had felt a bit unfair in the statement about her husband, but otherwise she had wondered at this man's arrogance in questioning and rearranging her life.

More than likely, every doctor present at this gathering tonight would also like to rearrange her life. The sole unhesitating medical supporter she had found so far, the doctor who had taken her through the hospital, was not a member of this board.

The meal finished, Edna was introduced with little more than the words and attitude, "Now we'll hear what you have to say." And she wondered if they did hear, as she explained the program she was advocating: better care of mothers and babies, to be achieved through birth control efforts in relation to the hospital's maternal-child health outpatient clinic. She offered to help in such an undertaking.

There was no response. Frightened and taken aback, she sat

down. Polite applause hardly ruffled the silence. No questions were asked. She picked up her purse and gloves, murmured, "Thank you, gentlemen," and left the room.

When she reached the refuge of her car, she burst into tears. Failure loomed on the horizon. Was her departure from Montana to be repeated here? She had used facts and figures and an appeal to the deepest humanitarian instincts—but she seemed to have been unable to move the doctors. And she *had* to win their support.

After a while, she started the car and drove slowly around the town, recognizing a few of the landmarks which were beginning to be familiar: the hill where the University of Tennessee stood; the Tennessee River; the fashionable residential areas with Indian names of Cherokee and Sequoyah; the market house where folks from the surrounding hills brought fresh vegetables and flowers, butter, eggs, herbs, shelled nut meats, and all kinds of homegrown produce to sell. She paused to wipe her eyes again.

The people she had already met here—white or black, wealthy or needy—were essentially kind, friendly; an old-fashioned sense of neighborliness still shaped many of the patterns of life. There was so much she had hoped to accomplish here, yet her first major effort had aroused no reaction. After tonight—would she have to give up her job?

Weary and dejected, she turned back to her hotel. The clerk came forward quickly as she approached the desk. "Someone has been trying to reach you on the phone. It seemed urgent. He left this number for you to call."

The caller was that doctor who had been her host at the board dinner. "Mrs. McKinnon, you've just won approval of the program you outlined. We took a vote and it was unanimous. Now we want you to help us set it up."

Astonishment gave way to relief and excitement. She began to cry again. This would be one of the first birth control hospital clinics anywhere in the country!

The next day she went to work with renewed energy and learned that only one doctor in the city had been trained in fitting women with diaphragms. He was willing to accept responsibility for the new birth control clinic, but he laid down a strict set of rules: no more than four patients at any session of the clinic, and each patient must already have had six children or more. Edna agreed unquestioningly to everything. "Do what you think best. Do what you can." The essential matter now was to get the work established in a hospital.

As she would do later, in many other places and situations, Edna launched support activity on several fronts simultaneously. Dr. Gamble insisted, and she agreed, that an effective nucleus of the general public, as well as the medical professionals, had to be enlisted to ensure any permanent birth control activity. Ultimately it was action, not organization, that Clarence Gamble wanted. This central principle of his life and work generated unceasing conflict between himself and national and international organizations leading family planning work. Sometimes Edna would be caught in the dilemmas and crosscurrents posed by this conflict between action and organization, but the sturdy groundwork of her approach and its success was being laid in these early years, and it gave her a later authority of experience which no one could deny.

With the doctors ready to cooperate and lead, Edna launched a personal educational effort in Knoxville and the surrounding area. Her public audiences included PTA meetings, men's luncheon clubs and women's circles, social sororities, professional societies, university sociology classes, medical and health associations, welfare organizations, and political gatherings. At one meeting, a group of nurses and social workers gave her a rousing vote of thanks for coming to Knoxville.

Privately, she presented her case to city and county health officers and found their response similar to that of the state commissioner: his department couldn't sponsor a birth control program at that time. But if Edna McKinnon stayed in the state a little while and educated people in the economics as well as the morals of the problem, then an announcement about birth control information wouldn't come as any shock to the public. As Edna left his office, she displayed her innate tact by asking the commissioner to please warn her if he heard of any single action of hers which went too far or ran contrary to the interests of his state health program. "My dear," he told her, with a trace of weariness which suggested how much he welcomed her help, "your work can't go too far to suit me."

Edna spoke with the conservative minister of one of the city's most fashionable churches. She left him a copy of the pamphlet, "Motherhood in Bondage," and felt that although she might not have won a total convert, she had forestalled a sermon of outright opposition to birth control. There were also conversations with the wife of a former governor of the state, a woman interested in suffrage who had known Jeannette and was now interested in birth control; and the directors of small settlement schools in the nearby villages of Pittman Center and Gatlinburg. These meetings were in accord with Dr. Gamble's suggestion that scattered clinics proved more effective than a single central unit which required long trips for the mothers. Certainly this was true for the Smoky Mountain area served by the Pittman Center School and the Pi Beta Phi Settlement School at Gatlinburg, where the need reached back into isolated mountain coves and hillside farms. The doctors and the teachers who worked there welcomed Edna's message and materials, since many mountain families numbered a dozen children, with a cash income of less than five hundred dollars a year.

In Knoxville itself, after she compiled a list of the leaders of various women's clubs and services, Edna telephoned the various presidents and officers and invited them to meet with her. Some of the ladies' reactions indicated the low regard in which birth control, as a general subject, was held. Some of the replies were amusingly personal. "Birth control?" a soft-spoken dowager said. "Why, honey, you're ten years too late for me!"

A more perceptive response came from a young matron named Mrs. Tom Ragland. A petite brunette, astute in her judgment of people and adroit in her political savvy, Martha Ragland was temporary director of social work in the Division of Institutions and Public Welfare. Up until this time, her interest in birth control had been balked at every turn, although she had won meager support in awakening public attention to the existence of the problem. Family position and income would have allowed her to fill her days with a busy schedule of Knoxville society teas, card parties, and luncheons had she not felt compelled to give more of her time and talent to the unsolved needs of a larger society. There were other friends, here and across the state, who shared her concerns, and wherever possible Martha Ragland recruited them to the cause of birth control.

One of the most influential women in the community consented to lend her name and support to the birth control clinic and its work, but warned that she could allot none of her valuable time or attention. Another promised to work for the clinic as long as her name was not publicly associated with the words "birth control." The president of a leading organization on whom Edna had counted for strong leadership declined the opportunity, explaining that there were so many debutante parties scheduled for the coming year that she doubted if her group would be able to squeeze in much welfare work. Yet it was a member of that same organization, in a neighboring city, who phoned Edna secretly one day and asked for information about effective birth control methods and where she could get the materials for her personal use.

From this initial gathering of women Edna formed the strong nucleus for a permanent committee. These individuals represented the volunteers whom Edna would work with wherever she went. Most of them were wives of professional, business, and educational leaders—educated, open-minded women whose sense of citizenship and responsibility had been stirred at some time during their lives. Actually, they represented one of the great undeveloped resources of America: womanpower, whose talents and interests were capable of simultaneously running a successful home and participating in the larger community.

Yet prejudice, custom, many of the same deep-seated fears and myths that restrained acknowledgement of any need for birth control, confined these women, too. While most of them would have neither recognized nor admitted that their comfortable, often luxurious lives were in any way circumscribed, they frequently entered a movement, such as birth control, with a dedication and zeal that suggested they understood, if only by intuition, some of the larger issues which should be summoning their energy and talent.

Knoxville was a landmark experience for Edna. As her efforts extended to other parts of the state, she sent Mayor George Dempster a carefully selected gardenia boutonniere with her card of appreciation. He was as surprised and pleased as many others would subsequently be by Edna's thoughtful and original gifts. Several years later, when she sent Martha and Tom Ragland's little girl, Sandra, a golden-haired, beautifully dressed doll, the child immediately named her doll Edna McKinnon. Obviously, Edna was the most glamorous person Sandra had known.

Wherever she went, there were unexpected trials—as well as friends. In Chattanooga she called on a woman whose influence would be highly regarded in any effort to initiate birth control work in that city on the Georgia border. But when Edna introduced her topic, the stranger turned on her with a venom that was alarming. "How dare you mention such a subject to me?" she demanded.

Taken aback, Edna stammered, "I don't understand. I'm sorry. Please—"

The woman burst into tears. Edna sat quietly for a few moments. Then an explanation poured forth from the woman: "You'll have to overlook my anger. You see, I had four children. My husband threatened to leave me if I became pregnant again. When we were expecting our fifth child, he fulfilled his threat and walked out on me—and on our four children with the fifth one on the way. If I had known anything, just anything at all about birth control, it would never have happened." Edna nodded. "My husband and I really loved each other—" The woman dried her eyes. "That is, we did until there were too many children."

Edna sympathized and said, "Then you'd be willing to help other women, wouldn't you?"

"What could I do?"

"You could give me a list of names, names of ladies who are prominent, who would help win public opinion and support for a clinic where women could go for help in controlling the size of their families."

"All right. If you won't tell people I was the one who suggested their names."

Edna gave her promise. Back at her hotel, she telephoned each woman on the list. In her most cultivated voice, she told each that she was working on birth control but did not wish to discuss it on the phone. "Would you come to the hotel and have tea with me?" Many of them accepted her invitation.

When they arrived and saw other friends there, they were often surprised. "Oh, you're here?" But they were visibly relieved to find themselves in each other's good company. As she had done before, Edna extracted from this group the core of a committee which soon became active in securing a clinic.

Nashville and Memphis, too, were turned into centers of birth control activity. The chief of medicine at Vanderbilt University assured Edna that he was strongly in favor of birth control. In the Bluegrass area of Tennessee, which was famous for its walking horses, he noted, "I don't see why we can't give as close attention to breeding humans as we do to breeding horses!"

When Edna wrote Dr. Gamble in November for funds to help support a Memphis clinic, he answered in a way and with reasons that she was to find characteristic throughout later ventures: "I think it would be a mistake to let the financing of the clinic come too easily. The need for local money-raising proves very educational, even though the process is difficult at first." He suggested that Edna's first offer to communities should be for free supplies: foam powder and diaphragms. If this proved inadequate, the furnishing of a nursing service could be discussed. Finally, if there were no alternative to paying doctors to participate, a three-month experimental program might be financed.

By the first week in December, Edna had talked with ninety-three physicians, spoken to three medical meetings, and helped establish five clinics in the three divisions of the state. Their very names—Maternal Care Clinic, The Motherhood Advice Bureau—indicated both their yearning after broad public support and the nature of their clientele. Edna worked with Negro doctors and nurses, too, especially in Memphis, although this city was also bound by the patterns of legal and traditional segregation that existed across the state. Wherever there was a white health problem—infant mortality, high incidence of TB, and malnourishment—there was a black health problem doubly, triply acute.

In February, Edna learned that an important tri-state medical meeting was scheduled to be held in Memphis. What a perfect occasion for communicating the birth control message to great numbers of doctors from a large area. She approached the directors of the convention about securing exhibit space but learned that she was too late for a booth. Undaunted, she approached one of the doctors who was sympathetic to her cause. He advised her simply to turn her room into an exhibit area. She could show her film there and set up her display, and as long as she didn't advertise on the lower level she could devise ways to circulate news of her program.

Without delay she had visiting cards printed which gave notice that "Scientific Motion Pictures" and an exhibit on birth control would be open in room 470. On the door she tacked a printed sign: "Contraceptive Methods. Admission by Badge Only. Displays of Birth Control Clinical Research Bureau."

With no assistance but that of a young medical student she had hired for three afternoons to run the projector, Edna showed her films, answered questions, scientifically explained the uses of the contraceptives displayed on her dresser. And she confronted, even among doctors, the variety of attitudes that ran the full gamut from professional compassion to callous indifference toward the suffering involved in lack of birth control and leering humor over the sexual aspects of the subject. After all, here was an attractive lively woman engaged in most unorthodox work.

Then and there she learned to cope with the snide laughter and stale jokes that would persist through her years of work, to put off sly hints which demeaned her very purpose. She must not alienate anyone by reacting with anger or impatience. Assuming her most lofty, ladylike air, she responded to any suggestive remarks or questions in disarmingly naive tones and disingenuous words—or with the purposeful objectivity she had learned years before as the lone woman in her criminal law class.

When a medical book salesman from one of the downstairs exhibits asked with a smirk if she gave personal demonstrations, Edna replied, with a shrug of her shoulders, "Well, this is the first time I've ever done anything of this sort and quite frankly I don't know *what's* expected of me. Right now, I'm trying to run this machine and I can't even do *that* very well."

Everywhere she went, people enjoyed her company, were charmed by her alertness, intelligence, and quick responsiveness. Men reacted to her quickly—but there were times when they were somewhat awed by her, too, awed by her energy, her wit, her independence in undertaking by herself work so controversial and indelicate (yes, downright indecent in some opinions).

At her Memphis meeting, however, there was at least one doctor who felt that her program was worthy of wider distribution. He invited her to come to Kentucky and promote the cause of birth control. This invitation pleased Dr. Gamble mightily. Another of his strictest tenets of faith, which never relaxed as his work spread from state to state and then from country to country, was that no outside worker should stay for long in any one place. The pattern was to make an introductory visit, become familiar with the situation, the people, the problems and potential, and initiate such programs and/or organizations as were possible; move on to another territory; then, after an interval, come back, evaluate what was being done and make new suggestions, lend assistance, and leave once more to return again periodically, as might be useful.

Dr. Gamble told Edna, "What a lot of scalps you do collect. The Tennessee accomplishment is magnificent. If you were twins the whole country would soon become depopulated!"

Later the following year, while Margaret Sanger's Research Bureau and the American Birth Control League, which Margaret Sanger had founded, were in the process of being merged into a single organization that would eventually be known as the Planned Parenthood Federation, the great lady herself came for a tour of Tennessee. Wide-set eyes expressive as always, stage presence dramatic and effective, Margaret Sanger spoke across the state to standing-room-only audiences. Edna had returned to Tennessee from work elsewhere so that she might precede Margaret Sanger's arrival in each city and make certain of the most effective use of her presence. At several of the gatherings, people were turned away for lack of room.

When Margaret Sanger returned to New York, she immediately wrote Clarence Gamble that from one end of Tennessee to the other, Edna McKinnon was spoken of with great admiration, loyalty, and respect. "The little extra courtesies that she does so graciously, the small gifts, and the like, are all paid out of her own pocket which she can ill afford." Mrs. Sanger admitted that she was telling Dr. Gamble this because it was really his good judgment that gave Edna her chance. "And she has not failed you."

Clarence Gamble was not contemplating failure. In fact, before Edna had even considered moving on from Tennessee, before she had received the invitation from a Kentucky doctor to bring her message there, Dr. Gamble was thinking about recommending that Edna go to Alabama. "Does this alarm you?" he asked in a letter. "I have a medical classmate in Birmingham who is very cooperative. I nudged him into starting a clinic there."

The result was that in the spring of 1938 Edna went to both Kentucky and Alabama. Each of these states brought a very special and enduring friendship into her life. In Louisville, Kentucky, she met Mrs. Charles Tachau, and in Birmingham, Alabama, she became acquainted with Mr. and Mrs. Charles Zukosky.

Jean Brandeis Tachau was born into a family tradition of public responsibility and service. Supreme Court Justice Brandeis was her father's brother. The economist William Henry Taussig was her mother's brother. The renown of these two uncles was only the most public evidence of a private sense of social commitment that influenced the young woman. A gifted musician, she combined an interest in the arts with concern for social problems, one of which was the need for birth control. As the first president of the Kentucky Birth Control League, she had drawn on her long interest in juvenile problems and legal justice to awaken concern for this cause. She was an intelligent, dedicated woman, not at all sure that she wished to welcome some outsider who was being sent into her territory for some purpose as yet unknown.

Jean Tachau went to call upon this person who had telephoned that she would be in charge of an exhibit at the Southeastern Surgical Congress assembling in Louisville, and that while there she would very much like to meet Mrs. Tachau, if it were convenient.

For her part, Edna was eager to meet the person who could apparently wield crucial influence in the success of birth control work in Kentucky. When Jean Tachau appeared, a trim little lady in a well-tailored red tweed suit with white gloves, they exchanged greetings, and Edna concluded that she was the coldest woman she had ever met. And Mrs. Tachau found Edna's exuberance disconcerting. Warily they discussed the birth control exhibit at the Surgical Congress.

The exhibit developed into a stunning success. Its standing-room-only audience clogged the hallway outside the space where the film was shown at scheduled intervals; it drew hearty approval from the medical adviser to the Kentucky Birth Control League. Within a few days, Jean Tachau invited Edna to her home for dinner. This was the signal of social acceptance; it was also the beginning of a long personal friendship. At dinner Edna met Jean's husband, Charles Tachau, and their three children, Charles, Eric, and Jean. All of them were attracted by this lively, compelling woman who might have some of the sophistication and know-how of New York but who also created an aura of the openness and freedom of her native Montana.

Edna told them that her own son, if he had lived, would be just the age of fourteen-year-old Eric. Eric and Edna—it became a special alliance which would last through years of friendship.

After dinner, Mrs. Tachau excused herself to attend a rehearsal of the Louisville Symphony Orchestra, of which she was a member. Edna and Mr. Tachau had the opportunity for a long conversation. Charles Tachau told Edna of his wife's years of fairly lonely work promoting birth control, and of her desire to enlarge its scope and effectiveness. Would it be possible for Edna to come to Louisville for a while and help achieve this?

Of course, this was exactly what Edna wanted to do, what Dr. Gamble directed her to do, what the Birth Control Federation hoped she could do. And now the invitation could come from within the state. She assured Charles Tachau that she stood ready to help in any way she could.

In May, Edna returned to Louisville—and to the Tachaus' spacious, hospitable home—where she spent the next six weeks in intensive and enlightening activity. She came to know some of the powerful, attractive leaders of the Bluegrass and its increasingly cosmopolitan city. First among them was Barry Bingham, urbane and knowledgeable owner and publisher of the *Courier-Journal*, the morning newspaper that was a state-wide institution. The day Jean Tachau took Edna to his office and introduced her to Barry Bingham, he was engaged in helping raise a $400,000 fund for the enlargement of the state's feeble-minded and child care institution. Edna used this as a springboard for their conversation.

"For about a dollar a year," she said, "we can protect a woman against unwanted pregnancy. If we could spend only a tiny amount on birth control, we could alleviate much of the expense of this very institution you're trying to help."

Barry Bingham called in his editor, Mark Ethridge. Ethridge, who had previously been the courageous and liberal editor of a paper in Macon, Georgia, was a knowledgeable southern newspaper professional who had known Edna's sister Jeannette. He immediately understood the thrust of Edna's argument, and he approved the purpose of her work. He pledged his support to the Kentucky program and that support remained steadfast. A short while later, when Mary Lasker, wealthy widow of the founder of the J. Walter Thompson Advertising Agency, paid for a full-page ad calling attention to the necessity for birth control, the *Courier-Journal* was deluged with subscription cancellations, mostly from Catholic readers expressing outrage. However, neither Mark Ethridge nor Barry Bingham, nor the latter's wife, Mary, who was on the board of the Kentucky Birth Control League, backed down.

After a brief flurry, it was discovered that most of the cancellations were quietly reinstated.

Bingham also offered free time on a radio station he owned, and Jean Tachau and Edna put together a birth control program. They deplored their presentation as "terribly innocuous" but were pleased when it aroused a measure of public interest. Simply bringing the subject out from under wraps was progress.

No one and no place was immune from Edna's introduction of the subject of birth control. Invited to attend a large fashionable horse show and the inevitable round of parties which followed, she met many people who could be helpful to her cause. She skillfully turned the conversation in that direction as often as she possibly could without becoming a bore. She wanted to make discussion of birth control not only permissible but fashionable.

She discovered that the horse farm aristocrats and the hill country farmers and miners she was soon to meet had one thing in common: all they needed to know was that their neighbor thought so, too. One acceptance of an idea or a cause led to another, each easier than the one before.

Beyond the Bluegrass, the people of the Kentucky mountains were considered a world unto themselves. In the early 1930s, Clarence Gamble had given financial help to the Mountain Maternal Health League, based in Berea. There the work of one nurse, Lena Gilliam, had been especially outstanding. By car and horseback Lena had gone into the back country of three mountain counties and had visited over five hundred families. A mountain girl herself, whose mother had died of tuberculosis after giving birth to a large family, she was able to break through the natural reticence of mountain women and relieve them of fears and anxieties that had shaped their entire lives.

Some of the agonizing conditions and needs of the region were set forth in a brochure which the League published at Berea shortly before Edna arrived in Kentucky. When Edna studied that brochure, she learned the facts of a harsh way of life: many of the families visited by the League nurse earned a total cash income of less than two hundred dollars a year. While the land could not maintain its present population at even subsistence level, the number of people to feed was steadily growing. In 1936, when the cities of the southern mountain area had only 332 children under five years of age for every 1,000 women of child-bearing age, the region outside the cities had 618, and some rural Kentucky counties recorded the incredible number of 900.

The parents often did not want so many children. Deep as their love for their babies was—"and in these mountain communities family affection is conspicuously tender"—the mothers made tragic efforts to ward off pregnancy as failing health or growing poverty threatened them. Too isolated, sometimes too shy to be able to consult a doctor, they had recourse to the "feminine hygiene" medicines which they found advertised in their "wishbook"—the mail order catalog. When these failed, there were attempts at abortion by large doses of drugs or by the still more dangerous use of some household implement not at all designed for surgery. And the pamphlet concluded: "Still the babies come!"

Edna and Jean Tachau discovered the accuracy of the League's description when they made an extended trip through the mountains that spring. The paradox of poverty and riches, need and blessing, hope and despair, was brought to sharp reality in their experience. The natural world of eastern Kentucky's Appalachia was bursting with new greenery of trees and shrubs; dogwoods glistened white as spring snow along the hillsides; watercourses half-hidden under thickets of rhododendron and laurel rushed clear and sparkling down slopes and valleys to join the rivers.

Yet in mining villages and isolated county seats scattered along the rough, winding roads, an incredible squalor existed. Edna looked at the dust-blackened hovels crouched in narrow valleys near a coal tipple, and at the ill-kept cabins perched on hillsides too steep for the corn cultivation that had washed away all semblance of thin topsoil, and she felt almost overwhelmed by the proportions of the need here.

As she talked with doctors and nurses who served at least some of these needs, Edna drew on her deepest reserves to inspire leadership in inaugurating programs and local clinics where women could receive proper care as they sought desperately to control the size of their families.

The words of one eighty-year-old doctor rang in her ears. He received Edna on his front porch, just before he left for a day's practice at his work-worn office. After he had listened attentively to her presentation about birth control he sighed, "Mrs. McKinnon, if only you had come sixty years ago. Your message could have saved so many lives!"

In the mountains of Kentucky, as in Nepal and dozens of other places later, Edna was brought face to face with the reality of population and ecology. Here it became unbearably clear that man could not "conquer" nature. He could change its balance, exploit or study it, but in the end he would himself be "conquered" or nourished by the land and its resources. Perhaps that was why, as Jean Tachau liked to point out later, so few of those who became committed to the cause of birth control ever deserted it. Either overtly or instinctively, they recognized the central importance their work carried for fulfillment of personal, individual lives, and for survival of human society in the largest social sense.

The ambivalence of her joy in the beautiful countryside and her despair for the many people who barely existed amid such surroundings was communicated in one of her numerous reports to Dr. Gamble. He liked communications, both the sending and the receiving. Occasionally, there would be as many as six or seven letters a day from him, causing Edna to wonder at the postage involved, considering his habitual frugality. At any rate, no matter how long or tiring the day had been, throughout the years of her work she tried to keep a steady flow of daily mail to satisfy his curiosity, his sense of participation. Near the end of that spring she wrote to thank him for letting her do this work: the mountains, the air, the countryside were all so harmonious and magnificent. Yet, she said, when she saw the forlorn cabins scattered along the way, she could find consolation only in the hope that her work could bring some fundamental, permanent aid to their plight.

For those on Dr. Gamble's "antistork payroll," as he called it, there were often overlapping jobs. During that same spring and early summer, Edna also became acquainted with Alabama and two people who had helped further the birth control work there: the Charles Zukoskys. They had come into family planning through acquaintance with a friend of Clarence Gamble's. A wealthy heiress in Minnesota had offered five thousand dollars to any state that would undertake a program in birth control. Dr. Gamble had prevailed upon a former classmate at the Harvard Medical School, Dr. Clifford Lamar, to set up a birth control clinic in Birmingham. Now Dr. Gamble wanted Edna to go down and see if the director, with the incentive of this possible five thousand dollar windfall, would not move out from his initial effort and inaugurate a statewide program.

Bernadine Zukosky, active in the Brimingham birth control clinic, waited with mixed feelings near the elevator of Birmingham's Tutwiler Hotel for her first meeting with Edna McKinnon. This new presence in the precarious field of birth control could play havoc with their struggling, little-known effort. She could not know that if Edna McKinnon had learned anything early in her southern experience, it was that she should not look like a social worker—at least like the stereotype of the social worker. It seemed that all kinds of barriers could be overcome if a first impression conveyed attractiveness, humor, and success rather than the grimness and hardship of constant struggle against uneven odds. When Edna walked from the elevator into the lobby, a friend standing with Mrs. Zukosky took one long, inclusive, knowing look at the erect, alert woman wearing a smart black and red suit and a jaunty hat and murmured, "She'll do. Yes, indeed, she'll do!"

Charles Zukosky had been a young lawyer in St. Louis who had moved to Birmingham to open the trust department in a local bank. His career had proved so successful that he remained in banking for the rest of his professional life and became a highly respected civic leader. As mayor of the elite residential community of Mountain Brook, he was the innovator of numerous progressive programs. His leadership in areas of race and social justice and civil liberties was founded on a deep-seated respect for individual worth and freedom. A quiet, soft-spoken, dignified man who moved with gentle, deliberate manners, Charles was something of a contrast to his slender, bright-eyed, articulate wife, Bernadine. They made a delightful couple. And they were devoted to the cause of birth control, maternal health, family planning.

They had supported Dr. Clifford Lamar from the beginning of his committee on birth control. After the committee had been at work for a while and Dr. Gamble wrote, "What are you doing for black mothers?" and sent one hundred dollars to get some work under way, it was Bernadine Zukosky who secured the black woman who would travel around the state and learn what the situation was among black women and judge if they wanted family planning. The result of that particular project was a collection of horrendous stories learned by the black nurse at first hand. Black women *were* planning their families—without medical help, and by the most primitive, painful, wasteful means of abortion.

Both the Lamars and the Zukoskys welcomed Edna and found her appreciative of the work they had done during the early years of their committee's formation. To accomplish what she wished, however, she particularly needed the support of the state's chief health officer. By a unique arrangement, Alabama's Department of Public Health operated under the medical direction of the state medical society. As Edna talked with the doctor about a full-scale birth control program in the department of public health, she found him to be neither fearful nor indifferent. He was conscious of the need for support, however, both professional and public.

"If I went around the state and talked with a number of leaders and found out their reactions, would that influence you?" Edna asked.

"Of course," he said.

"All right," she proposed, "you give me the names of some people whose advice you would follow."

The public health director gave her a list of sixty-three names. In her little black Ford, with suitcase and boxes of contraceptive materials in the trunk and back seat, she jolted across the roads of Alabama, from southeastern Dothan to the northwest boundary, from the northeast to Mobile on the Gulf of Mexico.

The first person she sought out was the state superintendent of public instruction. As soon as she had explained the program, he announced, "I'll support you any way I can. If we ever plan to educate the people of this state properly, we're going to have to cut down the high birth rate. I see the problem at firsthand every day."

Scattered from the capitol buildings to the county courthouses, others she contacted included religious and political leaders; presidents of clubs, lodges, and PTA groups; manufacturers; bankers; lawyers; editors; educators; and doctors. Wherever possible, she would be accompanied by a prominent person in the community who was interested in birth control. Out of the sixty-three names she was given, sixty agreed to put their names on a committee supporting the public health department's work in birth control.

There were varied reasons behind that support. Some of them involved the familiar concerns that prompted Edna's commitment. A few, however, grew from antihuman motives, such as those who hoped that birth control would solve the black-white problem, preferably by dwindling the black population. In their prejudice and naiveté, those people did not see that there was no such thing as a "nigger problem" or a "redneck problem"—only human problems, which had to be solved humanely or the total society suffered.

When Edna returned with her report, the public health director was impressed, and he dubbed her his "high-powered New York friend." She didn't like the title; she wasn't from New York, not really. But if she made the health department feel high-powered, that was fine.

For birth control work to be effective statewide, through the public health program, it needed not only the support of all the county medical groups but of strong lay groups as well. As it had been in Tennessee, this was Edna's next effort. In addition, a state league was formed, with the Birmingham organization as its nucleus. Members of the new groups—representing almost every county in the state—joined Edna in raising funds for their work.

An experience which resulted from their very first efforts taught Edna and her colleagues several important lessons. The local head of one of Birmingham's largest iron works had such a reputation for stinginess and lack of interest in civic affairs that no one wished to approach him for a contribution to this controversial cause. At last Edna decided that she would have to see him by herself.

As she walked into the office, his greeting was as blunt as everyone had promised his rejection would be: "What do you want?"

Edna replied with equal Montana bluntness tempered by her gentle, forceful tone of voice: "I want several things. I want your interest in a program that can help the workers here in your company. I want your interest in a program that can help the state of Alabama. Then I want a contribution. And I want you to set up a service right here in your iron works where your people can secure help."

After they had talked further, he asked how much money she wanted. "I wouldn't consider dictating the amount," Edna replied. "But I want you to think about it—because I want it to be a big amount."

He made no response.

"Another thing I want you to do," Edna went on, "is this: I want you to come to a meeting of businessmen at the Tutwiler Hotel." She gave him the name and date.

To everyone's astonishment, the cagey industrialist turned up at the luncheon. Dr. Lamar spoke to the twelve powerful men. Edna outlined briefly, enthusiastically, what had already been done in the state. When the time came for responses from the men around the luncheon table, the head of the iron works had his turn to speak. "The way I look at it," he said, "industry has a stake in this program. I find that if my men have healthy families they do a better job. If they're all worried about too many kids and sick wives, doctor bills, and loan sharks, they're no good to me. Maybe the best way for them to be satisfied at home is to have good birth control information." There was a pause before he turned to the president of the Birth Control League and said, "If you ladies come to me and ask for fifty dollars, I'll give it—and not think much of you."

With a nudge from Edna, the surprised president said, "Oh, we're asking five hundred from you."

"I'll give it."

It was not only the five hundred dollars that was important, of course. A barrier had been breached. One of the most powerful industries in the South—for its own reasons, reasons that would move other similar groups across the world in due time, had given its sanction to birth control efforts.

Not all of her forays were so successful, of course, and when there was special difficulty, Dr. Gamble might make a flying visit to Alabama. He brought fresh perspective, sound suggestions, and financial help, but most of all he brought the tonic of his unswerving conviction that the work in which he and his colleagues were engaged was important to the well-being of every individual in the world.

Whether she was in the black community of Tuskeegee or the steel town of Bessemer, whether she was suffering the infrequent personal depression of a dark, rainy day after having a tooth pulled or the professional sense of oppression from awareness of the immense job to be done, Edna never failed to be revived by Clarence Gamble's prompt response to questions, needs, or doubts.

Not that Dr. Gamble didn't have his flaws. He could take five long, precious minutes counting out the exact change for a taxi. He might ask a lady out to lunch—and take her to the nearest short-order stand while he explained the research and education taking place in the birth control field. In-fighting between national organizations and Dr. Gamble seemed incessant. To reduce it to the simplest explanation, they wanted him to channel his money and work through the bureaucracies they had established for what seemed to them most effective labor at both local and international levels. He, on the other hand, wished to have the freedom to explore different approaches, try new methods, and employ people who might not fit the orthodox rules and regulations. If opportunities for widening the field of work arose, he wanted to be able to respond at once without waiting for time-consuming board meetings and official approvals.

Clarence Gamble therefore invested his considerable gifts of money where and when he saw fit. He also enjoyed his role as a loner and dispute did not dismay him. There were times when Edna believed that he actually sought controversy. She was never sure whether he believed this might clarify issues and directions, or whether he enjoyed the prospect of keeping everyone's adrenalin flowing—perhaps it was a combination of the two.

When the Birth Control Federation of America (soon to be the Planned Parenthood Federation) was emerging late in 1938, however, and it appeared that Dr. Clarence Gamble might be frozen out of its plans and not included in future work, Edna McKinnon took up the issue with Margaret Sanger. The two women had engaged in a long conversation about the possibility that the new organization might not retain Dr. Gamble as a field director. Now Edna felt it a loyal necessity to put some of her thoughts into writing.

She pointed out Clarence Gamble's knowledge of America and his recent contributions from Ohio to North Carolina, Kansas to Alabama: he did not emphasize any one section to the detriment of another; he gave those working with him (always *with,* never *for*) freedom to use their judgment without leaving them out on a limb if difficulties arose; he was tenacious in sticking to the objective of getting direct, concrete aid to women without waste of time or money. Margaret Sanger, also a loner who could understand his spending his money as he wished, appreciated his emphasis on organization at the local level and subsequently agreed with Edna's evaluation of Dr. Gamble's contribution to their cause. Margaret Sanger said that, besides herself, Clarence Gamble had done more for birth control than any other individual.

At the end of her six months' initial effort in Alabama, Edna was sure that something the Zukoskys had told her was less true than it had been when she arrived. They had pointed out, "As far as child welfare laws and protections go, hogs and cholera are of greater interest to the government than people. There are laws to protect hogs, none to protect mothers and children." During her stay, no state laws had been altered, but attitudes were changed. And because of new attitudes, the foundation for important progress had been laid.

That foundation was based on three cornerstones Edna laid most carefully: endorsement by local medical associations; support of community and state leaders representing a broad cross section of people; and direct participation of key industries, not only as financial supporters but as centers for the program's dispensation as well.

Elated and convinced that this pattern could prove useful to other birth control advocates in other places, Edna wrote a carefully detailed report of the strides that had been made in Alabama and sent it in to the Planned Parenthood Federation. She received no response, no reaction. Perhaps the Federation's differences with Dr. Gamble, who had brought her into the work, influenced its apparent disregard of her success. At any rate, she was disappointed that her work did not seem to have more influence. And then she read a letter from Dr. Karl Menninger of the Menninger Clinic. Mary Lasker had secured a copy of Edna's report from Dr. Gamble and had sent it to the famous psychiatrist. Dr. Menninger praised the report and all it stood for and then expressed the fervent wish that workers like Edna could be functioning in every state in the union.

The schedule of travel, organization, and inspiration that Edna would keep for the next few years suggested that there were others who wondered if Edna alone might not achieve Dr. Menninger's wish by taking her work to almost every state. When she was asked to take other, more settled jobs, Dr. Gamble immediately advised her: "I really think you can accomplish much more for the mothers of the country as a mobile unit to be used where most needed. Such persons aren't easily to be discovered and with your skill are even rarer." As a mobile unit Edna was, indeed, a rare resource.

In South Carolina she won her credentials of acceptability when she was invited to be a house guest at one of the oldest plantations in the vicinity of Charleston. (From the expansive ranches of Montana to the moss-festooned plantations of the Deep South was a leap not only in time and space but in state of mind and style of life as well.) Later, from the capital at Columbia, she was again able to report that the South Carolina Board of Health had voted unanimously to allow birth control to be included in its program.

In Georgia, she repeated many of the activities that had been successful in Alabama. Yet each state was different, with different leadership and customs. For instance, no other state but

Georgia could boast of both Jessie Daniel Ames and Mrs. E. M. Tilley. Mrs. Ames was a Texas suffragette and feminist who had come to Atlanta to work with the Commission on Interracial Cooperation. She had organized the Association of Southern White Women for the Prevention of Lynching as an astonishing and effective weapon of protest and justice. Dorothy Tilley, Edna found, was the Methodist doyenne of the Southeast. Certainly she was a strong, well-known lay leader in that church. Each of these women, familiar with the daily problems of organization along with its necessity, heartily approved of birth control. They had seen the need for it firsthand in black shacks and tenant cabins as well as along the rural roads and rundown streets of white Georgia. Their advice was practical and down-to-earth and could only have come from a lifetime within the region. Mrs. Ames, for example, warned Edna, "Don't think everyone in Georgia or Mississippi who's polite to you is in favor of birth control. Down here, our manners—good or bad—don't always let you know exactly what we're going to do."

When another energetic southern woman, Josephine Wilkins, introduced Edna to the editorial writers at the *Atlanta Journal* and the *Atlanta Constitution,* Edna found both men cordial, willing to listen, and somewhat surprised by the success she was having in securing attention for birth control across the state. She ventured to point out to James Pope, editor of the afternoon *Journal,* that while he was surprised at the favorable reaction of other Georgians, they in turn probably did not know how *he* felt about birth control. He smiled and understood her point. They agreed that in birth control, as with many other subjects of controversy and conflict, such as race, lack of public discussion could be tragic. It relegated to the realm of the unknown and the mythical, realities that needed to be part of daily knowledge.

Ralph McGill, at the morning *Constitution,* was an even easier person with whom to talk. He laughed when Edna assured him, after their introduction, that it was not personal publicity she sought. His laughter turned to admiration as she pointed out that mention of birth control and family planning would be most effective if he could discuss it in his articles on housing, public health, democracy, government relief programs, and similar subjects dealt with in his widely read editorial column. As she left, McGill thanked her for the visit and requested that she send him any statistics or material about population which he could use to awaken public awareness.

All of her encounters were not so fruitful. In a small town south of Atlanta, she called upon a doctor who seemed not only too elderly to practice but also too deaf. After almost two hours of shouting, mostly in reply to his inordinate curiosity about the methods and effectiveness of every known contraceptive, Edna headed for the door. He followed her, suggesting in a hoarse whisper, "Well now, you come back and we'll see about starting this. By the way, young lady, are you married?"

Edna's diplomatic skills were tested in encounters with the inevitable county curmudgeon who could kill any birth control program in that area. In one of Georgia's largest towns, whose surrounding countryside had a special need for the birth control message, the local curmudgeon edited the town's only newspaper. When Edna offered to go and talk to him by herself, other leaders in the uneasy local group were only too happy to agree. "He can't do anything but throw me out," she told them, and phoned the editor for an appointment.

When she walked into his office the next day, she found him behind a barricade of books and papers scattered in tall piles over his desk. "Oh? Yes," he nodded, "I guess I did tell you to come today. Well, I'm just doing some research for President Roosevelt's Commission on Conservation of Natural Resources. I'm a member."

Edna eased into a chair as he went on. "Most people don't realize that right here in Georgia we have some of the greatest resources in the United States. But we're not conserving them. We have vast timber stands that could last for centuries. Our water supplies are tremendous. But we have to conserve them."

The lecture continued for a few minutes before he stopped short, peered at Edna to determine whether or not he had headed her off her subject, and said, "But this is a far cry from what you've come to talk to me about."

"No." Edna seized the opening. "Don't you know I've been

just sitting here on the edge of my chair while you talked? You've made my speech for me! I've come to talk with you about human resources."

"Oh?"

"All I'd like to suggest is this: what use will it be if you conserve all these other resources you mention and waste your human power? My story is purely conservation of human resources through birth control so that each child will have a chance to start his life and grow and become a sturdy part of the society and utilize wisely all that you're working so hard to conserve."

The editor leaned back in his chair a moment. "That's an idea," he said. "I'd never thought of birth control just that way. You know, this could make a terrific story."

Edna pushed on. She told him that some of his fellow townspeople wanted to start their work right in that town, and if the group were formed he could be the most important person, the key person in that county.

When his editorial appeared, strongly approving of the move to begin birth control work in the area, there was a general feeling that some degree of success was already assured. And the myth of the unalterably opposed leader was once again permanently shattered.

Success, of course, was often a relative matter. There was the carefully planned and presented talk which Edna made to an elite luncheon club one day. Later, one of the ladies told her that following lunch and her talk the members had been so interested in birth control that they could hardly get down to bridge!

As she moved out of the South into the Northeast and the West, Edna helped arrange, sponsor, and participate in an important three-day conference which was held in Atlanta. Its subject was "Tomorrow's Children."

Objectives of the conference had been clearly enunciated by Edna during its planning stage. They were to focus the attention of southern leaders on the fact that birth control could be used as one of the solutions to many of the region's problems, to bring to public attention their leaders' approval of birth control, to acquaint the nation with the fact that the South was aware of the need for birth control, and to give courage to public officials and civic leaders by letting them know that other major problems could find at least partial solution in effective birth control.

Many of the South's most noted figures participated in the discussion of "Tomorrow's Children." The need was best summarized in Louisville publisher Barry Bingham's keynote speech, in which he pointed out two facts: "The South stands ready for a second Reconstruction and this time it must build more soundly than before"; and "The South is not faced with a single problem which cannot be solved by intelligent analysis and careful planning."

Edna took her own capacity for analysis and planning with her as she worked in Maryland, New York, New Jersey, and Connecticut (where a nurse and two doctors were being prosecuted after a raid on a hospital birth control clinic). In Maine she was shocked to learn that one out of every eleven infants was born dead or died in the first year of its life. Although the Birth Control League of Maine had done good work, and the state medical society had put an early stamp of approval on the birth control movement, Edna welcomed an opportunity to enlarge and extend the work.

Idaho, California, Texas, Missouri, Colorado—the list lengthened to include thirty-two states which profited from her "persuasive tongue and intelligent planning," as Clarence Gamble described her contribution.

She skirmished with "the clutchers," usually women, who had founded and fought for early local birth control movements, but whose early ardor had gradually narrowed into a holding operation. Fearful of losing personal control of any remnants of prestige in "their" organization, they sacrificed activity and goals to the inertia of self-preservation. They felt threatened by any outside force working to broaden involvement and influence. Edna's first effort, then, was to convince them that she harbored no personal local ambitions. She put to good use the hard lesson she had learned in her own family: to subjugate her own prestige or success to that of others.

There were signal triumphs: in a city in northwestern New York where a large bank permitting a birth control exhibit was threatened with a boycott but did not yield, and the boycott failed to materialize; in a city in Maryland which allowed open discussion of birth control and watched incipient protest dissipate; and in Denver Edna won attention and approval at a men's luncheon group by remembering each name after only one introduction. Using every means available, she moved from state to state, always emphasizing the achievements of those who remained at the local level.

During these years, Edna asked a fellow worker one day, "Don't you just love to go into a new town and whip it into shape?"

"No," the friend replied. "It's hard, depressing work. There are too many setbacks."

But Edna disagreed. "It's the setbacks that give you the chance to dig in from another side, discover another approach!"

Reaction to her "digging in" was expressed by one who knew it firsthand, both in its early successes and during the return trips which brought fresh help and advice and insight. Bernadine Zukosky wrote to her friend and mentor, Dr. Gamble, "Edna McKinnon continues to work like one possessed and to have the success that seems to come only to the possessed."

The variety of her work included Washington and the federal government as well as the states. Her purpose was to get birth control included in the public health program of as many federal agencies as possible—the WPA, the armed services, and others.

One continuing effort centered around the Children's Bureau and inclusion of birth control in its maternal and child health program. The struggle was uphill all the way. Finally Eleanor Roosevelt, at the prompting of Mrs. Mary Lasker, agreed to hostess a Monday luncheon early in December at the White House. The director of the Children's Bureau would be the chief guest—and target. One colleague had described this director as "a congenital old maid," who should never have been in child and maternal work at all.

On Sunday, the day before the scheduled luncheon, Edna and the executive director of the Planned Parenthood Federation met at Washington's Mayflower Hotel with a number of distinguished people who would be present the next day. They would try to coordinate the effort to sell the subject of birth control to the Children's Bureau chief. Suddenly, a government official appeared at the edge of the group.

"Have you heard the news?"

They replied that they had not.

"The Japanese have attacked Pearl Harbor."

After the first flurry of shock and a rush to the radio to try to find out what was happening, Edna and her director realized that all plans for the following day would be changed. They telephoned Mrs. Roosevelt's secretary to assure her that they would understand cancellation of the luncheon. A short while later, the secretary returned their call. Mrs. Roosevelt had said there would be no cancellation of the luncheon; indeed, now there might be more need than ever for knowledge of birth control.

Washington, the nation, and the world were thrown in turmoil, however. Edna's own turmoil included not only upheaval in her work—the luncheon proceeded at Mrs. Roosevelt's insistence, although she had to be absent, and there was no alteration in the Children's Bureau policy on birth control—but included also the politics in Edna's immediate family. By a strange irony, Jeannette Rankin had been elected again in 1940 to serve her second term in Congress. After voting against United States entry into World War I, she had not run for national office again until twenty-four years later, when the country once more faced embroilment in world conflict.

During that Sunday night following Pearl Harbor, Edna received urgent telephone calls from her brother, Wellington, in Montana. "I can't reach Jeannette. Where is she? Are you hiding her from me? Edna, what is she going to do about this declaration of war?"

"Jeannette's on a train to Buffalo where she's gone to make a peace talk," Edna replied over and over. "I don't know what she'll do, Wellington."

"Well, keep her on that train—or be sure how she's going to vote. She can't be for peace again—after Pearl Harbor!"

Edna finally learned that Jeannette had been reached on the train and would return to Washington in time to cast her vote in the House of Representatives. More hectic calls between Montana and Washington. This time Wellington and Jeannette were too far apart to toss tumblers of water; indeed, they were too far apart to make any communication tolerable.

While Edna was at the luncheon at the White House making her appeal on behalf of an enlightened birth control program, Jeannette Rankin stood in the Congress and cast the sole vote against entry into World War II.

After her luncheon, Edna rushed over to the capitol where police were protecting Jeannette's office. Edna took Jeannette in her car and they drove out into the country. It was a long day.

There were criticism and attempts to humiliate Jeannette for her vote, but a curious sort of discrimination saved Jeannette Rankin and her family from the outright rage and ostracism that would probably have been visited on a man who followed her action. She was a woman, women were by definition unstable, impractical, and emotional. Thus, Jeannette's conscientious vote for peace was used in some quarters as confirmation of the stereotype that women were not ready for leadership in the hard world of "real politik."

And so, war—that old Malthusian agent of birth control—took center stage again and subordinated all other issues and concerns. But for Edna, the work for planned families continued. Statistics on high army rejections due to health and literacy problems were shocking. They confirmed the need for quality rather than quantity of life—the right of every child to be wanted, cared for, and educated.

Through these years of work Edna also combatted one of the oldest injustices embedded in the economy and mores of the society, the inequality of pay for women. Neither Dr. Gamble nor the Planned Parenthood Federation would act to raise her salary, which they acknowledged was too low.

"No mention, no recognition has been made of my worth— if I have any," she finally exploded. "And at no time have I been consulted as to policy, action, or any participation in the Federation. I have been ordered to go here and there and told to do a job."

With her instinct for innovation and her courage in taking

action, it was hardly likely that Edna was quite so downtrodden in her labors as she claimed—but it was indisputable that she did not receive a just salary. An important part of the folklore of American economics was the belief that women neither deserved nor expected cash remuneration equal to that of men. They received other, loftier, undefined rewards—or they were working for more or less of a lark anyway.

Edna protested against this folklore. She explained that she did not seek praise. But she judged that in accomplishment, hard work, loyalty, experience, and grass-roots development of the program, she was worth more to the birth control movement than any four of the young men who had been mentioned for certain executive positions. She did not want a title. "I *do* want equality in authority and salary."

Gradually, Edna's situation improved. And Dr. Gamble's efforts to provide vacations so that she might spend some time with her daughter, Dorothy, eased some of the difficulties of her employment. It was the injustice of getting her cheap because she was a woman that rankled Edna. After all, her work was to help enlarge the freedom of women everywhere. She wanted the process to be total, indivisible.

When a group of influential Chicagoans, whom she had met during work in that sprawling, varied city, asked her to come and settle down beside Lake Michigan and cease her activities as the itinerant evangelist of birth control, she was ready to listen.

Jean Tachau had said that during the late 1930s and early 1940s, Edna made the greatest march through the South since Sherman—and hers was constructive! Clarence Gamble had written, "We could use a dozen of you." And the Zukoskys surmised that if a job couldn't be started with Edna McKinnon there to help, everyone knew it simply couldn't be done.

Chicago would be a change from constant travel and from an official organization attitude that often irked her. Many members of the family planning organizations showered all their accolades on the volunteers who promoted the cause, and paid little or no heed to the mere workers who were on a payroll.

Edna had once offered Clarence Gamble a prophetic vignette of Martha Ragland and Dorothy Stafford, two of the ablest Tennessee women working in the birth control cause. Edna spoke of the unquestioned and enviable status which made them part of the social life of Knoxville. "There is something indefinable in their being looked upon as mere 'workers' that is distasteful to 'southern ladies.' Their social position entitles them to positions as 'board members' rather than F.W.s [field workers]."

It was precisely this sensitivity to nuances of individual and social relationships (nuances that might have been dismissed in some quarters as false or trivial) that increased Edna's effectiveness, especially as she went to work in foreign countries. No matter how inconsequential outsiders might consider a person's or a nation's small prides and customs, Edna never discounted them. After all, she had grown up with the pride and burden of being a Rankin in Montana, and she knew the pain and pleasure of being either over- or under-regarded.

During one conversation, in a slip of the tongue, Clarence Gamble—certainly Edna's friend as well as employer—asked how she happened to be attending a certain social function, since she was "a mere—" Then he caught himself.

"A mere worker?" Edna pounced on the slip with an alacrity that revealed her own sensitivity to the situation.

"You know what I mean," Dr. Gamble laughed.

But for long afterward, Edna often referred to herself, in conversations or letters, as "a mere—" And sometimes Dr. Gamble teased her by addressing her so.

A situation would arise, eventually, where lack of sensitivity to this matter of who was a paid worker and who a lady bountiful volunteer, would occasion a distressing and destructive crisis in Edna's foreign work.

Meanwhile, there was Chicago, eager to have her. She swept into the windswept city.

6

Inertia is the only mortal danger.

—Rene Dubos

I am concerned about the areas of the globe where people are rapidly becoming richer. For rich people occupy more space, consume more of each natural resource, disturb the ecology more, and create more land, air, water, chemical, thermal, and radioactive pollution than poor people. So it can be argued that from many viewpoints it is even more urgent to control the numbers of the rich than it is to control the numbers of the poor.

—Jean Mayer

O<small>NE MORNING</small> while Edna was executive director of the Planned Parenthood Association of the Chicago Area, an angry young woman presented herself at the desk of the clinic. The receptionist glanced at the stranger's tousled, unkempt hair, her threadbare coat and scuffed, rundown shoes—but it was the fierce despair burning in expressive eyes that arrested her attention.

"The welfare lady told me to come here. She said you could help."

"I hope so," the receptionist welcomed her.

Pride, bafflement, lack of familiarity with translating her innermost thoughts and needs into words stifled the visitor's conversation at first. But gradually her story emerged, a familiar one, yet unique nonetheless because it was happening to this one person at this certain time and in this certain way.

She was twenty-nine years old. In the space of seven years of marriage she had borne five children, each delivery accompanied by physical difficulty, and after the last birth the doctor had warned her that she must have no more babies. He had provided her with no contraceptive information, however. Her husband, a strapping young truck driver, accepted the doctor's warning and moved into a bedroom with the two little sons. The three little daughters slept in their mother's room.

Gradually the husband's absences from home began to lengthen. More and more evenings were spent out with the boys. As he began to drink heavily, it also became evident that out with the boys also meant out with the girls. Finally, there was less and less money coming home from his paycheck.

Irritable, frightened, and lonely, the wife who could not be a wife scolded and screamed at her husband who was seldom nearby and at her children who were constantly nearby. She felt trapped in a situation she could neither change nor escape. Finally, with only occasional dribbles of money coming into the household, she turned to the relief rolls for survival. It was the social worker assigned to her case who suggested that she call on Planned Parenthood for advice. Reluctantly, she brought her hopelessness and need there.

The receptionist led her to the clinic rooms. After an informative discussion she was provided with a contraceptive and given supplies sufficient for a number of months. Her earlier belligerence faded as she began to comprehend that here was help which might truly change her life. Still baffled, but summoning a shy, awkward appreciation, she departed.

A steady flow of patients, an endless recital of needs, and a persistent series of crises, crowded each day and week at the Planned Parenthood office, but those working there could not totally forget that particular young woman who had come with such rage and longing. They expected to hear from her, but no word came. She had appeared like a bolt of lightning and seemed to have disappeared the same way—abruptly and totally.

Late in the year she reappeared. The receptionist, famed for her ability to remember names and faces, did not recognize this brisk young stranger in well-fitting clothes with a ready smile. She gave her name and nodded at the receptionist's response. Her report was almost trite in its simplicity. It was also triumphant in the tested truth of daily experience.

She and her husband were living together again. His job was going well enough, she was a careful manager, and there had been no welfare assistance for months. Most important, they had a home once more, with normal husband and wife relations, free of the incessant fear of a pregnancy which might prove fatal.

For Edna, that experience stood at the heart of her work during the years in Chicago. It summarized the needs of thousands, and her organization's response to those needs. It justified her years of continuing effort to gain influential support for planned parenthood work, her campaigns to free doctors and nurses from their old legal bondage to Comstockery and its legacy and their own medical bondage to lack of training (no medical school in the United States offered a regular course in birth control). Above all, it confirmed her strongest personal motivation for work in birth control: creation of a good and happy family life.

She knew, with a knowledge gained through childhood wounds, the insecurity and anguish of growing up as the last member of a family which acknowledged it was too large, which implicitly admitted that her birth was more accidental than intentional. The usual childhood fantasies ("Perhaps I'm not really their child"; "Maybe I was a doorstep baby"; "Would they really miss me if I died?" and "Did they want another boy instead of me?") had played a larger than usual role in Edna's development as she grew up in Jeannette's and Wellington's shadows, groping for her own identity and work. That uncertainty had been compounded by the failure of her own marriage, a marriage entered in outrageous ignorance concerning the sexual relationship.

Because of her concern for this aspect of family planning, Edna became more and more convinced of the need to involve men as well as women in the program.

"Edna's boy-crazy," some of her friends in the office teased.

To which she replied, "It takes two to start a family! People talk about *women* planning their families—as if they could do this by themselves!"

Soon after Edna was sent to Chicago she was asked to speak to a luncheon group of fifty of the city's most influential men. She accepted immediately—and bowled them over. "That woman could sell a corpse on birth control!" one later said.

Employed by the Planned Parenthood Association of the Chicago Area, Edna adapted all the knowledge and skills she had acquired during her years as a roving antistork ambassador. Within the space of two months she had won the support of directors of important funds and agencies which had previously been hostile or indifferent to the cause of birth control. Business and professional leaders became active participants in the Association. Most important, the small, scattered, sometimes conflicting groups working in the field of planned parenthood in the Chicago area were welded into one organization with a renewed sense of purpose.

"Under her direction," an influential board member predicted, "we will command the respect of agencies, enlist the aid of men, and get unprecedented activity out of the volunteers."

Edna could expect such activity because she herself set the example. On the North Shore or the South Side, she spoke wherever she was asked. (A lady in Winnetka was shocked and intrigued: "Think of a lady talking about these things; and she *is* a lady. Perhaps it's time a lady said these things.") When a downstate appeal came from a woman with six children, Edna pushed forward arrangements to make certain that someone from the Association went to talk with her and take her to a friendly doctor for the information she needed.

Opposition pressures developed and she helped others withstand them. One volunteer who had done extraordinary work in the campaign for funds received threats. Mild at first, these threats grew increasingly sinister until the woman was compelled to accompany her child to school because she was fearful of kidnapping.

A real blow came after Edna had been in Chicago several years. An unusually attractive and effective socialite was elected president of the Association to succeed the young lawyer who had helped so much to move the group into fresh activity. This woman was a serious and dedicated worker, who had been suggested for eventual national leadership. Her husband was, of course, well-known, one of the rising stars in industrial Chicago. Edna welcomed the prospect of the influence this leadership could wield in breaching stubborn barriers.

Then the company informed its bright young officer that his wife's prominent position in the birth control movement could cause ill will among customers—not all customers, of course, but enough to be troublesome. There were also members of the board of directors who were offended by her activities. If she could not be less conspicuous, relinquishing her role as president of Planned Parenthood, her husband might be forced to become less conspicuous in the company and relinquish his slated role of president.

Such an ultimatum infuriated Edna. "Of course you'll stand your ground," was her attitude to her friend's dilemma.

"Of course I can't," was her friend's reply. "I'd be responsible for ruining my husband's career."

And an enthusiastic worker for Planned Parenthood was lost to the Art Institute and the Opera Guild and other noncontroversial causes.

There were alternate successes and failures with the doctors and nurses, too. The reorganized and strengthened Association was able to secure a notable medical advisory committee, but still it seemed to Edna they were unsuccessful in getting birth control information into some of Chicago's largest hospitals. Edna approached the doctors individually, in groups, in their societies—any way available at every opportunity offered. Some of their responses stunned her:

"I would never under any circumstances give a woman a contraceptive until she'd had several children," the head of a hospital department of obstetrics and gynecology vowed.

Edna silently asked, "And who gave you the power to determine 'several'?"

"You would have me advise mothers with newborn babies about birth control?" another asked, surveying Edna with horror. "I can't imagine anything worse than telling a woman who's going home with a little bundle of joy how she can keep from having another one."

Edna longed to reply, "You've never taken a little bundle of joy home—and had the joy dissipated by anxiety that you can't look after this baby properly or provide for it sufficiently because there might soon be another on the way."

But she did not argue with these opinions, only persisted: keep the hospital birth control clinics open, encourage doctors and nurses, build and solidify public approval, and secure a firm financial basis. She pulled the Association out of debt and gradually increased its annual budget to seven times the amount it had been when she arrived.

In 1948, an early breakthrough on radio came in Chicago. Edna worked hard to achieve the first crack in the wall of public silence that surrounded birth control work or family planning. Finally, the program director of one of the major radio stations, a woman, agreed to interview Edna—if a script could be submitted well in advance and if there would be a promise of no deviation from that script.

Edna agreed, submitted a talk and questions and answers which she felt were bland but better than nothing, and appeared for the scheduled program. One of the chief executives of the station was waiting in the studio. He would be on hand to signal the control room in case any unforeseen objectionable words or statements were introduced.

The program went on the air. Because Edna could not use such terms as "birth control" or "abortion," she spoke of "child spacing" and "protection of the health of mothers and babies through postponed pregnancy." But even that innocuous discussion broke the silence. The radio station received only two hostile letters and these were from chronic protestors whose objections carried no weight. Many supporters of the clinic wrote of their approval of the program. And thereafter, mention was made from time to time, on Chicago radio, of the need for and the problems of birth control.

During Edna's years as executive director, outstanding figures in the birth control movement came to Chicago. Dr. Philip Hauser, a sociologist who had become an early and expertly informed advocate of population control, was one of the finest speakers Edna ever heard. She could especially appreciate his ability to marshal strong facts and complex figures and present them in a manner the public accepted and remembered. Throughout her career her association with Dr. Hauser and her respect for his effectiveness would continue.

Dr. Gregory Pincus fortified and inspired the volunteers and staff members at an annual meeting. He and another friend of Edna's, Dr. John Rock, a devout Roman Catholic, were in process of developing the Pill—a contraceptive destined to become the most important agent of birth control in the mid-twentieth century.

As other organizations and national leaders increased support for population control, Edna's circle of interested colleagues and fellow workers continued to expand. Some of the men she had approached in her earliest travels around the country, awakening their attention to the need for birth control, began to make significant contributions. Among these were Will Clayton, the cotton magnate Edna first talked with in Texas, introduced by a mutual friend, Mrs. Agnes Nelms. And there was Joseph Sunnen, a St. Louis financial tycoon, who was introduced to the work for planned parenthood through Mrs. Arthur Stockstrom and Edna. His interest grew until eventually he invented an aerosol type of cream contraceptive called Emko and became one of the most generous contributors to family planning organizations.

Edna was a friend of Tom O. Griessemer, the able lawyer employed by the Hugh Moore Fund to help insure the success and frame the first constitution of the International Planned Parenthood Federation. The Hugh Moore Fund itself had an unusual history. Founded in 1944 by the man who was co-inventor and developer of the Dixie Cup (the first publicly accepted and distributed paper cup, with an attendant impact on public health), the Fund's initial purpose was to promote world peace. By the early 1950s, however, the problem of population—basic to peace and every other world issue—was receiving more and more of Hugh Moore's attention and resources. When the Hugh Moore Fund published a pamphlet entitled "The Population Bomb," which also introduced the phrase "population explosion," two new terms entered the popular language and public consciousness.

One of the outstanding persons who came to Chicago, creating a glamorous interlude in the daily round of clinic work, office detail, public education, and fund raising, was Lady Rama Rau. As president of the Family Planning Association of India, this handsome woman was one of the respected leaders in her country. Her suspicion of some of the simple contraceptive methods suggested for Indian women—such as use of salt solutions—was sharp evidence of her alertness and opposition to any experiments carried out on her people. Intelligent and forthright, wearing her saris with regal grace and authority, she was one of the world's most articulate women, bridging the gulf between the ancient patterns of social custom and religious tradition and the modern pressures of new freedom and altered relationships.

97

Edna had become acquainted with Lady Rama Rau during a journey made midway through her dozen years in Chicago. It was a journey important not only because of its immediate results but also because of its portent for Edna's future. For it was while he was attending the International Planned Parenthood Federation conference in Bombay, India, that Dr. Clarence Gamble began to consider more intently the neglected population realities of many Asian and African nations. And it was in Bombay that Edna had her first contact with some of the peoples and problems she would come to know firsthand within another decade.

Her trip to India came about in this way: late in the summer of 1952, Margaret Sanger wrote Edna that in December an international conference on planned parenthood would be held in Bombay. The occasion would be historic. Edna definitely must attend. Dr. Gamble, who visited Chicago a few days after the arrival of Margaret Sanger's letter, agreed that Edna should be present at the worldwide conference.

During the spring, however, Edna had taken a trip to Europe and now she had neither sufficient funds nor vacation time to make the visit to India. But when she read Mrs. Sanger's letter to her Chicago board of directors, a member responded, "Well, you're going, aren't you?"

"Actually I don't see how I can—" Edna hesitated. She knew that Jeannette would be on an extended visit to India at that time; she remembered a plan Dr. Gamble had suggested by which she might finance her trip. "Of course, if the board were willing to give me a leave of absence without pay, I'd be glad to go."

They agreed, and agreed also to advance her money for travel and expenses, which would be paid back out of each month's salary during the next year. Olga Baxt, who had been recruited by Edna for the board soon after her husband was transferred to the Chicago executive offices of Sears, Roebuck and Company, volunteered to fill Edna's place in the office. This was an important boost, because Mrs. Baxt was one of the most keen and capable workers for Chicago's Planned Parenthood Association. She brought the efficiency of professionalism to her generously donated time and talent.

As plans proceeded, two of Edna's close friends on the board, Mrs. J. Harris Ward and Mrs. John Nuveen, decided to go along to the conference, too. A high-hearted triumvirate, they flew by way of Honolulu and a successful planned parenthood conference there arranged by Mrs. Ellen Watumull, a long-time benefactor of the cause. Then they went to Tokyo, where they joined Margaret Sanger and Dr. and Mrs. Gamble.

In Tokyo Edna became acquainted with Dr. Yoshio Koya, director of the Japanese Department of Health and Welfare, whose important birth control research work in three quite different villages of his country had been promoted by Clarence Gamble. On at least one occasion Edna took Margaret Sanger's place on the platform and spoke to a throng of Japanese women only recently liberated into public appearance outside their homes. Her very first attempt at reciprocating the exquisite courtesy of her hostesses led to great laughter. When she was presented, she made a deep bow and discovered this was a man's bow rather than a woman's bow. But this mistake established an easy informal atmosphere and Edna felt an immediate sense of rapport with the audience. After she had spoken briefly, Edna asked for response from the Japanese ladies: what were *their* thoughts, *their* experiences in family planning? So far they had heard only about the United States. Now she was ready to hear about them. The floodgates opened as woman after woman stood and spoke her thoughts. The interpreter was busy—not interpreting Edna to the Japanese women, but interpreting them to her. This brief and novel interval, characteristic of Edna's sense of sharing and courtesy, brought her a special sense of satisfaction.

The route to Bombay, much of it traveled with Margaret Sanger, gave Edna her first glimpse of the extremes of life which seemed particularly pronounced in Asian countries: dinner in Hong Kong at the elaborate home of a wealthy Parsi who was promoting planned parenthood work; noise, heat, barking dogs, and the fetid pressure of crowded people in Bangkok; Singapore as guest at the mayor's mansion; and Ceylon, with its novelty of elephants as picturesque plodding beasts of burden and its exotic capital Kandy. She arrived at Bombay and the conference with a heightened vision of the teeming millions of the world, an expanding awareness of the necessity for work in planned parenthood. Could there be anything more brutalizing, more inhuman, than the results of worldwide *unplanned* parenthood?

In Bombay, Edna met for the first time the powerful triumvirate of Indian leadership: Prime Minister Jawaharlal Nehru, Lady Rama Rau, and Dr. Sripati Chandrasekhar, one of Asia's most vocal and eloquent spokesmen for family planning. As India's minister of state for health and family planning, Dr. Chandrasekhar would visit the United States a few years later on a lecture tour discussing his nation's program of voluntary sterilization. Edna maintained a long acquaintance with both him and Lady Rama Rau.

Edna's friend Dr. Gamble participated in the conference as one of the international speakers as well as an adviser on future plans of the Federation. Meanwhile, as usual, he was also laying some personal plans of his own. Before leaving the United States he had secured the names of American doctors working in various missions scattered throughout India, and he sent many of them invitations and expense money to come and meet with him during the Bombay meeting. From this group he recruited a number who would carry out small projects investigating the feasibility of various contraceptive uses in their villages. Fitting women with diaphragms was too expensive and complex a means of birth control to be effective on the mass scale necessary in India. Yet official methods sponsored by the Family Planning Association of India favored the diaphragm and Lady Rama Rau began to display increasing irritation toward Dr. Gamble's efforts to discover simpler, yet effective, methods. She did not know or would not acknowledge that as a trained physician and dedicated philanthropist he had carried on similar work in the United States for many years. She denounced his investigations and assistance as experiments using her people.

Relations between Lady Rama Rau and Dr. Gamble remained strained for years to come. She wanted his donations but felt they should be made directly to her planned parenthood organization to use as *she* saw fit. He wanted to promote planned parenthood in India but felt that his money should go into programs *he* believed important. Here, as elsewhere, he also asked for extensive reports yet provided insufficient funds for secretarial help or supplies. Frequently overworked doctors or nurses or staff members had little time or patience for lengthy correspondence. His insistence heightened his reputation of being difficult to work with, and in countries such as India his demands were sometimes impossible to meet.

In Bombay, however, Edna believed that Clarence Gamble's mind was opened irrevocably to the tremendous need for work beyond the United States. Sponsorship of his scattered projects among the missionary doctors was his first international undertaking. On this trip, he also met Margaret Roots for the first time. Mrs. Roots had reared a family and like many other middle-aged widows was left essentially aimless. She had left her native Canada to join the Royal Geographic Society in London. While there she took an extensive trip which had brought her to India, the firsthand discovery that too many unwanted children were being born, and introduction to Clarence Gamble. Swift as always in his judgment and decisions, Dr. Gamble engaged Mrs. Roots to join his personal task force. She became Pathfinder's first international field worker.

As Edna had done in the United States in the late 1930s and early 1940s, so Margaret Roots would travel and organize and break paths for birth control work in foreign countries during the 1950s and 1960s. Dissimilar as they were in style and personality, Edna and Margaret imparted the same message. As Margaret Roots entered one strange city or province or village after another and asked, "What is your most valuable resource?" the standard reply came, naming a crop or mineral. She would shake her head. "No. Your children are your most important crop. Your people are your most valuable resource." Then she was ready to discuss the quality versus quantity of the people crop.

For her part, Edna was momentarily pleased that Dr. Gamble was diverting his interest farther afield. She was deep in her work in Chicago and proud of the sturdy federation she was helping to build there. She had deliberately avoided association with Dr. Gamble wherever possible because she was succeeding in an important organizing effort, and his reputation was too often for disorganizing. She and the Gamble family remained devoted personal friends. Sarah, Clarence's wife, was one of the most gentle and genteel persons Edna had ever known, and their lively, individualistic children, with whom Edna enjoyed a special rapport, offered her rewarding friendships during holidays by the sea in Maine or at their home in Milton, Massachusetts. But there were times when Edna disagreed with Clarence Gamble, and she was one of the few people frank enough and selfless enough to tell him so when the situation warranted. However, at this moment in her life, she was content to be his friend and once-removed colleague rather than his field worker.

Following the IPPF conference, Edna remained in Bombay to visit Jeannette and spend a month traveling with her to other parts of India. Jeannette's familiarity with the huge subcontinent was the result of a half-dozen lengthy visits to study Gandhi and his peace movement. There were those in the U.S. who considered Jeannette Rankin one of the authorities on something called "nonviolence"—an old concept that had had an early prophet in Henry David Thoreau. Yet this "nonviolence" came to American attention as a new and strangely alien movement, advocated by a wizened Indian in a loincloth who defied the power of the British empire.

Thus, as they had once in an earlier decade walked together down Washington corridors lobbying for peace and birth control, Jeannette and Edna walked through the sprawling cities and the swarming villages of India. Here was splendor and beauty of royal proportions. But here, too, was the sweating, emaciated, groping truth behind the warning, "population explosion." Here was the ignorance and hunger breeding too many people, too many wars. More than half a million villages, not to mention the great cities. Fourteen percent of the world's people living on slightly more than two percent of the world's land. A maternal mortality rate almost six times as high as that of England. Fascinating—terrifying—and potentially overwhelming. But the Rankin sisters from Montana refused to be overwhelmed. They would go on working.

Jeannette took Edna to many places off the beaten track. One of these was the British rest site, or summer retreat, of Almora, situated over six thousand feet high in the mountains, where Jeannette had been a recent summer guest of friends. Here Edna was up before six o'clock one morning to watch the sunrise over the jagged peaks of the distant Himalayas. The swelling light, growing from a faint pink blush to a rosy flood and finally to a full crescendo of daylight, was one of the most unforgettable sights she had ever experienced. It came almost as a sublime prelude to a fearful test.

The next day, on the drive down the steep mountain road from Almora, Edna suddenly said, "Jeannette, I can't see!" Both of them were seized by alarm.

Her blindness at first was total. After a short while, however, she realized that part of her vision was returning. Only her right eye was affected. She could see, if somewhat imperfectly, out of the left eye. Back in New Delhi, Jeannette decided that since they knew no doctor in the vicinity, it might be advisable for Edna to wait for any diagnosis or treatment until she was back at home. The dread mishap that haunts every traveler— serious illness far from familiar surroundings—had befallen Edna.

The swiftness and finality of the blow to her vision tested Edna's deep religious faith and her naturally high spirits. She thought of the sight of the morning sun on the Himalayas, one of the final scenes she had beheld. She reconsidered her sense of frustration over the way the members of the IPPF had disregarded her in Bombay. Could this rudeness have contributed to her trouble? She thought of her bright and talented daughter, of her many faithful friends in Chicago and of the work yet to be done, and of how distressed each of these people would be by her plight.

Cutting short the visit in India, she returned to Chicago, haunted by the possibility of something happening to her one good eye. An oculist diagnosed her trouble as a detached retina. Deciding against an operation, which the doctor did not recommend without serious reservation, Edna adjusted her habits and actions—but not her life—to the loss of half her vision. She would forge ahead.

She met the full schedule of talks which had been arranged in the Chicago area about the Bombay conference and her subsequent visit in India. She carried on her full load of work for the Chicago planned parenthood organization. Except when her brother, Wellington, in odd and cruel attempts at humor, occasionally referred to her right eye, Edna managed during the rest of her life to forget this misfortune. And because she overcame any urge for self-pity or self-consciousness there were no reminders to make friends or strangers uneasy. In fact, most of them never knew of any trouble with her eyes. She took this loss as she had taken others and put it behind her. She would not let it distract her from work or discourage further travels.

Her aims in Chicago continued along the lines she had already established. How and where could a larger number of birth control clinics be opened to reach an increasing number of people? How could doctors be moved to volunteer more advice and information to their female patients who needed or wanted birth control assistance? How could ugly rumors and whispering campaigns, the most destructive of all propaganda devices, be swiftly and effectively scotched? How could financial support and necessary leadership be ensured on a long-term basis? Above all, how could more people be made aware of the individual needs, the world need, for family planning, for defusing the population bomb?

With the efficient office assistance of Chieko Hata, the small, quick girl of Japanese parentage who had answered Edna's early advertisement for a secretary and remained through the years to assume increasing responsibility, Edna and her able board welded the Planned Parenthood Association of the Chicago Area into a force to be reckoned with.

She maintained an appearance of dauntless optimism and stylish taste. Her hats—often purchased in the early hours of an annual sale held by one of Chicago's most fashionable and expensive milliners—remained so famous that she could be identified on a flight from Chicago to Louisville.

"I'm waiting for a woman wearing the maddest hat you ever saw."

"Yes. She sat in the second section just behind me."

On such a visit to the Tachaus in Louisville, Edna could no

longer sit cross-legged on a great four-poster bed and play cards with the children. The children were now grown. But she did play gin rummy with Charles Tachau, and when glaucoma impaired his eyesight and his sense of good humor, Edna could say, "You're going to have to stop using this glaucoma, Charlie. You've worn Jean out, and if you're planning to have an operation you should go ahead and stop worrying everyone." His acceptance of her outspoken advice indicated how closely she moved in their inner family circle.

But the Chicago work was taking its toll. Frustrations and disappointments delayed work that seemed to Edna more than urgent—in fact, long overdue. In addition, there was the attitude that had assailed, on so many occasions, her personal dignity and ebullient effectiveness. Difficult to describe, its reality was as tangible as a crystal glass barrier, a cellophane wall. It involved a discrepancy in attitudes toward paid workers in the planned parenthood movement and those who were volunteers. That discrepancy was symbolized in Dr. Gamble's "a mere—" meaning "a mere worker," but at every turn there were those ready to emphasize the gulf of caste between those whose time was paid for and those whose time was given. Reduced to its bluntest terms, it was the distinction some wished to make between the employers and the hired help.

Among Edna's friends were those belonging to some of the most distinguished social and industrial families of the Chicago area. As informal, first-name friends, she did not want to identify them by their power or prestige; and yet on certain occasions, at unexpected moments, the feeling emerged: there was a difference between "staff" and volunteers, and it was a difference of inequality. Such moments revived her sense of painful childhood inferiority to her older sister and brother, when she had often wanted to fail, to be ill, or to be incompetent so that Jeannette and Wellington would notice her, give her affection and attention.

Remembrance of this role of the underling had kept her keenly sensitive to the feelings of those who were volunteers; from the earliest days, in every way she knew, she built up their importance and tried to diminish her own. She appeared in few publicity pictures; her ideas were distributed over someone else's signature. Skillfully and subtly, she built up others—at her own expense.

But this did not mean that she was immune to the snobbery based on false values, as all snobbery must be. An aristocrat in the truest sense of the word, Edna Rankin McKinnon could walk with anyone of any age, race, sex, class, nationality, or profession—and never be less than herself or make the other person less. Yet those who could claim only the shaky superiority of money were often rude in the most casual, perhaps unintentional, ways. She had felt the sting of that rudeness from some of Margaret Sanger's innermost circle of friends, from certain members of the Planned Parenthood Federation hierarchy, and now even from some of her beloved friends in Chicago. Money was not only an insulator, it could also breed callouses.

There was also the frustration arising from the chasm between technology and attitude. Attitudes toward birth control were changing, and Edna could see the fruits of her own work there. But the technology of birth control—methods, doctors' training and their willingness to lead in the careful, medical use of birth control—lagged far behind. Edna sometimes felt she was beating against an impervious barrier.

Edna remembered Dr. Gamble's dictum that no one should stay too long in the same place. From October 1946 until mid-1958 she had been in Chicago. During that time, the Association had tripled in size and increased its budget seven-fold. Clinics had been opened in most of the hospitals, although Edna had despaired of the gulf between what they were doing and what they should be doing. And the public had been made aware that a movement for planned parenthood, birth control, family planning—call it by whatever name—*did* exist. The organization was on its way, and perhaps she should be on *her* way.

With emotions as mixed as her reasons for the decision, she resigned. Some of those with whom she worked felt that the world came to an end when she departed. While the forcefulness of her personality and the drive of her purpose had undoubtedly alienated a few incompatible spirits, there were none who wished to deny that Edna left behind the stamp and impetus of her unforgettable magnetism and unquenchable enthusiasm. Perhaps it was all summed up in a single small incident. One day in the middle of Edna's years in Chicago, Grace Nuveen returned home from a board meeting of the Chicago Planned Parenthood Association. "I won't work like a slave for Edna McKinnon any longer," she vowed to her husband. "I will not be driven by her to do more than I can."

Her husband quietly replied, "Isn't that why you hired her?"

When the news of Edna's departure from Chicago became public, two old friends—Eleanor Pillsbury and Jane Canfield—approached Edna about an important new task to be done. Mrs. Pillsbury's husband was a member of the famous Minneapolis flour family. Years before, their company had not yielded to threats of boycott when Eleanor Pillsbury assumed prominent leadership in birth control work in Minnesota and the nation. Both her work and the company had survived and grown. Mrs. Cass Canfield's husband, president of Harper and Brothers publishers, was chairman of the IPPF and a long-time leader in the birth control cause. These two women wanted Edna to accept the challenge of helping publicize and implement the Draper Report, especially among United States Congressmen.

This report was named for General William H. Draper, Jr., who had served as chairman of a committee appointed by President Eisenhower to evaluate the effectiveness of United States foreign economic aid. The third part of the report, published in 1959, discussed population control as an important, indeed critical, aspect of foreign aid and economic growth. No other official government report had ever taken a stand on birth control, and therefore the Draper Report made news—and controversy.

Edna recognized the report's potential as a means of real breakthrough on the whole subject of birth control. She accepted the persuasive offers of the Planned Parenthood Federation to promote the report, under the direction of William Vogt, executive director of the Federation, who had sounded one of the earliest alarms on population in his book, *The Road to Survival*.

Edna moved to New York and set to work studying every detail of the report and planning approaches which might secure congressional attention and support. But the Draper Report was destined to languish. President Eisenhower rejected its recommendations on population and said that the United States Government should stay away from birth control. The Catholic bishops denounced any possible governmental implementation of the report's warnings and suggestions. The Planned Parenthood Federation withdrew Edna's assignment. She helped gather a National Clergymen's Advisory Committee until her six months' contract expired. Again, she felt both thwarted and satisfied: pleased that she had been able to make any contribution at all to the use of this landmark document; unhappy that its urgent message would not be acted upon immediately.

During her stay in New York, Edna came close to embarking on another venture. An executive in one of the country's largest electrical manufacturing companies, a leader in Ivy League educational circles, handsome and righteous, was fascinated by Edna—and she by him. They enjoyed being together, and when he asked her to marry him, she decided to accept. Misgivings crept in when she learned that he had discussed the possibility of their marriage with his minister, who had decided he couldn't perform the ceremony because Edna was divorced—and then had taken the matter to the bishop, who said, after hearing a description of Edna, "Marry her right now."

As they actually approached marriage, small revelations of their differences in habit and thought assumed larger importance. The final straw was small indeed: a pair of gloves. Edna's fiancé could not find the kind of gloves he wanted for the wedding. She went shopping with him on several fruitless searches—until the humor, the triviality, the absurdity of the whole enterprise overwhelmed her. She could not spend her life adjusting to such inconsequentials; she was not sure he could adjust to the things she believed of consequence. Amicably, with a mutual sense of regret and respect, they broke off wedding plans.

Edna also decided that at age sixty-six she was finished with any work in family planning—it had not been as great as she could wish, but it had not been inconsiderable either. Back in

Montana, where her daughter was now living with her husband, an English professor, and their two talented sons, Edna could fulfill some lifelong plans. The first of those plans was to go with a friend on a leisurely journey around the world. There would be long visits to lovely Kashmir, to Kandy, which she remembered so happily from her Bombay trip, and to other exotic places that might attract their attention along the way.

Before Edna left for Montana, Clarence and Sarah Gamble took her to dinner at the Ritz-Carleton Hotel in Boston. Several months earlier, they had invited her to their hospitable home in Milton, where she had often visited in the past, and had introduced her to Margaret Roots, whom Gamble had met at the Bombay conference, and Edith Gates. Both women were working for birth control in foreign countries. Now Dr. Gamble wanted to ask Edna to undertake a job for the Pathfinder Fund. One subject upon which Dr. Gamble and Edna had always agreed was the inconsequence of her age. Her sixties were no more subdued, no less productive, than her twenties and thirties. Why not disregard the fact that she would soon be seventy? If Edna wanted to travel, why not for the Pathfinder Fund?

Dr. Gamble had established the Pathfinder Fund in 1958 to continue his previous work of introducing family planning in places outside the United States where no efforts at effective birth control existed. Its name defined the fund's role—it would open paths for others to follow and develop. And the Gambles believed that Edna would be a great pathfinder abroad, as she had been at home.

After thanking them for their confidence, Edna declined, describing her leisurely plans for the year ahead.

"You'll be bored to extinction on that trip," Dr. Gamble warned. "You can't just visit in those foreign lands without any purpose."

"Oh, no, I'll love it," Edna replied.

"You'll hate it." After a pause he asked, "Would you rather work for the International Planned Parenthood Federation than our Pathfinder Fund?"

Edna said no. Part of Edna's refusal was prompted by her

ambivalent feeling toward Clarence Gamble. In Chicago she had learned the importance of strong organization; yet from all that she knew of his work in the United States and all that she had heard of his work abroad, she was aware that Dr. Gamble often avoided the orthodox organizations. Some of his enemies—and they were numerous and vocal in the in-fighting that afflicted the birth control movement—argued that he subverted other organizations and called him a troublemaker.

Yet—Edna's interest in Asia and other distant continents had been stirred by the Bombay conference, which she never would have attended without his prompting and advice. She also knew from her earlier experience of Dr. Gamble's work in the South and across the United States that his Pathfinder Fund might have virtues not found in other organizations. The more she considered his offer, the more she reconsidered her refusal.

Edna came back to him with her own proposition. She would go ahead with the proposed trip with her friend, but along the way she would visit various projects sponsored by the Pathfinder Fund to see whether the criticisms she had heard of Dr. Gamble—especially from the IPPF—were valid. She would also try to assess how well each Pathfinder project was fulfilling its purpose.

Dr. Gamble agreed. "I'll give you the names of the people with whom we've worked in various countries. And I'd like it if you could send me reports. Otherwise, you will be completely separate from me. I'll be glad to buy your ticket and pay your expenses as far as Singapore," he offered.

"If you did that," Edna told Dr. Gamble, "I'd be able to take my daughter, too. We could go together, with my friend, but I would not be in your formal employ."

Dr. Gamble offered one other suggestion. Mrs. Constance Goh Koh Kee, an eminently wealthy and influential lady from Singapore who served as head of planned parenthood work in the Southeast Asia region, was visiting in New York. "Why don't you go and talk with her and ask if you can work as a volunteer in Singapore while you're visiting there? It would give you a chance to know the country and I'm sure she could find plenty for you to do."

Thus Edna called on Constance Goh Koh Kee, whom she had first met in Singapore and Bombay, a sophisticated Chinese woman ready to welcome the offer of a volunteer assistant. She immediately began to make plans for what Edna might do in Manila, Saigon, Hong Kong, and Singapore. The old challenge reasserted its pull; Edna felt a tide of energy rising to meet it. The Gambles had been right: this was the way to see the world, with a purpose, meeting people who were making a difference in their country's life. She and Mrs. Goh Koh Kee parted with mutual assurances of friendship and plans for future meetings in Mrs. Goh's home.

Edna returned to Montana where she was stunned by the sudden death of the very friend with whom she had planned to take this trip. She and Dorothy would go ahead, however.

It was the first step in travels that were to take her far in space, in time, and in achievement. All the positive thrust and sensitivity of Edna's nature, all the knowledge and skill of her experience, were to culminate in her adventures with the Pathfinder Fund during the decade of the 1960s.

7

Less than five dollars invested in population control is worth a hundred dollars invested in economic growth.

—President Lyndon B. Johnson

The only way we can preserve and nurture other and more precious freedoms is by relinquishing the freedom to breed, and that very soon.

—Garrett Hardin,
Planned Parenthood News, May 1969

Pathfinder was to open paths, not reach final destinations.

—Edna McKinnon

O<small>NE QUALITY NECESSARY</small> for birth control work, as Edna had long since discovered, was adaptability. This was no field for pompous stuffed shirts or rigid bureaucrats. Edna's initial traumatic experience in her overseas Pathfinder work was a misunderstanding resulting from just such inflexibility in an organization which seemed more jealous of its hierarchy than zealous in its cause. The episode left lasting scars on Edna's memory and on the family planning cause in Southeast Asia. It occurred at the end of her very first survey trip in 1960 and changed the direction of her work in Asia.

Ironically enough, the immediate misunderstanding arose from the old dichotomy between volunteers and paid workers, but the underlying cause was rooted in unresolved differences between Dr. Clarence Gamble and the functioning of his Pathfinder Fund, and the large, prestigious International Planned Parenthood Federation with its more conventional methods of work and procedure. With the population bomb exploding around the world—so momentous a challenge to meet and so comparatively few to work on it—differences and quarrels among groups dedicated to similar goals seemed an extravagant waste of time, energy, and money. But Edna was caught between conflicting forces. She never failed to defend and appreciate the pioneer work and unique contribution of Dr. Gamble, but her sense of fairness made her understand that his unpredictable and unorthodox ways of operating could often frustrate many associates. In fact, she herself sometimes felt she was the victim of his unique approach to people and to problems.

A disastrous example of this was his failure to mention to

Mrs. Constance Goh Koh Kee, after he sent Edna to meet her and her companion, Mrs. Amstutz, in New York, that he knew anything about Edna's plans to travel or work as a volunteer in Singapore and the surrounding area. Likewise, he did not divulge to Edna that he, too, had seen Mrs. Goh Koh Kee and Mrs. Amstutz at their New York hotel and that he had promised Mrs. Goh a grant for work in the Southeast Asia Planned Parenthood Association, of which she was president.

In addition, because of IPPF distrust of Dr. Gamble, Edna and Dr. Gamble had agreed that she would be completely disassociated from him during the 1960 trip with Dorothy. He was paying for her transportation but she was not formally in his employ and she would be free to make such judgments as she wished about Pathfinder projects and the IPPF programs. As a volunteer worker under Mrs. Goh Koh Kee's direction, she would meet leaders in various parts of the Southeast Asia region. Dr. Gamble even had some cards printed with her name and a title—Representative of the Southeast Asian Region of the International Planned Parenthood Federation—and her address at the Planned Parenthood clinic in Singapore.

With the cards and a two months' itinerary Mrs. Goh Koh Kee had helped arrange, and with an eager Dorothy by her side, Edna set forth on her new adventure.

All went well at first. As they visited countries and programs in various stages of development, Edna felt that she was returning to an earlier period in her own work, when she had learned through trial and error lessons she believed might be useful here on the other side of the world. Start with a positive attitude (a "No" answer was no answer); reach the top echelons of leadership so that the public would have confidence in the idea of family planning right from its inception; build up strong lay support for the leaders; approach both leaders and public with an idea they could accept (if not population control, with its impersonal overtones, then maternal and child care and happiness, which would benefit everyone).

In Tokyo, Taipei, Manila, Hong Kong, Saigon, Bangkok, and Kuala Lumpur, she and Dorothy were greeted by governmental, educational, and social leaders. Everywhere Edna visited clinics, spoke at luncheons, dinners, and public gatherings, interviewed medical personnel and volunteers in various family planning programs, and evaluated the strengths and weaknesses of each situation. Wherever the place, whatever the situation, Edna's attitude toward those she met was similar to that of her fellow countryman Will Rogers, who said he never met a man he didn't like. Edna never encountered a people she didn't like; and her new Oriental friends charmed her— especially the solemn, friendly children.

Outside of Hong Kong, at an unusual community called Rennie's Mill, Edna observed a project, financed by Dr. Gamble, of house-to-house visitation and research in birth control. Out of some four hundred families in Rennie's Mill, three hundred and fifty-four had accepted birth control assistance. Edna was emphatic in her approval of the two local nurses who worked at Rennie's Mill and in her recommendation to Dr. Gamble that the undertaking should be supported for another two years.

One of Dr. Gamble's rules, perhaps the only really inflexible one, was that he would never finance a project for longer than one year at a time. This aroused the wrath of workers in many programs seeking his aid, especially when there was need for a sense of continuity and security, although during all of Edna's experience she never saw Dr. Gamble abandon any program that was showing real progress or results. His one-year rule prevented over-commitment to projects that might prove untenable, but his good judgment dictated continued support of any program that could eventually be taken over by one of the larger foundations or by the local people themselves.

Perhaps the effort at Rennie's Mill was made doubly impressive because she witnessed it at a time of growing frustration. Despite all of the official activities, Edna and Dorothy were still vulnerable before the human degradation of the thousands they had seen swarming in the alleys of Hong Kong and exploding in the slums of Manila. And in Saigon they experienced the strongest sense of failure.

The lovely capital city of Vietnam, with its spacious French colonial architecture and its gracious people, had not yet been degraded by war and gave only slight reminders at this time that conflict was raging nearby. Dinner on a floating restaurant opposite their hotel introduced Edna and Dorothy to many savory delicacies wrapped in grape leaves. A visit to the home of the American ambassador made them aware of the communication gap existing between American officialdom and the Vietnamese people. But it was at a luncheon that an educated Vietnamese woman pleaded for information, with tears in her eyes.

"My sister is dying of tuberculosis," she explained. "She has three children and another pregnancy will kill her. Isn't there anything you can do to help her?"

Edna could not reply. The answer lay in her head, in her reach, but the grip of old French laws and the Catholic cadres of Ngo Dinh Diem prevented her giving any help to this pleading woman—and to others around the table who waited expectantly, patiently.

In this encounter both Edna and Dorothy experienced a desolate sense of inadequacy—made more bitter by awareness of the fact that similar incidents would be reenacted in many places through the many years to come. They felt much as Margaret Sanger must have felt when Sadie Sachs begged for help in a New York slum a generation earlier.

Some of their encounters mixed humor with pathos. In Kuala Lumpur the local family planning group gathered all of its budget to organize one impressive gala for the visitors. The result was a night club production complete with a floor show which seemed intended to achieve results directly opposite to family planning! For once, Edna found no opportunity whatsoever for introducing the subject of birth control. She felt humiliated and frustrated by the squandered opportunity and funds.

During these travels, two particularly interesting men became Edna's friends: Dr. Yoshio Koya and Mr. Jimmy Yen. Dr. Koya, director of Tokyo's Health and Welfare Department, had been one of the earliest Japanese leaders to seek new postwar solutions to his country's population dilemma. In 1947 he had approached Dr. Gamble about support for a research project to determine Japanese attitudes toward family planning. Dr. Gamble and Dr. Koya devised a plan by which individual and family attitudes could be studied in three different kinds of villages: one on the sea coast, one in the lowlands, and one in the mountains. At the Bombay conference in 1952 Dr. Koya had reported on the conspicuous decline in the birth rate in those villages and on the accumulation of positive proof that the Japanese people was ready for birth control.

By the time of Edna's visit in 1960, Dr. Koya's accuracy in interpreting his countrymen's attitudes had been demonstrated. Government programs had provided legal sanction to make Japan a demographic phenomenon of the twentieth century, reversing its birth rate from 33.5 per 1,000 in 1948 to 17 in 1957. But he shared with Edna his concern over the number of abortions. His effort turned not toward outlawing abortion but toward educating the public about its drawbacks and ill effects compared with family planning. To Edna, Dr. Koya exemplified governmental leadership of the highest order.

Dr. Jimmy Yen had led several lives before arriving in Manila. Edna had first met him at the Evanston home of the John Leslies when she was director of the Planned Parenthood Association in Chicago. Dr. Yen's mass education movement in China had met with incredible success before he went to Taiwan and established the Joint Commission on Rural Reconstruction. This work he turned over to the Provisional Government when he moved on to the Philippines. Here he had begun a four-point program of livelihood, literacy, health, and self-government in the barrios, or villages.

Dr. Yen was now head of the Philippine Rural Reconstruction Organization and was carefully but surely seeking to promote family planning activities in this predominantly Roman Catholic country. Edna welcomed the opportunity to visit with him two of the barrios where his work was taking hold. At one of these barrios, Edna was fascinated as she watched the young man who was in charge of the community financial program. The people asked him for advice on spending or saving and on what products were the thriftiest purchases. He was investment counselor and consumer advocate in one.

Jimmy Yen spoke, too, of his desire for a college to train young leaders for the villages, natives who would return to their familiar areas and work as equals in partnership with the rural people. His ambition resembled that of a few leaders in the southern Appalachian region of the United States from which a million people had migrated during the decade of the 1950s.

Edna made the most of the beautiful dinner party hosted by Dr. and Mrs. Yen. Among their guests were influential Catholics as well as those of other religious beliefs, two successful professional women who were not hesitant about speaking out on the urgent need for birth control, and prominent citizens from government, medicine, education, and other related fields. This was just the sort of personal-impersonal occasion Edna enjoyed utilizing to its fullest potential. Conversation was animated, there was genuine exchange of ideas, and all those participating, including the host and hostess, seemed a bit amazed at the interest in family planning exhibited by everyone present.

Edna extended her effort in the Philippines. Under her prodding it was discovered that the Philippine Federation of Christian Churches had been studying family planning for three years. After two encouraging meetings under Edna's influence, plans were laid for a clinic and a budget. Preparations were made to submit a request for funds to Mrs. Goh Koh Kee, the regional director who had authorized Edna to promise help if there seemed any real possibility for progress in the Philippines.

Filled with information, plans, and enthusiasm, Edna arrived in Singapore toward the end of October. Mrs. Goh Koh Kee welcomed Edna and Dorothy to the crowded crossroads metropolis of Southeast Asia with its nearly two million people, its busy port, and its mixture of races and cultures from every corner of the world. Enjoying the luxurious Cathay Hotel, Edna and Dorothy became sightseers in the "city of the lion," fascinated by its color and variety.

Early the following week they parted, Dorothy to continue her trip around the world and to return to her family in Montana, Edna to stay behind for as long as her volunteer services in Singapore might be desired. First, she wanted to find a less pretentious place to stay. On Orange Grove Road she located a pleasant guest house with many windows and a veranda with a trellis covered by dainty yellow flowers on a climbing vine where her tea could be served and where she could enjoy a restful vista of green grass, large trees, and shrubbery.

With Mrs. Goh Koh Kee, Edna found herself caught up in a round of social activities where she was cast in the role of those volunteers who had at times in the past aroused her pride and temper. To Edna it seemed that Mrs. Goh's accomplishments as a hostess were both an asset and a drawback to her leadership in the family planning program. Generous hospitality often made teas or dinner parties prevail over basic organization. The clinics under her direction were well run, with professional help, but they had little sustained basis of support within the larger community. As Edna became more familiar with the situation, she began to understand that a paid executive who could work throughout Singapore and Malaya would coordinate and strengthen this potentially productive situation.

Edna began to formulate plans for securing such an executive, enlarging the budget for clinics, and broadening the work.

"Don't go too fast," her friend Mrs. Goh Koh Kee advised. "Give us time—"

And Edna tried to comply. With the support and cooperation of Mrs. Amstutz and Mrs. Marjorie Butcher, experienced local leaders in the work, she continued observing and suggesting. Mrs. Butcher, as the wife of an English resident, was able to share with Edna much of her knowledge of Southeast Asia and to impress on her the need for trained workers and more money for family planning. She and Edna spent many hours formulating plans for progress, during which Edna's experience in Chicago proved valuable. Mrs. Goh Koh Kee seemed pleased with their effort.

In the midst of this auspicious beginning a British member of the board of directors of the International Planned Parenthood Federation arrived in Singapore with his wife. VIPs, and very conscious of their status, they were making the grand tour of Far Eastern birth control projects and had already found Edna's footprints preceding them at several points. They were distinctly annoyed to be walking along any paths blazed by Clarence Gamble. In fact, it was the hostility they displayed which made Edna reluctant to mention that Dr. Gamble had even so much as paid her travel fare for this trip.

When the IPPF official and his wife, en route from the Raffles Hotel where Edna had picked them up to take them to tea at Mrs. Goh's, inquired bluntly if Edna were in Dr. Gamble's employ, she was taken aback and hastily answered, "No." Technically she was telling the truth, but as she was aware during the rest of the uncomfortable afternoon, the miserable night, and the week to follow, it was only a half-truth.

During the following days, as she worked with the Englishman on plans and budgets for the region, she also struggled to close the rift between his organization and Clarence Gamble. She wrote Dr. Gamble: "The thing that is so annoying is that both of you may be in the category of spoiled rich men's sons. Each of you wants your own way to a certain extent. But I'm convinced that each of you honestly wants planned parenthood to succeed."

It was means rather than ends that were causing the division, she informed Dr. Gamble. "Coordinated planning on *how* to make family planning available throughout the world is essential and the framework of national associations helps greatly."

Edna had learned in Chicago the value of strong organization. On the other hand, she had learned in her field work across the country the value of extracurricular efforts. "The setting up of little projects here, there, and everywhere as you have done them are the best things that have been done—and without them I say they can't lay the foundations. But why not *both?*"

Her role of arbiter was cut short when she decided that regardless of what the reaction might be, she must tell the IPPF director and Mrs. Goh Koh Kee the exact details of her arrangement with Dr. Gamble. She was hardly prepared for the storm which broke around her.

Accusing Edna of dishonesty and Dr. Gamble of subterfuge, the Englishman promptly advised Mrs. Goh Koh Kee that Edna was not a bountiful volunteer but a hired employee of Dr. Gamble. He suggested that Edna's ultimate goal might be to take over Mrs. Goh's job as director of regional family planning work. The latter's warm favor abruptly turned to icy rejection. She felt deceived by both Edna and Dr. Gamble.

There was also the unspoken matter of status: Mrs. Goh Koh Kee had been entertaining "a mere" worker as if she were a prestigious donor of her time and effort.

The heart of the conflict, however, lay in the continuing animosity of the IPPF toward Dr. Gamble and his insubordinate, free-wheeling, innovative Pathfinder Fund. While Pathfinder conceived of itself as a trailblazer, opening areas of the world where there had been little or no previous birth control work, financing initial approaches to discover which might be most successful, the International Planned Parenthood Federation accused Pathfinder of starting projects it did not finish and passing the responsibilities on to the larger organization. There were related problems of procedure and funds. The differences between the two organizations seemed to have deteriorated into really ugly institutional in-fighting. Edna was furious with Dr. Gamble for having placed her in such an ambiguous role, a twilight zone where anything she said might be half-true and half-untrue and neither would be convincing to strangers, especially strangers already conditioned to be antagonistic.

Southeast Asia had aroused Edna's interest and imagination. She wanted to remain long enough to make some impression on the region, to leave behind her a contribution that would permanently advance the cause of family planning. Now, in an outburst of anger, Mrs. Goh Koh Kee invited Edna to leave Singapore. Within a few days, she reconsidered and said to Edna, "You won't leave us, will you?"

Across the Singapore Strait, accessible to the metropolis of Singapore by a causeway, was a smaller city called Johore Bahru. Not long after her arrival in Southeast Asia Edna had visited there and found the nucleus of a good program with the possibility for a research project that could have consequences throughout Asia. The place was fascinating and the people had been extraordinarily cordial.

In Singapore the atmosphere remained tense and suspicious. Edna felt that her usefulness there was seriously impaired. Why not move the seventeen miles from Singapore to Johore Bahru? Following the dictates of her own sensitivity, which had been so mangled and betrayed in the recent incident, Edna discussed her plan with Mrs. Goh Koh Kee. The latter agreed that this would be an appropriate move, and suggested that after Johore Bahru, there were other places in the region where Edna might apply her talents. Mrs. Goh's irritation had softened considerably, but the attitude of the IPPF hierarchy seemed to have hardened.

Edna and Dr. Gamble worked out a new arrangement, one in which Edna became a paid visible member of the Pathfinder Fund field staff; yet the hostility of the IPPF remained. It would surface in small, disconcerting ways during the coming years. In a few instances its influence would be of major and negative significance.

From this time on, Edna was determined that such internecine jousts would not deter her from her work. At international and regional conferences in India and in Singapore, because of her association with the controversial Dr. Gamble, she was pointedly snubbed—sometimes by old associates and friends—carefully frozen out of deliberations in which she could have given and received valuable help. In certain communities and countries she discovered that local leaders who wished to be cooperative and friendly (and receive Pathfinder assistance) had been told that they must choose between the IPPF and Pathfinder. Edna invariably advised such groups to choose the larger organization, of course, and often helped beginning local groups formulate the plans and appeals that would bring admission to the IPPF and secure its financial support.

During these years her loyalty to Clarence Gamble did not waver, but increased. She went into country after country and encountered at the daily village level the limitations of a large organization that had no field workers but tried to carry out programs through central staff and local volunteers. No matter how able these were, the smaller and more agile Pathfinder Fund could be more responsive to immediate needs and problems. If, for example, the IPPF required that membership be requested by a country desiring its help—how could that country ask for help (or even know of its availability) without the elementary, introductory efforts of some group such as Pathfinder? Personally Edna believed that both IPPF and the Pathfinder organization, as well as other groups working for the same cause, had important roles to fill. She cared more for the success of planned parenthood as a whole than the success of any single agency. Whichever one she worked through, she would give it her best and overcome obstacles, real or artificial, natural or man-made.

During the next decade, her work did not seem to proceed chronologically but geographically. Her life divided itself not so much into months and years as into cities and countries. She went into Malaya, Indonesia, Fiji, and Tonga; Iran and Turkey; Saudi Arabia, Kuwait, and Jordan; and into four countries of Africa. She left each, only to return again—and sometimes again and again. Each became an entity in her experience—not in terms of dates, but in terms of what she found and what she brought to each place and people.

8

Familiarity breeds children.

—Mark Twain

In the first sixty years of this century the world's population has doubled, and we can look forward to a second doubling before the year 2000.

—Georg Borgstom,
The Hungry Planet

I N JANUARY 1961, Edna moved from swarming Singapore to the city of Johore Bahru, capital of Johore, southernmost state of Malaya. The move was in several ways a symbol of both defeat and victory.

Initial rapport with Constance Goh Koh Kee, head of the Planned Parenthood Federation for all of Southeast Asia, had been shattered and any constructive working relationship with the International Planned Parenthood Federation seemed out of the question at that moment. Edna's best efforts toward fence mending had failed. She was convinced that changes or advances she had suggested based on information and advice from Mrs. Amstutz, Mrs. Butcher, and others would greatly strengthen the work throughout the whole region; but with her motives under suspicion she could only follow the advice Mrs. Goh had given her in friendlier days and "go more slowly."

If she seemed a threat to some, there were others, however, to whom she appeared a blessing. On the day in mid-January when she arrived in Johore Bahru, she was greeted by Mrs. Eileen Kwok and Mrs. Renee Lowe with an offering of exquisite orchids. These two women, along with Dr. E. C. Pink, an English physician who had lived in Malaya many years with his Chinese wife, were leaders in the local birth control program. It was evident that they welcomed Edna's know-how and enthusiasm. Renee Lowe, of French and English descent, was married to a wealthy Malayan; Eileen Kwok, wife of a successful Chinese industrialist, was herself Chinese; both were cultured women dedicated to the improvement of their country through planned parenthood. They and Dr. Pink filled Edna with renewed hope for all that needed to be done.

Once again she believed she could win out over misunderstanding and discouragement. But with each new beginning in a new country, she experienced the old familiar apprehensions and tensions: the sense of inferiority implanted long before; fear of failure, nurtured by the rejection in Singapore that resembled in some aspects the traumatic rejection of her very first birth control effort in Montana. The only way she knew to abolish these fears was through work.

Malaya, to which she turned her total attention, was a challenge to all her talents and faith. A lush green country three-quarters of which was covered by tropical rain forests, its rich alluvial plains along the western coast were bounded by a mountainous inland laced with rivers, streams, and deep gorges. The variety of its scenery was duplicated by the diversity of its people. About half of the more than seven million inhabitants of the long, narrow peninsula were Malays; perhaps a third were Chinese; and Indians, mostly from Ceylon and southern India, formed the next largest group. In addition there were Eurasians, Europeans (mostly British), and a half-dozen indigenous groups including an aboriginal tribe inhabiting the central jungles.

While the Malay language and the Muslim religion predominated, there was the Mandarin of educated Chinese and numerous Chinese dialects, along with the Tamil spoken by the Indian population; and the Buddhist, Taoist, and Christian religions. Due to a century and a quarter of British influence, the common language widely used in hotels, offices, shops, and many commercial and social enterprises was English.

With the Indian Ocean on its western edge and the South China Sea on the east, Malay was a productive land of plantations growing more than a third of the world's rubber, mining the world's largest exports of tin, and cultivating rice, pineapple, and oil palms. Moreover, for Edna it was a fabled realm of childhood legends about the Sultan of Johore. It was also a country self-conscious and confident in its new nationhood, only recently freed from the so-called Emergency (it was pronounced with the accent on the third syllable) of the Communist guerrilla terrorism, and from generations of British domination.

In this charged atmosphere of change and progress involving many races, religions, and cultures, Edna sought to develop the cause of birth control. Two random facts suggest some of the background of attitudes against which she labored: one of the recent sultans had had forty-three children—unplanned parenthood run wild! And there was a Chinese phrase, "mui tsai," used to describe girls in their teens or younger who had been sold by their families into domestic service, which often included prostitution. Outlawing this form of slavery could not so quickly eradicate the low value set on life, female life especially. But balanced against such holdovers from a harsh past were the freshness and the eagerness for a better country that Edna found among the majority of people everywhere.

In Johore Bahru the daughter-in-law of the Sultan, Che Khalsom, arranged for Edna to live at the Government Rest House. This was a type of small hotel created by the British wherever they colonized so that their officials might find comfortable accommodations on vacations or on official rounds of duty. Now, of course, it was run by the Malayan Government, but there was still strong evidence of the British presence—especially at teatime and in the rugby field to be seen from several of the windows which overlooked the strait. Food at the Rest House was good, the frequent breezes refreshing, and the mosquito netting plentiful.

The hospitality of Johore Bahru was embodied in the person of Che Khalsom, who came to call soon after Edna arrived. During a conversation which lasted two hours, Edna learned that this intelligent, personable young English member of the royal family was not simply a figurehead president of her state family planning association, but a keenly interested leader. Her mother-in-law, the Sultana, royal patron of the association, also demonstrated her support by immediately giving a luncheon for Edna.

The luncheon was an interesting affair where, for once, the people—wives of some of Johore's leading citizens—were less fascinating to Edna than the surroundings. After all, it wasn't an everyday event for her to be entertained in one of the great Istana (palaces) of the Sultan of Johore by the Sultana herself. The feeling was a bit like eating in a museum, surrounded by elaborately designed, inlaid screens, silver ornaments, carvings in jade, and all manner of treasures—except for one article. The single exception to the sumptuous appointments was a row of lamps scattered down the length of the long table. Uncoordinated in color or design, useless due to a lack of bulbs, they sat in odd contrast to every other fantastic detail of the decor. Edna was at first startled and then amused at this paradoxical little glimpse of her new world. She was not one to miss a detail. Details could provide clues to larger subjects.

Pathfinder and Edna had two general goals in Malaya. One was to encourage and enlarge any existing birth control clinics and to initiate new clinics wherever advisable; the second was to discover ways by which all the women in a community could be informed of the available clinic services and persuaded to use them.

A few years earlier the first planned parenthood work had begun in Malaya. It consisted of a loosely knit national organization with headquarters in the capital of Kuala Lumpur. Besides clinic services in that city, there were also centers in Ipoh, Malacca, and Johore Bahru. With little money and no paid workers (Dr. Gamble had sent Margaret Roots to encourage some of the earliest work), the groups were generally weak and severely limited in their outreach.

There were numerous reasons for the failure of women to seek out birth control advice. Edna soon became acquainted with those reasons that involved attitudes and those that arose out of physical circumstances. Among the latter she discovered that many women simply did not know of the clinic's existence; that they had no one with whom to leave their small children, if they did want to visit the clinic; and that they often lacked money either for car fare to get to the clinic or for birth control supplies if they did attend. Finally, they were reluctant to ask for anything that might be considered charity.

Even more decisive were attitudes. Women did not use family planning clinics because they were afraid of their husbands' or relatives' criticism if they initiated any steps toward contraception; because they were sometimes too busy, sometimes too shy, to leave home on a certain day at a certain hour to go to a strange place for help; because of the inherited outlook throughout Asia that the more children a couple produced the more fortune smiled on them and the better their chances of comfort in their old age; because of the feeling that it was women's "fate" to have babies and that some religious restriction forbade family planning; and lastly because of apathy, ignorance, or laziness—which seemed afflictions common to most countries and societies.

How could these obstacles be overcome? One problem facing the volunteer workers was basic: how could the most people be reached within the limitations of the community budget? Clinics alone had proved insufficient. The decision was made to launch a house-to-house experiment. A pilot study of this highly personal approach would be carried out for a year in Johore Bahru. Meanwhile, birth control efforts would also be extended to some of the large rubber plantations surrounding the city.

The personalized method of calling house-to-house in kampongs and selected districts throughout the city seemed to offer obstacles as well as advantages. The one most feared at the beginning was the mother-in-law. She was a powerful force in Oriental families and her hostility could block any effective results.

The skills and personalities of those who would carry out this home program became of decisive importance. After some search, a woman was found who apparently possessed all the necessary qualifications. A Chinese midwife with years of public health experience, she enjoyed a wide acquaintance among many groups of people, especially other health workers. A widow who had borne ten children, her main assets were warmth, gentleness and wisdom, and the fact that she spoke several Chinese dialects as well as Malay. It was evident that she could surmount formidable barriers. There were, however, two drawbacks: she knew no English and she could neither read nor write.

To overcome this handicap, a team was formed—its second member a young Malayan woman with secretarial experience, trained at the Family Planning Association in Singapore, who spoke English as well as her native language. This arrangement proved to be successful.

Introductory efforts were begun in some of the villages that had mushroomed around Johore Bahru during the resettlement of the Emergency period. In each village assistance district officers, as persons of authority, were approached to provide the proper sponsorship deemed necessary to overcome the shyness of the women in meeting strangers.

In this village work, Edna received new lessons in patience. Johore was a Muslim state and Fridays were observed as the Sabbath; therefore, government offices closed on Thursday afternoons and Fridays and opened on Saturdays and Sundays. Chinese citizens, however, did not work on Sundays. In addition, during February—the month when the work was begun—there were several Indian feast days and the Chinese New Year to be celebrated. Being Malay fast month also meant that few women would come out in public during the afternoons—but since many village workers were busy as weeders and tappers on the rubber plantations in the mornings, the visits of the family planning team had to be made in the afternoons.

Accommodating to all the various customs and religions, the team persisted. As they entered each village they went to the town council hall first. While people slowly began to gather—in increasing numbers as the work progressed and their visits were repeated during following months—they set forth a display of materials and leaflets. The mimeographed statement of the religious hierarchy stating that it was permissible for Muslims to practice family planning was distributed to those who could read with the hope that they would pass the information on to others. Timid and hesitant as wild birds, the women had to be coaxed to come close enough to talk, to examine the birth control supplies, and to accept them. Many were pregnant—but they listened eagerly to the news that they would not have to spend the rest of their lives in this condition. A woman who had borne twelve children already—six of whom had died—seemed more typical than remarkable. Sometimes a woman followed the team to their car so that she could speak privately with them.

As work in the villages progressed, house-to-house calls in Johore Bahru were begun. Apprehensions about the mothers-in-law soon disappeared as it became apparent that frequently they were more eager for their daughters-in-law to know about birth control than were the young wives themselves.

The home visits proved astonishingly successful. Bashful women who would emerge uneasily in public gatherings to learn the physical facts of conception or the methods of contraception, proud women who would never ask openly for help or materials, accepted in the privacy of their homes both education and supplies. The plan was to revisit each home monthly so that there would never be a lack of these supplies.

General misunderstanding about birth control proved enormous. One woman in a district on the edge of Johore Bahru came out each day the birth control team was in her neighborhood and shook her fist and muttered imprecations. A few months later she appeared one day at the clinic in the general hospital in Johore Bahru and explained that she had been angry at the family planning workers because she had used the foam tablets and they didn't work. Pressed more closely for an explanation, she admitted that she was already pregnant when she began using the tablets. But now she had had her baby—and wanted to give the foam tablets another chance.

There were real failures. Because the foam tablets tended to deteriorate rapidly in a damp atmosphere, the climate of Malaya made their storage and distribution a major problem. One woman who had accepted a diaphragm and jelly refused to talk with the family planning worker on a follow-up visit: she had been severely beaten by her mother, who opposed birth control. In certain town areas rumors arose that the medical team were really only sales ladies in the employ of drug manufacturers. Finally, there was the old power of word-of-mouth, for good or bad. No method could be guaranteed one hundred percent effective, and unfortunately those with whom a method failed, either through intrinsic flaws or the fault of the user, seemed to be considerably more vocal than those who were well satisfied with the results.

Birth control work on the rubber estates out in the country developed in two ways. First, a full-time, trained midwife carried instructions and supplies directly to the homes of plantation workers. Second, women were brought from their homes to the estate's central dispensary, where they received instructions and supplies.

Success at these estates seemed essential to real birth control progress in Malaya, for if rubber were the lifeblood of the country's economy, the people who produced the rubber were that economy's muscle.

Visiting at one plantation where the British manager and his wife lived high on a flower-covered hill over-looking the workers' village and rubber-processing plant in the distance, Edna was told of the constant efforts which were made to improve the quality of the rubber trees. She thought, as she had once before in Georgia when a hostile editor had been discussing conservation of natural resources, that what was good enough for rubber trees was surely good enough for people. Human ingenuity and foresight controlled and perfected production of certain trees while reproduction of their own kind was neglected and encouraged in haphazard prodigality.

Tapping of the trees for valuable latex was done by men, women, and children from the age of twelve. Babies in Malaya, the saying went, cut their teeth on the tapper's knife. Thus children could be an economic asset; there were many on the rubber estates.

Not all pregnancies resulted in assets, however. At Ulu Tiram, a Tamil nurse and midwife, trained in birth control at the Johore Clinic, had convinced the skeptical estate manager of the necessity for her work. The Englishman had become distressed over the number of abortions, miscarriages, illnesses, and deaths among the rubber families as the grim record came to his awareness through the family planning workers. His wife, a trained dietitian, went to the Johore Clinic where she talked with the informed and persuasive volunteer Renee Lowe. As a result, the estate manager's wife began to assist the midwife in her work of going to the workers' homes with the birth control message and devices.

At Tebrau, on the other hand, the estate manager's wife was herself a member of the Family Planning association and a nurse with midwifery training as well as birth control education in Singapore. She encouraged the women on the estate to come to the dispensary where she assisted the family planning team and volunteer workers in talking to small groups and distributing supplies.

Every phase of the work—in new villages, on rubber estates, among kampongs and depressed districts within Johore Bahru, and at army and police barracks—brought unexpected problems and progress. But Edna's work was not confined only to these local areas. She also traveled over the state of Johore. At Kluang, sixty-five miles from Johore Bahru, she and Renee Lowe spoke to a group including seventeen planters who had gathered to see what practical steps could be taken in birth control work in their area.

At the extreme southern tip of the Malay Peninsula Edna went by river boat to call at two small, deprived fishing villages. From one location to the next—a schoolhouse, a town hall, a local leader's home—women had gathered since early morning to hear the liberating message she brought.

Everywhere there was a continuing need to involve men more directly in the work. As Edna discovered in her pioneering across the United States, success was usually halting and less than complete when only half of the human birth control equation participated in the program. At the end of the first year's work in Malaya she concluded that far more education of men was essential before family planning would be widely accepted.

"It will help," she told her associates, "if men are made to feel that they have initiated the idea of child spacing. The women have clearly shown that they are moderately interested, but are either too afraid, too shy, or too clever to broach the subject to their husbands."

Renee Lowe, secretary of the Johore FPA, had also turned her wit and attention to this subject. Edna encouraged her to write her ideas to Dr. Gamble and among these were some on involvement of men through entertainment.

"Since, in the Far East," Renee Lowe wrote, "women's emancipation is comparatively recent, the logical approach is to make the men feel that family planning is their responsibility and moreover to their benefit financially, since ethics carry little weight. To this end we have in production film slides (black and white on brilliant orange) by a former newspaper cartoonist—Chinese." These slides were to be presented in English, Chinese, Tamil, and Malay.

Evaluating the use of films at various rubber plantations, Mrs. Lowe described the conditions under which birth control apostles had to promote their cause: "In the afternoons the women and men tappers sit about in front of their quarters but there is a general atmosphere of apathy—they are tired after a long day and our enquiries are a tedious business. It struck me then that a good family planning film, part entertainment and part educational, would draw every man and woman on the estate and, to encourage attendance, perhaps a comic film for children could be included."

One place which offered an opportunity to spread the family planning message to estate workers was a baby clinic. Even here, as Renee Lowe described, "the atmosphere of howling babies and consoling mothers is not sufficiently relaxed or leisurely for ideal family planning work."

When visits were made to the homes, the team of workers found it difficult not to arrive at inopportune times. Often the woman was preparing a meal and had to divide her attention between food and the message of birth control. Usually there were other people present, and this lack of privacy was inhibiting. Always, in Malayan homes, the women had to get the permission of their husbands before or after they accepted any birth control supplies, and if the husbands were not at home when the midwife called this could lead to delays and postponements.

Despite handicaps, the work progressed. Where 112 new patients had visited the birth control clinic at the general hospital of Johore in the preceding year, during the year when the house-to-house project was under way there were 1500 new callers. Definitive statistics at some of the plantations were difficult to determine but the widening influence of the work was evident and cumulative. Counting both Johore and the plantations, an estimated 4,730 people were personally informed by an Asian worker about family planning—half of that number were spoken to individually and half in groups.

Realization mounted that this personal approach, although effective, was too expensive from the standpoint of the time it consumed and the lack of workers available to carry it forward as a permanent program. Much had been learned about attitudes, needs, and effective approaches. But other means of communication had to be devised, too.

Although the Ministry of Health had never given official approval to the experiment and research, they were impressed with general results and findings. This approval resulted in permission for the FPA to have a table at each of the Maternal and Child Health Centers in the community. As women left the health centers they found it necessary to pass this table where volunteer workers, or those previously engaged in house-to-house calls, would be ready to provide information and refer them to the clinic, or, in the case of those already practicing birth control, renew their contraceptive materials. As this innovation caught on and there were many pauses at the FPA table, the eagerness of women for knowledge and help was once again demonstrated.

Shortly after Edna began work in Malaya, the cause of family planning received an important boost. An IPPF official visiting in Kuala Lumpur held fruitful meetings with various ministers of the government, including those of finance and health. A government pledge of one hundred thousand Malayan dollars (about thirty-three thousand American dollars) was made to the family planning program. The money would come from the Welfare Lotteries Board, a national lottery which raised money for hospitals, charities, and related causes. Its financial support meant that family planning could make real strides.

Edna promptly set about formulating purposes, goals, and fund apportionment to city and rural, large and small, and old and new groups. To secure any of the money, she knew there would be a certain amount of red tape involved, and she wanted to cut it to a minimum, leaving the local groups as free as possible to do their real tasks: reaching the people and running clinics.

During the various periods in the early sixties when she was in Malaya, Edna did not devote all of her attention to organizational, clinic, and field work. A large part of her goal here, as everywhere, was to create at the highest possible level a favorable official climate regarding family planning. Through auspicious publicity, varied educational channels, appeals to social and economic pressures, and the scope of her own persuasive forcefulness, Edna brought prestigious and powerful support to the birth control movement. There was no rod by which to measure the importance of that support, but without it, in the parts of the world where she was working, there would have been little possibility for the survival of a viable family planning program.

The key to Edna's contacts with the royal family of Johore was the Chinese couple Eileen and Philip Kwok. Handsome, wealthy, sophisticated, they were also deeply interested in the welfare of their emerging nation, and Eileen Kwok was one of the most loyal workers in the Family Planning Association. The orchids with which she often graced Edna's room were the gesture of a coworker who was a personal friend as well. The Kwoks were favored members of the inner circle of the Sultan's and Sultana's social life and through them Edna participated in numerous royal functions. Two such events gave her special glimpses into, first, the paradoxes of kingly luxury in a time of change; and, second, the unusual command performances sometimes expected of planned parenthood workers.

On the first occasion, Edna was invited with a select group to attend a housewarming (or Istana-warming) at a palatial new residence the Sultan had only recently acquired. She wore her best dinner gown and delicate evening shoes. Driven by the Kwoks' chauffeur in their elegant Jaguar, Edna arrived at the entrance to the palace. As they approached they were stopped by a guard and told that the gate was locked. Driveway repairs of some sort were under way and it would be impossible for cars to deliver the guests inside the grounds.

In her flowing dress and fragile slippers, Edna reluctantly climbed out of the car. It appeared that the only way around the tightly closed gate was an opening at one side which boasted a deep mudhole guarded by two more sturdy watchmen. As Edna approached, she saw that these two were literally picking up lady guests and passing them around the gate to deposit them on the rocky path leading up to the palace. When her turn came to be hefted over the mud, in a fashion more expedient if less gallant than Sir Walter Raleigh's cloak, Edna enjoyed the absurdity of a situation in which her evening bag contained the beautifully engraved Sultan's card of invitation, while her shoes had to be lifted out of the mud at his entrance.

Only slightly the worse for wear, Edna arrived at the party, found that she was to be one of four eating dinner at the Sultan's table; and, with Eileen Kwok's encouragement and leading questions, she spent much of the time entertaining the Sultan with accounts of her work in birth control. He was amused, an achievement considered more than sufficient approval by all except Edna, who was unaccustomed to royal privilege and felt that some explicit encouragement would be nice. Between the mudhole and the celebration of the new Istana, however, Edna found the evening instructive and delightful.

Equally enjoyable, in a different way at a later time, was a dinner dance at the great palace. For this elaborate celebration of the Sultan's birthday, Edna wore a short, swirling, turquoise blue chiffon dress and gold shoes with five-inch heels. The rich gleam of the shoes matched highlights in her thick, carefully coiffed gold hair; the blue-green shades of the chiffon accentuated the clear blue color of her wide-set eyes. She was ready for whatever the evening might bring—she thought.

After an elaborate entrance down the central staircase, the Sultan and Sultana led their guests into a long banquet hall where the tables sparkled with silver and crystal reflecting the lights from magnificent chandeliers which dripped in frozen splendor from high ceilings, like perfect icicles under the brilliant winter sun. Following the banquet, the guests moved into another room, slightly less ornate but boasting a large dais at one end. This set aside for dancing, while the Sultan, his prime minister, the crown prince, and other princes and ministers sat in a front row of chairs with other guests scattered around the room.

Edna joined a cluster of the women, dressed in their long gowns of rich brocade or finely handwoven fabric, with simple flat slippers or sandals, and watched the Malayan dancing. A row of men lined up opposite a row of women and carried on most of the gyrations while the women moved more subtly to and fro in rhythm to the music. Suddenly the crown prince was standing before Edna. He requested a dance. In such a situation an invitation became a command performance. She found herself on the dais at the head of the line of women.

In her sleeveless, low-cut cocktail dress and high heels, she felt bare and naked beside the ladies totally swathed from throat to ankle moving about in low sandals. There was nothing to do but make the best of her forward position, and under the gaze of the royal spectators she twisted and turned and moved back and forth following the gestures of the other women.

Her partner, the prince, on the other hand, was following no one else's gestures. His response to the music grew more enthusiastic, his gyrations became wilder and wilder. Before the dance had ended, a young minister of travel, whom Edna had met through the Kwoks, broke in on the prince and saved Edna from becoming involved in even more abandoned whirlings.

At last the music stopped. Seizing Edna by the hand, the minister of travel turned to the Sultan and others sitting within a few feet of the dais and announced: "If *this* is family planning, I'm all for family planning!"

Whereupon the Sultan and entourage arose, applauded, and when Edna extended her arms in an impulsive gesture of appreciation and goodwill, they all shook hands with her.

She went back to her seat with the other women, embarrassed over the sense of herself as a public spectacle, pleased over the fact that she had helped publicize, focus attention on, and find important favor for her cause.

Not all of Edna's social life, or her education, was formal. She learned about customs and clothes and food in a variety of ways. One evening after she had worked in Malaya for some time, Che Khalsom called Edna. The prince, her husband, was away and she was lonely. Would Edna come and have a steak dinner with her? When Edna arrived at the Istana she was taken to the children's dining room, a more informal and intimate spot than the palace banquet halls. As the door was opened, a wretched odor poured from the room. It seemed to be the revolting smell of ancient sewers. To herself, Edna noted, "Wouldn't you think the royal family could afford decent plumbing?"

But after she and Che Khalsom had been in the room a short while the stench seemed to disappear, which was fortunate considering the delicious dinner which was served. When time for dessert arrived, a maid entered bearing a large platter. "It's our durian," Edna's hostess explained.

Then Edna realized that the permeating odor which had been so offensive had come from this fruit which was being cut in the kitchen when she arrived. The durian was one of the favorite fruits of Malaya, Indonesia, and Southeast Asia. About the size of a small round watermelon, with a thick hard greenish skin and tough spines, it was difficult to handle and worse to smell. "The odor of latrines at New York's old Third Avenue elevated," Edna decided. But once cut, the seed inside was oval-shaped, somewhat larger than a silver dollar, and covered with a custard-like coating which was delectable. Holding the seed firmly with a fork, the custard could be scraped off and eaten easily in all its delicate goodness.

The real import of the durian lay not in its delicious flavor, Edna discovered, but in the fact that it allegedly rendered men sexually potent beyond belief. Nine months after the durian season, there was reputed to be a dramatic rise in the birth rate among those who had access to the fruit. The durian grew on large trees, taller than the mango tree, with ample leaves. The heavy fruit supposedly fell at midnight when it was just at the peak of its ripeness, and in wealthy households a servant was stationed beside the tree all night during harvest season to retrieve the fruit as soon as it plopped to the ground. Edna was told of one landowner in Malacca who had three durian trees of such quality that he would allow very few people to even taste their fruit. The pedigrees of durian trees were discussed at length. But because of its renowned aphrodisiac virtues, women were not supposed to like the durian. Edna did, however, and made no pretense otherwise. Once she had overcome the smell, which dissipated after the fruit had been cut, she savored the rich custard of the durian seeds.

The morning after her dinner with Che Khalsom, however, she received a phone call from the princess. "The servants are all furious with you."

"What have I done?" Edna asked.

"Being a woman and a foreigner, you weren't supposed to like our durian dessert. The servants had looked forward to eating all of your portion themselves. But we didn't leave them very much!"

As Edna encountered the folklore surrounding the durian everywhere she lived in Southeast Asia, she began to wonder if she should recommend to Dr. Gamble that one effective means of birth control might be to chop down all the durian trees!

The first place Edna had visited in Malaya, when she and Dorothy were en route to Singapore, was the capital of the country, Kuala Lumpur, in the state of Selangor. It was there that the local FPA had thrown the lavish, inappropriate, well-nigh disastrous party for Edna. The night club program, complete with belly dancer, was not conducive to any discussion of birth control. Its purpose, to entertain visiting dignitaries, seemed geared solely to the traveling salesmen in rather different fields. Edna had been appalled and had shocked Dorothy, when they were back at their hotel, by dissolving into tears of frustration over the evening's waste.

There was more cause for tears than she realized. Not long afterward it became apparent that the group had squandered all of its money on this party. In addition, Edna's visit to Kuala Lumpur was followed shortly by a call from the IPPF representative. Having spent much effort and all the bank account on Edna, however, the FPA of Selangor did not feel ready for another social blast after such a short interval. Both the IPPF dignitary and the struggling association were angry, especially when the latter learned by the grapevine from Singapore that Edna was not a powerful volunteer worker but was, instead, a professional employee, while the Englishman was an "authentic" VIP.

Distressed and baffled by the situation, Edna wrote Clarence Gamble a description of the ill-conceived social function that was threatening the success of her work. To her surprise and gratification, Dr. Gamble sent funds to repay the FPA treasury for the outlay it had made on Edna's party. The Kuala Lumpur

144

officers were greatly pleased. This very practical gesture, combined with Edna's willingness to undertake difficult, detailed organizational work, soon closed this breach.

Kuala Lumpur was a flourishing metropolis of 350,000, in which the Moorish-style architecture of government buildings and the spires of minarets on the Old Mosque in the heart of the city were reminders of an age-old history, while gleaming skyscrapers and modern commercial buildings arose in mute testimony to the urgency of the present and future. Golden domes gleamed in splendid contrast to functional high-rise wedges of glass and steel, while darting motorbikes illustrated a new tempo in the city's pace. Malay kampongs, Chinese and British residential areas, Indian shops all flourished in the city bounded on three sides by hills, at the juncture of two rivers, with tin mines and rubber plantations in the surrounding suburbs. The city boasted the nation's Parliament Houses, Ambassador's Row, and Malay's modern university.

During numerous visits to Kuala Lumpur over three years, Edna's closest associates became Dr. L. S. Sodhy, the minister of health, and Mrs. Rosalind Foo, whose home was in Ipoh. As president of the FPA Federation for Malaya and for the state of Selangor, Dr. Sodhy was the key figure in all national work. A slim, thirtyish Tamil Indian with regular features, dark hair, large brown eyes, and a courteous manner that was confident but not aggressive, he was an outgoing, friendly man eager to succeed in his responsible position. Edna came to him as a welcome aide and a potential threat. Selangor was his territory. Edna's work in other states delighted him. But not on his home turf. He stressed his eagerness to have family planning groups in each state of Malaya, but it was apparent that he did not relish the prospect of advice or assistance where he was in charge.

In the capital, Edna visited clinics, made suggestions concerning film slides and office procedure, accompanied the health van out to estates in the surrounding countryside, and discovered that the nurse conducting the house-to-house birth control program had solved the problem of being considered a drug manufacturer's saleswoman by the simple expedient of wearing a white uniform and her staff nurse's blue belt. Edna found that in many departments of the University of Malaya resources were available which could further the cause of family planning. She contacted professors and introduced ideas for studies of attitudes and other projects. At Taman Osakan Women's Training College Edna spoke about family planning to members of the staff and some of the women receiving health education. She also furnished a supply of literature in Malay and completed arrangements for many of the trainees to come to the clinic.

With Dr. and Mrs. Sodhy, she attended a meeting of influential labor leaders from various rubber estates and was impressed by the skill with which the doctor explained family planning and fielded their questions.

Through friends at the hotel where she stayed, Edna met the representative of the Rockefeller Foundation and his wife, Dr. and Mrs. Clifton Wharton. When Mrs. Wharton invited her for dinner, Edna encouraged the interest they expressed in family planning. She felt that the work of every U.S. government agency and philanthropic foundation must take into consideration the birth rate of the country where it worked—or suffer serious consequences.

When the U.S. ambassador's wife, Mrs. Charles Baldwin, telephoned, Edna made a special effort to accept her invitation. Che Khalsom of Johore had written Mrs. Baldwin about Edna's arrival in Kuala Lumpur and the same day Rosalind Foo had telephoned Mrs. Baldwin to tell her about Edna. The result was a luncheon which gave unofficial but warm welcome to Edna's family planning activities in the country.

Rosalind Foo, a delightful Chinese woman who introduced Edna to many key people in Kuala Lumpur, became one of her closest personal friends. Y. K. Foo was a successful Malayan tin manufacturer. He and his wife had a family of six daughters. Their home was in Ipoh, capital of the state of Pérak, in western Malaya, between Kuala Lumpur and Penang, but their interests ranged over a broad section of the country.

Petite in appearance, Rosalind Foo had demonstrated an amazing capacity for hard work. To the cause of family planning she had brought not only prestige and enthusiasm but attention to daily details. As Edna accompanied her on trips to villages outside of Ipoh, the network of clinics Rosalind Foo had created became more impressive. She had also been able to secure for the family planning program a grant of seven cents per planted acre from a number of the rubber estates in Pérak, and this brought considerable revenue into the local FPA.

In the city, Mrs. Foo visited the clinic regularly, made sure that it was open at the designated hours, and inspected its maintenance and sanitary conditions. After she helped secure a van for work in the countryside she assisted in scheduling its use for maximum effectiveness. There was no aspect of the work that this animated Chinese woman did not stimulate, guide, and encourage. She worked with Dr. Sodhy at the national level and with patient midwives at the village level and was successful with each.

There were scars from Malaya's past, however, which could not be healed by even so sophisticated and extroverted a person as Rosalind Foo. Edna was astonished one night, early in their acquaintance, when the Foos were taking her to dinner at a hotel. As they entered the large former British private polo club, Rosalind paused and said, "Before Malayazation, we wouldn't have been allowed in here." And then she swept through the door with a flourish. For years, the accounts of Malaya's struggles with Great Britain and its efforts to guide its own destiny had been only news stories to Edna. All at once that struggle was crystallized by a tiny lady with a luminous air of verve and generosity who had known stigma and insult.

Edna had a rare skill in wedding common sense to diplomacy through practical ways that allowed the personal needs of pride and dignity to survive even as they accommodated the larger goal involved. While she did not find the reputedly sensitive Asian people with whom she worked any more susceptible to the follies of pride than fellow Americans she had come to know abroad and at home, Edna believed that the nature of her work, the absolute need for its success, and her presence as a woman in foreign cultures required that she be particularly responsive to personal feelings as well as programs or organizations.

One such success came in Penang. As head of the entire Southeast Asia organization, Mrs. Goh Koh Kee, along with

Dr. Sodhy, asked Edna to go to Penang to see what could be done to improve a difficult situation which had developed there. Some years before, a prominent doctor in the province had heard Margaret Sanger speak in Japan. The experience had stirred him so deeply that as soon as he returned to Penang he proposed a planned parenthood organization.

Unfortunately, it remained only an organization. There was no clinic, no materials—just a group of interested people. Every once in a while there would be some publicity. Mrs. Goh Koh Kee would come from Singapore and give a talk, offer some plans, the good doctor would agree, and then—nothing would happen. Now Mrs. Goh Koh Kee and others were asking, how could something be made to happen?

Edna went to Penang. When she reached the doctor on the telephone, he assured her that he would be happy to call a meeting of his planned parenthood group. He mentioned the following Tuesday at nine o'clock. Edna told him that she would be at his office at nine o'clock Tuesday morning. No, he replied, he meant nine in the evening. And the place would not be at the office but at his home. Such an arrangement seemed odd, but Edna had grown accustomed to odd situations.

Rosalind Foo had sent Edna a list of names, people in Penang who might be interested in family planning. A young woman doctor Edna had met in Johore Bahru, originally from Europe—who had been in Malaya for many years—also worked in Penang. She was eager to make some progress in birth control but had been thwarted by the inertia of the doctor who was titular head of the local organization. Other names were suggested and Edna contacted each individual. After every conversation she telephoned the doctor who was head of the family planning association and asked if that person had been invited to his meeting. "No, but it's a fine idea," was his unfailing reply.

On Tuesday night at nine o'clock, a half-dozen concerned people appeared at the doctor's home. They had been approached by Edna and invited in the doctor's name. Edna suggested to the little gathering that they lay plans for a general meeting for the whole province of Penang with speakers invited from Ipoh and Kuala Lumpur to tell about the new national organization. The doctor was delighted with Edna's suggestion for a larger meeting and the possibility of national financial help from the Welfare Lotteries grant. He was apparently relieved, during the following week, when she set July 4 as the date for the meeting, and proceeded with arrangements without disturbing him.

A tentative outline for organization, with a slate of officers, was pulled together. A woman was found who would be willing to stand for president and do the actual work while the doctor who was even now only a figurehead president would be promoted upstairs to become an even more glorified figurehead as honorary chairman. There was an able and interested woman who agreed to carry out the organizational work in Penang as soon as funds could be secured from Kuala Lumpur.

With these arrangements quite firmly made, Edna could not tarry for the July meeting. Dr. Sodhy, in his official capacity as state public health officer, and Rosalind Foo, as an enthusiastic and experienced volunteer worker in planned parenthood for her state, agreed to come to Penang and speak at this important initial function. Edna felt confident that all would go well.

The assembly was a great success. An organization was formed, officers were elected, and no one was more satisfied with the outcome than the doctor who had just been acclaimed by the title Edna proposed. When Edna was asked, back in Singapore, why she hadn't just dismissed him, she was dismayed.

"That would have been impossible. We can't afford to lose any supporter," she said, "and most certainly not an important leader in the medical profession. Now he's in a top position where he's happy and can't do any harm. The group is in a position to go ahead and do everything. Everybody's happy."

The Association did go ahead. At the end of their first year's work, Edna was invited back to Penang as the guest of honor at an anniversary dinner. More than the formal address, or her own brief speech, it was the annual report that she found interesting: during that first struggling year, twelve birth control centers had been established in public health units on the island of Penang. This was tangible evidence of the vigorous program that had been built on her foundation. And no one had been rejected or offended in the reorganization. Support had multiplied, not divided, as had often been the case in such episodes.

Shortly thereafter, another event left Edna with a much diminished sense of satisfaction. That outcome, once again, was the result of her extravagant enthusiasm, her eagerness to find the source of a problem, and then move rapidly toward a solution.

Following the news that funds would be allotted from the Welfare Lotteries board, the struggling planned parenthood groups scattered among five of Malaya's largest cities agreed to attend a meeting in Kuala Lumpur and decide on some method of distribution for the forthcoming money. Since Penang was only then in the process of realistic organization, it was not qualified to send a delegate to the meeting, nor did it have the budget to do so. Edna believed, however, that even if the able European doctor who had shown such leadership in the work in Penang were not a delegate, she could play an important role in the convention. Edna offered the assistance of the Pathfinder Fund in paying her travel expenses if she would go to Kuala Lumpur. The young woman accepted.

But Edna's whole effort was soundly condemned. Malayan leaders in birth control work felt that Edna had circumvented their orderly procedure. They accepted the presence of the doctor, she participated in the sessions and made a notable contribution—but Edna was reproached, both openly and covertly, for not waiting to encourage her presence until Penang had applied for acceptance in the national group and become a full-fledged member.

Such niceties, involving delays and wasted time, were anathema to Edna, although intellectually she knew that she must adapt her drive, her rhythms of life, to the people among whom she worked. Here in Malaya was continuing evidence of her great asset-turned-liability: her eagerness tripping her over the customs and habits of other people until, instead of going forward, she faltered.

Each setback due to this sense of urgency left her momentarily discouraged. Would people never understand the reason for her pushing, propelling, insistent drive? All they had to do was look about them in the crowded streets at the crushing throngs and the neglected faces to discover the incentive which compelled her. But there were processes and patterns to be followed, as Mrs. Goh Koh Kee had warned her. Once again, Edna resolved to synchronize her timing with Malaya's.

It was not to be. Early in her work in this country she had seen the need for a full-time, trained worker who could go into all parts of the country setting up clinics and winning public support for family planning. She had found it difficult to convince the organization's officials to meet this need, however. Dr. Sodhy was eager to have FPA groups in every state, but he had little free time in which to implement his goal.

There were differences, too, over whether such an executive should be a man or a woman. Dr. Sodhy insisted that precisely the right person must be found—due to the newness of the job and the complexities of firing a new but unsatisfactory employee. Edna replied that a beginning was the most important thing; perfection was not a realistic standard of employment.

When the Welfare Lotteries board had first announced their appropriation to the FPA, Edna became concerned lest the lack of a unified, well-defined purpose lead to a dissipation of funds. As minister of health for the state of Selangor, Dr. Sodhy had massive needs and commitments confronting him. Only one portion of his time and attention could be devoted to family planning. In an effort to be useful, Edna took a map of Malaya and notes on the family planning programs in various areas, and allocated portions of the Welfare Lotteries money where it seemed most likely to be useful.

Her idea was to provide professional assistance which could strengthen the struggling programs already under way. Then, the following year, with progress demonstrated in these areas, a larger amount of money could be requested to extend the services to other parts of each state. By this plan, associations which were stumbling along could be brought to a more professional pace. When Edna invited Dr. Sodhy to dinner and presented her suggestions, he seemed pleased and impressed.

As the opportunity arose, Edna proceeded to help several of the states make application for a share of the Welfare Lotteries money. She suggested to the new group in Penang that they could find financial support from their national capital if they laid out acceptable plans for a birth control program.

In the state of Malacca on the strait with the historic seaport of the same name, where Portuguese, Dutch, and Chinese influence intermingled, Edna found a young doctor acting as president of the family planning group with the able help of a Chinese woman. They welcomed Edna, cooperated with her suggestions, and accepted her assistance in formulating a report for a budget to fill some of the particular needs of Malacca. When a meeting of the national FPA was held in Kuala Lumpur, the young doctor took along the request Edna had put in proper form. At that meeting, Johore Bahru and Malacca were the only states with such a plan for a paid worker, a detailed program, and related budget proposals. The doctor was elated when he returned to Malacca with all that he had asked.

At a subsequent meeting of the FPA, Edna was dismayed to learn that she was out of favor with some of its members. Although she and her friend Eileen Kwok had arranged to room together, in the official gatherings there was an atmosphere which puzzled and troubled her. Then Edna learned that Dr. Sodhy had confided to the FPA treasurer, an Englishman from Kuala Lumpur, that Edna was ambitious to take the treasurer's job. Whereupon she sought an opportunity to explain to the conference the purpose behind her plans—which had seemed to her too clear to need explanation. After she had presented them in broad outline, the treasurer was quick to rise to his feet and acknowledge the soundness of her motives and her approach.

Such incidents seemed to be trivial, organizational in-fighting at its most obvious, but because Edna was in a foreign country, involved in delicate relationships concerning major issues, she felt that no difficulty or misunderstanding was small. Each night she returned to her room alone to think, to plan, and to pray for strength.

Rumors that she wished to become treasurer of the Malayan FPA, because she organized proposals concerning money, were rendered as groundless as earlier rumors that she wanted to be executive director of Southeast Asia because she offered specific suggestions concerning organization. Eagerness to accomplish as much as possible in a limited period had led her to push and prod when she should have waited, encouraged, and enticed. To people accustomed to a different time schedule, her zeal seemed surely to be born of some hidden motive.

On the other hand, her organizational skill and her ready attention to any problem that arose were not to be scorned. Dr. Sodhy was anxious to have family planning work extend to the more remote states on the eastern coast. Edna agreed, but when he suggested that she should visit the eastern cities at the beginning of the monsoon season, she suspected that he was also retaliating for her insistence that the country should have a paid national director for family planning.

Edna hesitated, but when Dr. Sodhy appeared adamant, she went to secure a plane reservation to Kota Bharu, the northern-most city on the east coast, where the Gulf of Siam and the South China Sea meet. Airline officials were skeptical. Bad weather was brewing; there had already been difficulties on several flights. Yielding to her insistence, the clerk sold her a ticket.

Above thick jungles and intricate rice paddies which made Malaya appear a lush green paradox of wilderness and cultivation, Edna crossed the peninsula to the capital of the state of Kelantan. Economically poor, ninety percent Malayan, Kelantan was rich in history and culture. It considered itself the cradle of Malayan culture, which was reflected in its dance, art, and such highly refined craftsmanship as the making of batik.

When Edna landed at its capital city of Kota Bharu, a committee that had been notified of her plans was waiting at the airport. They welcomed her with relief: hers was the first plane that had landed for two weeks. Shortly after her arrival, the monsoons closed in and no other plane came into or went out of Kota Bharu for two months.

Among those most eager for birth control to become successful in the city was the president of the little FPA group—a man who turned out to be the father of eighteen children! Edna learned that six of these, all sons, had been adopted and educated before he was married. Each son was still living in Kota Bharu. They were doctors, lawyers, and businessmen. After he married, he and his wife had twelve children, each of whom was receiving an advanced education. Proceeds from a benefit performance at one of the FPA president's theaters in his motion picture chain had helped the family planning group survive until more substantial financing could be secured. Before Edna's arrival the group had even selected a woman they hoped to hire as a paid worker. Edna spent several days talking with her and working with the committee.

Here, as in other places, Edna set about creating an orderly pattern of work to establish clinics and stimulate public awareness. There were the fundamentals of securing a headquarters and officers and staff.

When such a beginning was well under way, she made ready to go on down the coast. With the weather at its wildest, she disregarded constant alarms and warnings and set forth in a jalopy that seemed akin to vehicles she had seen in old movies about searches for hidden treasure in the mysterious East. With an unlikely assortment of fellow passengers representing many ages, nationalities, and levels of agreeability, she jolted along the roads from Kota Bharu to Kula Trengganu to Kuantan.

Torrential rains had swollen streams to rivers and turned rivers into raging floods. After a long pause and debate at one bridge threatened by a swift, deep current, the old bus rattled across and reached its destination. A short while later the bridge went out.

In four different states along the less developed eastern coast of Malaya—weathering the monsoon rains, tramping through mud when passage for cars seemed dubious, meeting new people and old problems—Edna organized and reorganized, planned and prodded. From Kuantan on the east to Kuala Lumpur in the west, her return route crossed Malaya's dense green jungle heartland. Communist guerrillas had terrorized much of this central area until a short while before, and there was still a sense of unease among many travelers. Again disregarding warnings of trouble from nature and man, Edna found a bus which would take her on this last leg of her mission. Across the tropical terrain of Malaya she rode with a polite but crowded and shifting load of fellow passengers who were almost as varied and as interesting as the striking landscape.

Weary and waterlogged, Edna arrived back in the bustling capital and telephoned Dr. Sodhy.

"Where are you?" he asked.

"At my hotel here in Kuala Lumpur."

"You couldn't get anywhere?"

"I've been gone four weeks! I've been to the four states along the east coast. Each one is now organized, applying for a national license, and ready to go to work. If I may, I'd like to bring in my report."

There was a slight pause. "Of course," Dr. Sodhy replied, "and I'm glad you're back. I've been very worried."

By the time Edna finished her work in Malaya, there was not a single state on the peninsula where the Pathfinder Fund had not initiated, reorganized, or strengthened the family planning organization.

Edna felt that she had failed in some of her personal relationships, perhaps—through over-eagerness, misunderstanding, organizational rivalries. She had been unable to persuade Dr. Sodhy to approve a full-time organizer, a national paid director who could help each of the separate states in a unified, professional way. But she believed the work had been worthwhile: she had made loyal friends in this fascinating, beautiful country, friends who would continue to build strong clinics and reach the women who needed them. Knowing that at the current rate of natural increase it would be less than twenty years before Malaya doubled its population and knowing that she had made some contribution toward diminishing that possibility also gave her a feeling of achievement.

There were memories of busy Singapore where population seemed the most apparent and often appalling fact of life, of the isolated rubber estates where routines of life and attitude had to be interrupted to bring a knowledge of birth control, of dancing before the Sultan of Johore, of orchids in her room as a token of affection, and of private reprimand as a result of offended pride and suspicion.

During her first year in Malaya, Edna had asked the hostile English representative of the IPPF about going to Indonesia to promote birth control work. His reply had been disconcerting. "I wouldn't wish Indonesia on my worst enemy. It's a hellhole. But why don't you go?"

With an invitation like that, how could Edna resist? She departed with a farewell from Constance Goh Koh Kee in Singapore: "Indonesia is all yours. Good luck!"

9

_____

If children could be harvested, all Balinese would be wealthy.

—Donna K. and Gilbert Grosvenor
quoting a Balinese man,
National Geographic, 1969

The greatest reward for doing is the opportunity to do more.

—Dr. Jonas Salk

During the decade of the 1960s, Edna made many journeys between Singapore and Indonesia. But one stood out above the others. It occurred at a time when relations between Singapore and the islands to the south were particularly strained; there was little communication and less commerce between the two. Indonesia's family planning program relied on shipments from Singapore for its contraceptive materials, and there had been no receipts for some time. This could be a decisive blow to the struggling effort of birth control on the islands.

Edna, visiting in Singapore, suggested that she would be going to Indonesia and if the Singapore agency would fix up a package for her to take along with her personal baggage, she would see that it reached its destination. Her invitation was readily accepted. Indeed, the morning she was to leave she discovered that her "package" consisted of two huge cartons, each approximately three feet square. Not one to remain dismayed for very long, Edna sallied forth with them to her point of departure.

Over a period of months she had become acquainted with most of the customs officials and they with her. They readily passed her suitcases, unopened, through inspection. But two immense unlabeled boxes were another matter.

"What is this?"

"Oh, just part of my baggage," Edna replied as matter-of-factly as possible. There was silence. "Something for my own personal use," Edna added.

But the young inspector was not satisfied. "We'll have to see what it is." And he drew out a knife to slash open the cartons.

"Wait!" Edna said. "I'll tell you exactly what the contents are. They're condoms."

A startled pause, while other officials began to show interest in this unusual conversation. "But I thought you said this was for your personal use."

"Well, it is—in a way," Edna replied airily.

"How many do you have?" the inspector asked.

"Three or four thousand, I suppose."

"And you are staying how long?"

"A month."

Waves of laughter suddenly filled the air. A deep pink flushed Edna's neck and face as she joined in the hilarity at her absurd situation. She was allowed to take her personal supplies to Indonesia.

For five different periods in 1961, 1962, 1963, and 1968, ranging in duration from six weeks to six months, Edna worked in the islands which a colleague had called "a hellhole." He referred not so much to the weather, although, being British, the high humidity and drenching rains of the east and west monsoon seasons might have had undue effect on his judgment, but to a sense of chaos which prevailed throughout Indonesia. Tales drifted back to Singapore of mistreatment of foreigners; travelers along country roads risked attack by roving guerrillas.

It was a far-flung country of more than three thousand islands strung like stepping-stones along a volcanic route from Asia to Australia, with a population in 1961 of ninety-two million. More than two-thirds of these were crowded on the single island of Java. An area only slightly larger than the state of Pennsylvania, Java was one of the world's most densely populated pieces of real estate. Throughout Indonesia there were scattered a hundred thirty ethnic groups speaking two hundred dialects. Establishment of Bahasa Indonesia as the national language had sought to impose some unity on this fragmented Babel.

Oil-rich, rubber-rich, fertile Indonesia had been ruled by the Netherlands for more than three centuries, until World War II. Then it had been occupied by the Japanese for three years. Following the departure of the Japanese, the Indonesians had sought the departure of the Dutch as well. Bitter negotiation and bloodshed had resulted, until in 1949 the Netherlands relinquished all claims except to part of New Guinea. Achmed Sukarno had become president of the new republic—fifth most populous country in the world—still torn by strife among its major islands, plagued by guerrilla warfare and banditry born of the general upheaval. It did not seem to be a likely place for a lone American woman to further the controversial work of family planning.

Among Edna's resources, however, were those numerous acquaintances she had made during previous years of birth control work. And very few people who had met Edna ever forgot her. Now she reached back in her memory and recollected the name of a young Indonesian woman who had come to Chicago while Edna was executive director of the association in that city. In Indonesia the police enjoyed the same social status as the military, and as the wife of the chief of police, this very intelligent woman held a role of real leadership potential.

Mrs. Kartina Soejono had come to Edna's Chicago office to learn about family planning. Edna had spent some time with her and then asked one of the volunteer workers to entertain the visitor. Mrs. Soejono, with her winning charm and remarkable use of English, had made a great hit with the Chicago couple who were her hosts, and she had been impressed in turn by their American hospitality.

As Edna's plans to go to Indonesia developed, she discovered that a visa was difficult to obtain without some Indonesian to vouch for her, and she remembered Kartina. Edna wrote of her plans and her need for a sponsor and received an immediate reply. Kartina Soejono would be delighted to have Edna visit Indonesia and she would do everything possible to improve the journey. Using this letter, Edna was granted her visa with a minimum of red tape.

Amid the civil eruptions and social disruptions of changing Indonesia, housing in the capital city was limited, and Edna turned once again to her friend. The reply was warm but not altogether reassuring: Kartina was working on the problem. Edna should come ahead and there would be some sort of arrangement for her—perhaps not as nice as they could wish, but there would be something ready when she arrived in Indonesia.

If she had listened to the uneasy predictions of many of her associates, if she had heeded the rumors of danger that lay ahead, Edna would never have gone to Indonesia in the summer of 1961. She would have missed one of the most rewarding ventures of her life, one of the most outstanding triumphs for her work.

Her arrival in Djakarta was enough to allay her apprehensions—and amuse her, too, for it was in precise contradiction to the atmosphere she had been led to expect. A pleasant employee of the airline met her at the foot of the plane's steps and asked if she were traveling alone. When Edna said yes, the young woman took her typewriter and filing case. "It is too heavy for you to carry," she told Edna, and led the way into the waiting room. "Now you will sit down in here and I will see what I can do for you."

With Edna's passport and the letter from Mrs. Soejono and other papers, the guide disappeared. When she returned shortly, all was in order, and she led the way through customs where Edna's typewriter was registered, her bags were checked without inspection, and she exchanged some money into Indonesian rupias.

As she was finishing this transaction, Edna turned and saw Mrs. Soejono approaching. "Edna! I have wonderful news."

Her friend had discovered that the widow of one of the country's great leaders for independence, Haji Agus Salim, who was called "the father of his country," had a room which could be made available for Edna. What more auspicious beginning than as a resident in the household of one of the most distinguished and beloved families in all of Indonesia, whose relatives were scattered throughout the entire country?

The Salim house was a large Dutch-style home, and Edna was given the largest room in the house. Although it was spacious and boasted a washbowl with running water and a high ceiling, it had only one tiny window in one corner, which left the room almost stiflingly airless. The high four-poster single bed had a throne-like appearance, and the white sheet trimmed with lace that was its sole covering suggested the weather that Edna might expect during her stay there.

That very first night she did not expect so many visitors—in the form of mosquitoes. And, as far as Edna could see, they had no way of leaving, even if encouraged to do so. She had come prepared with insect repellent but it proved ineffective. After a while she lit a wick that had been placed in the room; its smoke was supposed to eliminate mosquitoes. It did not even discourage them.

Finally, just before daylight, Edna decided in desperation that the coil of smoke must be brought closer to her bed and she set it on the sheet beside her. For the first time that night she fell asleep—to be awakened in a couple of hours by a dense cloud filling the room. And the smoke was not from the insect coil; it was from the mattress, which had caught fire and was smouldering. A large hole, about six inches wide, was already burned in the mattress.

Frightened and embarrassed, Edna called the Salim household to her rescue. They were immensely courteous and kind. The only concern of the Salims was whether or not Edna had been burned. Money could replace the cost of the mattress and sheet (Edna wondered what Dr. Gamble would make of *that* on her expense account), but the greatest cost was her sense of utter chagrin at such apparent carelessness in someone else's home.

In addition to the airlessness of her bedroom, Edna's character was put to a daily test by the bath. Typical of those in upper-class Indonesian homes, it nevertheless offered a primitive institutional sort of accommodation. It was a square room with a reservoir holding water in one corner. Constant dripping from a single faucet kept the reservoir filled and the water perpetually at room temperature. The person wishing a bath dipped water from the reservoir and sloshed it over her body out of bucket-like bowls whose handles across the top made them tipsy and awkward to handle.

From this do-it-yourself shower, water ran across the floor to a drain in another corner. The tile floor underfoot remained wet with a slimy slipperiness that ranged from merely unpleasant to mortally dangerous.

Here, as elsewhere, Edna discovered that no householder ever told a foreign guest how to use that reservoir of water. One poor Western girl who came to visit the Salims climbed into the reservoir (a feat in itself) to bathe, and of course ruined the water for everyone else's use.

But mosquitoes and baths were only incidentals in Edna's stay with the Salims. More important was their reaction to her mode of life. Mrs. Salim, the widow, revered by family and friends, was cared for and waited upon as an imminent candidate for the grave. She never ventured out of her home alone. When she and Edna compared ages one day, it was discovered—to everyone's amazement—that Mrs. Salim was three months younger than her guest! Yet here was Edna galloping around the world dispensing a new gospel and means of freedom. The fact that she went everywhere and anywhere *alone* was particularly incredible to this family.

Her mode of transportation also startled the Salims and other Indonesians. When she was not called for by some coworker in family planning, and she often had such assistance, Edna employed a betjak. The betjak was a three-wheeled pedicab—a bicycle in which the passenger was carried along in a sort of swinging basket. In Indonesian (the only Indonesian she spoke involved street addresses), Edna would tell the betjak cyclist where she wanted to go and they would wheel off down the street. Such action would have been unthinkable for an elderly Indonesian woman. But taxis were expensive; they would have given her Indonesian friends the impression that she was an American millionaire; besides, Edna hardly thought of herself as elderly.

The ease with which she made itineraries and then followed them also seemed to astonish her Indonesian friends. The country's train and plane schedules were reputedly in such disorder that any plan was considered automatically subject to change or cancelation, with or without notice. Confidently, Edna went her way and found some means of opening that way whenever it was threatened by delay.

When her work in Indonesia expanded, she traveled to more areas of the country than most of the natives themselves had ever visited. She tried to take others with her whenever possible. Such travels offered excellent educational opportunities in the field for those who were beginning in family planning work. They also broadened and deepened friendships.

The person with whom Edna wished to make first official contact after her arrival in Djakarta was Madam Subandrio. The wife of the foreign minister, Indonesia's second in command at that time, Madam Subandrio wielded influential power—not only because of her husband's position but also because of her own authority. She had spent six years in London when her husband was an ambassador to the Court of St. James, and during that time, although she was already an M.D., she studied anthropology and received a doctoral degree in that subject.

At a women's all-Asian conference in Ceylon in 1957, Madam Subandrio had met Margaret Roots, of the Pathfinder Fund, and persuaded her to come to Indonesia to discover what might be accomplished in the field of family planning. The answer was: very little. Despite the huge rice crop harvested in its green valleys and terraces, Indonesia had to import hundreds of thousands of tons of rice each year, using precious foreign exchange. Contraceptives, considered luxury items, carried prohibitive import duty. This high tax on contraceptives curtailed their import so drastically that any interest aroused in birth control was lost because there were no supplies available.

After Mrs. Roots left, the Indonesia Planned Parenthood Association was formed, but it was frustrated in its purpose and feeble in its practical achievement. Now, in 1961, Madam Subandrio was assistant to the minister of health for Indonesia and she was still working toward a program of family planning. At the suggestion of the IPPF, but as the paid representative of Clarence Gamble's Pathfinder Fund, Edna had come to see if something could be done to help Madam Subandrio realize her ambition for the birth control program.

But after Edna's arrival in Djakarta, no word came from the assistant minister of health. She had been informed of Edna's arrival, but she made no move to meet her. The stifling air of her room oppressed Edna, despite the Salim family's friendliness. As always, she felt that she should be about her job, working every day. Each venture into the streets, each exploration of the capital city, heightened her sense of urgency.

From a little Dutch trading post, Batavia, had grown this metropolis of almost three million people, Djakarta. Spread over a wide area, with many red tile roofs and a man-made canal left as reminders of Dutch rule, it had an open, colonial appearance. Downtown streets were a maze of bicycles, automobiles, and betjaks during rush-hour traffic. Mosque domes, high-rise office buildings, lean-to shacks, tree-shaded colonial dwellings, gleaming new hotels, and business enterprises under construction all coexisted in a mixture of contrasts.

The rains which turned vegetation lush and green left the streets (made of volcanic ash except for such stone or chert or gravel as was imported) pitted with large holes and ruts which yawned in perennial stages of repair. The tall palms, banana trees, fragrant frangipani, colorful hibiscuses, cannas, bamboos, and dozens of other trees, shrubs, and flowers, all seemed to reflect in their abundance the almost excessive fertility of this tropical island—a fertility which, carried to the extreme, could lead to poverty and barrenness.

Edna enjoyed the natural fruitfulness of Djakarta and the island of Java, but she was sensitive to the pressures of its noisy streets—vendors and horns, beggars and sirens—and the needs of the population exploding around her. She was also sensitive to the excessive nationalism which prevailed everywhere. It was understandable that a people only recently relieved from centuries of foreign rule and ownership should want to obliterate many reminders of that alien presence, but it was also unfortunate that hypersensitivity to any outside influence could limit many worthwhile projects and relationships. Edna's warmth and tact would seldom be put to a more severe test, or win a more significant victory, than here in Indonesia.

During her wait—and she was determined to begin her work here with the right person or not at all—Edna was invited to a reception at the American embassy. There she finally met Madam Subandrio. This powerful woman was cordial and friendly, and as they parted at the end of the evening Madam Subandrio invited Edna to her home for dinner two nights later.

That dinner marked the beginning of Edna's work in the country. Present were members of the incipient family planning association, alert and intelligent women almost totally thwarted in their purpose. The only clinic in existence was run by Dr. Koen Martiono at the Ministry of Health and it could offer only intermittent services due to irregular flow of supplies through customs.

After dinner Edna turned to Madam Subandrio. "What would be possible for you, what would you choose, if you could do whatever you really wanted in this group?"

"If we could expect a regular supply of contraceptives and know that they would come routinely, we could do a real program of family planning," Madam Subandrio replied.

"But with such a high duty," Edna said, "how could you get them into the country?"

"I am now the deputy minister of health. If they were sent directly to me, personally, at my office in the Ministry of Health, and if I could be sure of their arrival, I could arrange to bring them in as regular medical supplies."

Edna seized the opening. "Could you really? If that's the case I can promise you all the supplies you need."

This was the first, practical sort of assistance Dr. Gamble sought to give. Even when Madam Subandrio's estimate of amounts she would need for the first year seemed astronomical, Edna assured her that it could be managed. "But how will so many supplies be distributed?"

"Right through the Department of Public Health."

"But how," Edna asked, from long years of experience, "do you know that the Public Health officers will be willing to carry out such a program in their localities?"

Madam Subandrio hesitated, and provided Edna with the opening she sought. Instead of arriving in Indonesia and announcing that she wished to go around the country establishing a birth control program, Edna had waited for this moment when spontaneously, in the natural sequence of events, she could offer her help. "I will be in Indonesia for a while. I want to travel all over your beautiful land. Would you like for me to talk with some of the Public Health officers as I go around? I could tell them about your plan and ask if they would cooperate."

Madam Subandrio and the others on her committee greeted this offer with enthusiasm. In fact, their enthusiasm was so stirred that they turned to discussion of the location of their family planning centers. Certainly the majority would have to be on the two most populous islands, Java and Bali. Then the committee listened intently as Edna described the house-to-house programs being tried in Malaya. They explained that in Indonesia a strict law prohibited the offer of any medical service except through organized clinics. Home visits by nurses, who could take the foam tablets with them, would be permissable, however. Edna was interested to learn that a charge must be made for any materials offered. This small charge would encourage use of the contraceptives as something of value. In addition, a revolving fund could be built up for reorders.

Edna also told the group about the Welfare Lotteries board in Malaya and its grant to the family planning work. A similar lottery existed in Indonesia, run solely by the government. Before any help could be expected from this source, a successful program would have to be under way.

Finally, several members of the committee described dissatisfaction with the contraceptives themselves. Besides being difficult to import and expensive, they deteriorated rapidly in the tropical weather and were hard to store. There was discussion of the possibility of Indonesia manufacturing its own contraceptives. Since the present minister of small industries was former president of the FPA and a doctor, he might be interested in such a manufacturing project, especially if some foreign capital might be found to make initial investments. Edna told them of her friend Mr. Joseph Sunnen of St. Louis, who had carried out a successful project in Puerto Rico by local production of the aerosol type of contraceptive, Emko. The committee agreed to investigate the possibility of opening a similar industry in their country.

With ideas flourishing and optimism high among the little Association's executive committee, Edna saw in this good beginning the inevitable necessity for that key person—an able, paid executive director for a nationwide organization. As she returned to her room at Mrs. Salim's, she decided that it had been a very promising evening.

The very next morning Madam Subandrio arrived at the Salim residence and began formulating a list of names and addresses for doctors and health officers scattered across Indonesia in places where it seemed worthwhile to investigate the possibility of establishing a family planning program. With this list, Edna was off—from one tip of Java to the other, and to the nearby islands of Sumatra, Madura, and Bali.

One of the first hurdles to be overcome was a public belief that the government was opposed to family planning. President Sukarno had made numerous speeches against birth control. There was a common theme running through his talks: with three thousand beautiful islands, many of them unpopulated, what need for birth control existed in his country?

Shortly before Edna arrived in Djakarta, however, while she was still in Singapore and Malaya, President Sukarno had met with Ayub Khan, the President of Pakistan. At this meeting, Ayub Khan had said in a public address that his country was turning its attention to family planning. Pakistan was experiencing such a startling population increase that some measures for control were becoming mandatory. Following the Pakistani leader's remarks, Sukarno took the platform. He asserted once more that Indonesia did not need a program of birth control—*but,* family planning might be welcome as a means of health protection for mothers and babies.

Edna grasped this statement as an answer to recurring unease about the government's attitude. And along the way, Madam Subandrio assured her that the President knew—from indirect sources—all that was being done. If he had not approved, she and Edna and the others would not be continuing with such success.

Another question that demanded attention involved religious approval of family planning. Although strains of animism and mysticism and the influences of Hinduism and Buddhism were strong throughout Indonesia (especially in Buddhist Bali), nine-tenths of the people were followers of Islam. In Bandung, one of the first places Edna visited, the director of the municipal health department brought up the relationship between the Islamic religion and family planning. Edna explained that Pakistan and Egypt, Muslim countries, were sponsoring official family planning programs. In Malaya, where she had worked most recently, government leaders of

169

the Muslim faith favored it and provided some of the leadership. Certain Islamic religious leaders of international renown had also issued public statements supporting family planning, and Edna informed the director of these. He seemed convinced by her explanation, which he could use to answer those who might approach him about the compatability of their religion and their contraceptive practices. Then this health officer went a step further and committed himself to establishing a family planning service in his central clinic.

On a later trip, a lawyer who was also one of the most consistent workers in the country's FPA, Mrs. Nani Suwondo, was asked to prepare a statement on the Islamic religion as it related to family planning, including quotations from some of the spiritual leaders. When this was finally prepared, it proved useful for distribution in cities and villages throughout the islands.

Edna received rapid confirmation from Dr. Gamble that the Pathfinder Fund would provide supplies if a way could be found to distribute them. Once again, Edna welcomed the efficiency and satisfaction of working in a situation where decisions could be made promptly, without lengthy delays for committee meetings, board approvals, and shifting of responsibilities. She was able to seize a local opportunity and move ahead while the interest was fresh and keen.

And move she did. Released from the confines of her one-window room and any doubts she might have had about Madam Subandrio's support and cooperation, Edna set forth across a country of stark mountain ranges and thick green jungle, terraced rice paddies, rubber and tea plantations, red-roofed villages, forests of teak, ebony, camphor, and sandalwood. It was an incredibly beautiful, fertile land, and Edna found its people open-minded and openhearted. Wherever she went—before formal audiences gathered to hear her speak, to companions on a train, in private social gatherings, or at large public functions—Edna managed to mention family planning. From casual encounters, important invitations resulted: to speak before a group of government officials or explain methods to a gathering of midwives, to meet a United Nations official who could open doors and promote good will or talk with the representative of the *Hope* ship mission which might include a program of family planning. Everyone had something to contribute, and with her vivacity, wit, and imagination, Edna meant to see that as many people as possible, wherever possible, had the opportunity to make their contribution.

As her work progressed, Edna tried to keep in mind the advice Madam Subandrio shared with her one day, advice too often overlooked by many enterprising Westerners seeking to work in and for, rather than with, Asia.

"Indonesia," Madam Subandrio said, "needs to work out its program in a way suitable to Indonesia and at the pace which fits into other activities in this country. Help is welcome and necessary—but in ways and amounts that can be put to effective use. Pressure to do more than may be done properly is wasteful—and useless."

Aware of her own strong motivation and sense of urgency, which had led her into unfortunate mistakes in Malaya and had helped undermine her relationship with the powerful Mrs. Goh Koh Kee, Edna did her best to harness her own time schedule to that of the people around her. She was successful here because many of these people, too, sensed the need for her work and were eager for her to go ahead at any pace she chose, if it brought results. They recognized that by proceeding at her own pace she was neither questioning nor threatening their own way of life.

Her travels took her from northern Sumatra to tiny Bali and covered the heart of this world's largest tropical archipelago, almost a quarter of it jungle, much of it crisscrossed by rivers and mountains, brilliant with fragrant flowers and flashing birds, exotic in delicate and complex dances, costumes, and festivals.

The first city where Edna called after Djakarta was Bandung, capital of the province of West Java, near the site where discovery of the half-million-year-old Java Man had once been hailed as the missing link in scientific studies of evolution. The bicycle-crowded city had also been the site, only six years earlier (in 1955), of a historic assembly of twenty-nine Afro-Asian nations to discuss world problems and their role in world developments.

Surrounded by rice fields and tea plantations—water buf-

falo patiently plodding in the rice paddies, women with colorful turbans and hats picking the tea leaves which flourished on
cooler slopes—Bandung itself sat on a plateau of 2,200 feet,
surrounded by high mountains. After Djakarta, its climate was
refreshing. The city boasted, too, the Institute of Technology
where President Sukarno had earned an engineering degree,
and its schools reflected the astonishing fact that in the few
years following the war Indonesia had nearly quadrupled its
number of teachers and students—until national literacy had
climbed from a low of only seven percent to more than fifty
percent.

Jogjakarta, on Java's southwest coast, was in many ways a
startling contrast to the other cities Edna visited. It was also one
of the most memorable. For more than a thousand years it had
been a cultural center of the Javanese, the nation's largest ethnic group. Both historically and artistically it was the metropolis of central Java. Its silverwork and the intricately dyed cot-
tons known as batiks were famous. Museums (some in the
Sultan's two-hundred-year-old "kraton") preserved objects of
the past culture; schools of puppetry, dance, and design kept
traditional arts alive for the future; while bustling markets—
for the batiks, silverware, carvings—guaranteed that the
unique arts and crafts would be part of the present economy
and culture.

Outside of Jogjakarta, perhaps an hour's drive, on a mound
surrounded by thick jungle, was the great Buddhist sanctuary
of Borobudur. Built by Indians in the eighth century and later
abandoned until the famous British governor, Raffles, and
later the Dutch rescued it from oblivion, its ancient walls rose a
hundred thirty eight feet in a series of nine ascending terraces.
Its size dwarfed the cathedrals of Europe. Bas reliefs of incredible number and detail transformed the lower galleries into a
history in stone of the life of Buddha. The three top terraces
were adorned with bell-shaped stupas, or shrines, each enclos-
ing a statue of the sitting Buddha. The crumbling yet enduring
monument of carved stone, in its silent setting of blue mountains and emerald foliage, seemed a reminder of man's spirit
eternally yearning toward understanding.

Also in the vicinity of Jogjakarta were the Prambanan

temples. The largest of these, a hundred ninety feet tall, provided a majestic backdrop for the performance of the great Ramayana ballet drama staged on nights of the full moon from June through October. Five hundred dancers and musicians presented the epic on six successive nights. Attending that Ramayana presentation was one of the most memorable experiences of Edna's life. It opened to her a rare insight into the spirit of the people with whom she worked. It thrilled her with a sense of participation in the most spectacular drama she had ever witnessed. In the vast open-air theater, with the ancient temple in the background drenched in light from the full moon and the sweeping floodlights, Edna became one of the enchanted spectators caught up in the story of Rama.

Rama was the son of a king in northern India between the twelfth and tenth centuries B.C. The epic of his life struggle between the forces of good and evil probably had its beginning sometime after 1000 B.C. and assumed its present form a few centuries before the Christian era. In the dedicated search of this young Hindu prince for virtue was incorporated one of the oldest universal stories of mankind. In the Ramayana's music of two gamelan orchestras and two choruses, its dance composed of hundreds of participants, its pageantry of rich and elaborate costumes and intricate staging, the theater as religion, the drama as instruction and revelation reached a summit of impressiveness.

For six successive evenings Edna watched as this spectacular production unfolded the simple and moving account of Rama's wanderings, his defeats, and his final victory over the forces of, evil. She marveled that this drama could be staged using ordinary people from all walks of life. Participants and audience alike were part of the Ramayana; farmers and officials, children and sages, all found a common bond in this experience.

Attendance at the Ramayana was rather expensive and Edna was pleased to be able to afford this luxury as a token of appreciation to her host and hostess in this part of Indonesia.

In addition, she discovered that the impression she had gained during those magical evenings—an impression of being part of all Indonesia—was more than a fleeting notion. Wherever she traveled, when she told people that she had been to the Ramayana, she was accepted. It became a symbol of compatibility, a bond of spirit between her and her Indonesian friends.

In Jogjakarta, however, Edna experienced one of the few early rebuffs to her work in Asia. It came from a doctor who felt that under existing conditions little work was possible in family planning. But the fascination, the spirit of the culture she encountered there kept her from giving up. Before her work in Indonesia was completed, that doctor and that city had become staunch participants in family planning.

She went to Surakarta, also called Solo, a city of more than a half-million, the artistic center for batik, gamelan music, and shadow theater; to Malang in the interior; to Semarang on the coast; and to Surabaya. Surabaya, once surrounded by rich sugar-producing fields, once the center of Java's greatest Hindu kingdom, the capital of East Java Province, had now become the country's chief naval base and one of its commercial centers. After the history and pageantry of Jogjakarta, Surabaya seemed like an intrusion of the twentieth century, with its freighters and warships lying in modern docks and its nearby naval base. But this provided Edna with an opportunity to promote birth control clinics in the naval health facilities, where she found a response remarkably similar to that she had known years earlier in promoting birth control in army and navy hospitals in parts of the United States. After initial hesitancy, there was cooperation based on increased knowledge of the facts and the need for family planning.

Surabaya was also the point of departure for Madura, the island famous for its bull racing. Edna listened to descriptions of how carefully the handsome bulls were bred and cared for in each of the island's districts and about preliminary competitions before the final championship team was determined at the final harvest festival. And she thought of some of those places in the United States, too, where prize animals received more care and attention in their procreation than did the community of humans. On Madura, as alsewhere throughout this part of the world, children—wiry, brown-skinned, solemn-eyed, and shy—seemed to overflow every door and street. Edna wondered how many of them had eaten, during their short lives, as many as the three or four dozen raw eggs fed each day to a pedigreed racing bull.

Northwest of Java lay Sumatra, eleven hundred miles of jungle-clad volcanic mountains, green and gold rice terraces, and a wealth of petroleum, rubber, palm oil, and legendary spices. At its southern seaport of Palembang, the derricks and refineries of American oil companies reminded Edna that Indonesia held the largest oil reserves in the Far East—and that these companies provided medical facilities for large segments of the population—more than fifty thousand in Palembang alone. She initiated efforts to enlist their support for family planning.

Padang, on the opposite coast, offered a strong contrast. Surrounded by highlands and lakes, a shipping point for copra and coffee, it lay in the country of the Minangkabau, a fiercely independent mountain people who had given birth to some of Indonesia's greatest independence leaders. One of these was Hadji Agust Salim, at whose home Edna lived during that first visit. A conservative Muslim community, slow to accept the message of birth control, Padang emphasized for Edna the variety that made up Indonesia's history and culture, especially in the contrasts between Java and Sumatra.

The third and northernmost town she visited on Sumatra was Medan, a provincial capital, center of a scenic lake resort country, bustling with people of many tribes and nationalities. The ornamental costumes of its women, the lavish embellishments of its mosque, its tree-shaded streets, and its surrounding fields of tobacco, sisal, rubber, and palm embraced much of the beauty and productivity of the whole of Sumatra.

And then there was Bali. Was it legend, myth, or truth? As someone had said of the Ramayana, it was all and it was neither. It was paradise—with problems. It was the middle world, that land area where men worked to please the gods, between the sea (which was considered a haven for evil spirits) and heaven. Religion was the central force of life. Edna discovered that there were thousands of temples on this one small island, household shrines, and altars in many fields so that the gods of various crops might be placated.

It was a land of rigid caste—the Brahmin priesthood at the

top and then, in descending order, the governing class, the tradespeople, and finally the common throng—and also a land of easy laughter. Evil and friendly spirits waged constant struggle for domination of the human world, and the spirits of animals might be part of that contest between darkness and light. A parasol could be a mark of dignity, and the stern countenance of a stone deity might be softened by the petals of a hibiscus bloom adorning one ear. It was a land where everything seemed to grow and flourish without effort, and yet there was prodigious work to be done.

Bali: dancing—processions, festivals, and constant ceremonials—above all, surrounding all, dancing. Cockfights and sculpture and carving. Ducks in the paddies, pigs on the road to market, golden-colored cows. Looming over the landscape was the shadow of volcanoes which might erupt after centuries of slumber, as did Gunung Agung, "the navel of the world," in 1963, while Edna was on one of her last visits to Bali, scorching thousands of acres of land with molten lava and smothering other thousands of acres beneath heavy ash.

More impressive than the scenery were the people. Bali was a Hindu enclave in a Muslim nation, intellectual and proud. Gentle and gracious families went about the drudgery of their field work with eloquent dignity. Women carrying weighty burdens of rice or fruit atop their heads or in baskets slung from bars across their shoulders walked easily, erectly. Women seemed to bear most of the burdens. They also labored in the rice fields along with the men. Yet they bore children, too, in abundance. There were five children in an average family. Two million people lived on this tiny fragile island of two thousand square miles.

And behind the waving palms, the thatch-topped, mud-walled family compounds, and the rhythms of musical rituals, was the reality of a land of two million inhabitants with eighteen doctors and two dentists. Along with perhaps one hundred midwives, they were responsible for the island's births and health—although most of the babies were born with the aid of only a relative or friend.

It was not the Bali of *South Pacific* that Edna came to cherish, but the beauty and endurance of industrious people who were up at four o'clock in the morning to go to the rice fields or the rubber plantations, where they worked until noon or shortly after and then returned home to practice their art or craft: painting, carving, dancing, playing a musical instrument, or shaping stone. It was the Bali of graceful and practical women who seemed in constant procession to the temples with their enormous baskets of fruit, where they did not waste the offering as a whole but left only tokens—a piece of fruit, a flower, a handful of rice—on the altar. It was the warmth and tenderness of families who never excluded their incredibly happy babies from anything, but who committed their care to older brothers and sisters—sometimes only slightly older—who grew up with an infant slung across one hip.

And it was from the standpoint of the family's welfare and happiness that Edna spoke with the Balinese about her work. They were utterly astonished at the whole concept of birth control. Edna discovered on her first visit to Bali that there were no words in Balinese to convey the idea of birth control.

On the plane to Denpasar, she sat next to an educator who learned—as most of her acquaintances did sooner rather than later—about Edna's work. The woman suggested that the first person Edna should contact on the island was Dr. A. Djelantik, head of all public health work in Bali. With his name and that of Dr. Esther Wrowar, gynecologist and director of the maternal and child health program, which had been provided by Madam Subandrio, Edna arrived in Denpasar.

When she went to talk with Dr. Djelantik, she found a leader of the highest caste, descendant of one of the former rajahs of Bali. He had been sent to Holland for his education, where he married a Dutch girl who was a nurse. Together they returned to Bali to establish a charming home on the outskirts of the capital and to devote themselves to public health.

Edna spoke of family planning to Dr. Djelantik and he smiled. "No one has ever talked to me about family planning. But I think it would be impossible because our government is opposed."

Edna dug into her handbag and brought forth the clipping from the Singapore newspaper in which President Sukarno's statement at the meeting with Pakistan's President had been quoted—that family planning was necessary, not for population control but for health reasons. Edna also showed him credentials from Madam Subandrio, national minister of health, and explained her idea of receiving contraceptives without duty and distributing them through various health departments throughout the country.

"This is interesting," Dr. Djelantik replied. "It could be a sound health measure. I would not have the faintest idea how it would be accepted on this island because, frankly, the term has never been used here so far as I know. Would you be willing to speak to a group of our doctors and tell them what you have told me?"

Edna agreed. While she was waiting for the doctor's meeting to be arranged, Edna went to call on the Governor of Bali and his wife. Her friend, Mrs. Hadji Agus Salim, had written Edna a letter of introduction to this young couple.

When Edna finished telling them of her work for family planning, the governor turned to his wife and said, "Our home is a good place for her to start, isn't it?"

The wife laughed and nodded. "Yes. We have nine children, but we've only been married six years."

Even with her background of experience Edna was startled. They explained. "We have three sets of twins."

At least Edna felt she had the reassurance that they would not be hostile to her work.

When Dr. Djelantik called for her to speak to the doctors, he asked if it would be all right if he asked a few others, too. "You may invite all of Denpasar," Edna reassured him. "This is the sort of work that needs to be explained."

Between fifty and seventy-five community leaders gathered to hear Edna. With Dr. Djelantik interpreting, Edna made short statements and then listened as the doctor uttered a lengthy stream of words. From the reaction of the audience she gathered that what was being said was absolutely startling to them. But they began to understand, and the interest mounted. At the close of Edna's talk there was a stream of questions from the floor. After an hour and a half, a man stood and asked, "How are we going to follow through on this program?"

Edna replied, "The ideal thing would be to form a local organization, with officers, meetings, and a program of education. Such a committee can be helpful to the public health department in receiving supplies and distributing them, and in supporting clinics and circulating word of their existence."

Someone else spoke. "Why don't we organize such a group?"

This last query, and a subsequent flurry of activity, took place in Bahasa Indonesian, the national language. Presently Dr. Djelantik turned to Edna and reported, "The wife of the governor has been elected president of our new family planning organization, and she has accepted."

After a few minutes he gave another return: "My wife is the vice president." The wife of the director of Garuda Airways was made the secretary, Ibu Ujrah Sagan became treasurer, and Dr. Esther Wrowar was appointed medical adviser. It was a varied and capable group.

The whole affair was incredible. Here, on the island of Bali, most improbable of places to be promoting birth control, her very first public discussion had resulted in a family planning association. Even Edna had never dared hope for such a speedy schedule.

Of course she returned again and again, usually accompanied by the beautiful and brilliant Nani Suwando. By the very next year Edna found that the little group formed that first night had not been a figurehead committee, existing in name only. It had been responsible for establishing three dispensary centers, with listings of addresses and days and hours for these dispensaries published in the local news.

One of the centers was located in the general hospital. Another was located in the governor's mansion on the main street of Denpasar, where the governor's wife served as supervisor. Edna felt that this center did not receive as many callers as it might, however, because of general reluctance to visit the official government mansion on this personal mission. The third clinic, however, was in the office of Dr. Djelantik, adjacent to his home. Mrs. Djelantik, a trained nurse and midwife, conducted this clinic. Not only did she serve patients but she also conducted a training course for married midwives who seemed especially well suited to this phase of public health service. From Denpasar these midwives would go out to other cities and villages of the island.

It was during her second trip to Bali that Edna participated in an event which permitted her to gain a genuine sense of identification with the people and their attitude toward the basic realities of life and death. A major purpose in all of her travels was to know and become part of each country, and when she was invited to sit with the royal family and witness the ceremony of cremation she accepted.

As it turned out, this was one of the last of the great royal cremations. It had been in preparation for six months and represented a cost of more than a million dollars. For this was not a mournful formality but one of incomparable celebration. Gamelan orchestras—gongs, xylophones, and drums—provided the haunting music, and youthful dancers of supple grace expressed the felicity of the ceremony. Even the richness of the elaborate costumes reflected its mood.

The ritual itself was unlike anything Edna had ever experienced. Two enormous towers had been constructed—one slightly taller, for the dead rajah; the other for his wife who had died shortly after he did. Atop the higher tower was the immense replica of a black bull; atop the lower the figure of a white cow. An entire day of the ceremony was required for these unwieldy towers and figures to be carried up the hill to the summit where the cremation would take place. More than a thousand people, Edna estimated, strained and labored in joyous participation.

Atop the hill, the bodies of the rajah and his wife were lifted into a kind of pavilion, to which throngs of people were then privileged to carry wood, constructing a massive pyre. The figures of the bull and cow, draped in some rich material resembling velvet, were carefully placed on top—a feat in itself, considering their ponderous weight.

When the fire was finally lit, the thousands of participants became onlookers as the flames leaped high, devouring the wood and the bodies and the figures of the animals.

Perhaps the most joyous moment of all came the following morning, when the ashes of the dead were taken to the seashore, and a bearer was rowed out across the water. As the ashes were scattered to wind and water, symbolizing release of the soul, the oneness of life and death reached a happy culmination and this celebration—in such contrast to Western observance of funerals—reached final fulfillment.

To Edna, all the rhythm and festive sense of the Balinese was integrated into this experience, and she felt that it reaffirmed her own concern that all life should be wanted, should be cherished—birth, no less than death, a celebration.

During one of Edna's final visits to Bali, a stranger she met at one of the clinics approached her with shy dignity. As one of the workers interpreted for Edna, the woman said, "Do you know? We call you 'the angel.' "

Edna smiled in some embarrassment but the woman explained, "For the first time in our lives we live and work free of the fear of pregnancy."

Not all of her journeys were rewarded with such instant and sustained success. But throughout Indonesia she met remarkable individuals who ensured that family planning would take firm hold in that populous land. In Djakarta there was Dr. Koen Martiono, one of the first people she had met at Madam Subandrio's. Dr. Martiono was in charge of the clinics for all maternal and child health programs, and promoted the work at the lowest local level and participated in international conferences as well.

In Bandung, Edna's initial key acquaintance was with a fine woman, coordinator of the city's midwives, Dr. Zuleika Masjhur. She formed a FPA, agreed to receive supplies from Dr. Subandrio and see that they were distributed through maternal health care centers. In subsequent visits she arranged for Edna to meet the province's officials and receive their sanction for the work.

Also in Bandung there was Dr. Samedi, the health inspector for West Java, who had known nothing about family planning when Edna first talked with him. After her explanation he began to make plans for integrating family planning into pilot rural and city programs. During this planning, Edna discovered that Dr. Samedi's assistant had spent a year in public health training in North Carolina, where he had witnessed an excellent family planning program; he had also visited the Frontier Nursing Service in Kentucky's mountains. He and Edna could exchange reminiscences of work in those distant parts of the world.

One of Edna's goals in Bandung was to establish a family planning service at the army hospital, which was open to the public as well as to military personnel. Again, her experience in similar situations in the United States proved useful. The lieutenant colonel who was director of the child care division of the hospital was initially dubious of the need for such a program. Then he began to examine his records. He visited the prenatal clinic, where his reluctance turned to concern. Family planning work was inaugurated at the hospital. Eventually it would also be taken up at hospitals of the other military services.

In Jogjakarta there were delays. In Padang, on Sumatra, the strict traditional customs of an intensely religious people slowed any change to the sluggish pace of water buffaloes at midday.

Perhaps an encounter in Surabaya was typical of many, not only in Indonesia but in other parts of the world, where Edna refused to accept the reputed opposition of leaders and went after their support.

On her first journey to Surabaya, Edna did not carry a letter of introduction from Madam Subandrio to Dr. Saiful Anwar, although Dr. Anwar was director of provisional health services for all of East Java and one of the most widely traveled and respected men in his country. Edna's only introduction was to a doctor working on a research project in family planning. After lengthy conversation about this research, which impressed Edna as being time-consuming, expensive, and without practical application, she asked if he would not take her to meet the chief health officer.

"I must tell you the truth. Dr. Saiful Anwar is unalterably opposed to family planning. In addition, he is opposed to white faces. He does not like Westerners."

"Well," Edna said, "this creates a situation. Perhaps I should just leave."

"You can't do that. He knows you're here in Surabaja. It would insult him if you didn't try to see him."

"Then we must consider what to do," Edna replied.

That evening the research doctor telephoned. Edna had an appointment to see Dr. Anwar at eight o'clock the next morning. Edna did not sleep very soundly that night.

Dr. Saiful Anwar was, indeed, a highly educated, widely traveled man. When Edna was ushered into his office, he talked gently and courteously for an interval before he suddenly said, with considerable rancor, "So! You're here for family planning? Where are your headquarters? Singapore?"

"No," Edna replied. "Actually, I've been working most recently in Malaya."

"Malaya?" His surprise was obvious. "That isn't overpopulated."

"Heavens, no! Malaya is a beautiful country of only some seven million people. Seven million in a country about the size of Java."

"Well," Dr. Anwar said, "why family planning? Isn't that for population control?"

Edna took a deep breath. "You must understand, Dr. Anwar, I'm not particularly interested in population control. The Pathfinder Fund and I feel that if a mother's health is protected, if children are spaced to be born when the mother is well and the baby can be well cared for, the right number of children will take their rightful place in society."

"That is not what I've known as population control. I have been in the World Health Organization for many years, and all we hear there in Europe is how to cut down on black populations and yellow and brown populations," Dr. Anwar stated.

Edna was dismayed. She could not tolerate having her mission so misunderstood. "Before I ever came over here, Dr. Anwar, I had worked for twenty-five years among *white* people in America on this same family planning program for them. What I'm concerned about is the health of mothers and children. The color of their skin doesn't concern me in the slightest."

He looked at her steadily. "If that's planned parenthood," the doctor replied, "that's nothing more than plain public health." He paused. "How do you go about this?"

"In the beginning the Pathfinder Fund will provide any contraceptives you need in order to let individual couples decide how many children they want and can support. When you have integrated service into the public health program, each family will have the human right to decide how many children it wants. This would protect both the mother's and the baby's health."

"We have eighteen health centers right here in East Java. We could introduce the program into all of these." Dr. Anwar smiled slightly. "I have a new doctor in charge of maternal health who will be interested in this."

"I want to meet the doctor," Edna replied.

"You'll have to wait a little while. She's having a baby this very day."

"I'll be glad to come back anytime and help set up a program," Edna assured him.

She did return. The program was established and Edna was present the day the first clinic was opened in Surabaya. Dr. Anwar introduced her to patients as the person who had made the service possible. The very first woman she met haunted her: thin, stoop-shouldered, with a sagging stomach and dull eyes.

When Edna was back again a year later, Dr. Anwar said to her one day, "Mrs. McKinnon, the first patient who ever came to clinic is here. I think you remember her?"

Edna watched as the woman was given her supplies and left the clinic. She walked uprightly and there was flesh on her bones and tone in her skin. It seemed impossible that this lively human being could be the skeleton she had seen earlier.

When the woman spied Edna, she suddenly fell on her knees and kissed Edna's hand. Edna was even more embarrassed than she had been by the woman in Bali who called her "the angel." But the testimonial was similar. For the first time in all her years of marriage, this woman said, she was not nursing a baby or carrying a baby inside her. For the first time in all their married life she and her husband could be together without making a child.

Edna's eyes flooded with tears. The heat and the mosquitoes and the rains had not made her cry. Rebuffs and discouragements had not made her cry. Separation from her daughter, whom she often longed to see, and from friends she loved, had not made her cry. But this small grateful woman kissing her hand brought tears. The woman's words and sense of freedom were enough reward for all the hardships which seemed, in comparison to her gratitude, mere inconveniences.

There were many steps to be taken in building up the work. When Edna returned to Singapore after her first trip to Indonesia, she suggested to Mrs. Goh Koh Kee that training of nurses and doctors was essential. They needed instruction in techniques of contraception, how to talk with patients, and a multitude of small but not inconsequential matters. As a result, the IPPF and the Pathfinder Fund each paid for three public health doctors from Indonesia's cities to attend a doctors' seminar in Singapore. Two months later two more doctors and six midwives attended a training course there.

An example of Edna's consistent consideration for her friends and fellow workers occurred at this time. The philanthropic funds financing this training accounted only for the necessities. But Edna insisted that these visitors could not be brought to the shopping mecca of Singapore without being provided a small sum for personal spending. On her own authority she underwrote an allowance for shopping—small, but enough for at least one happy expedition to the markets. She was later repaid by Dr. Gamble, who understood her thoughtfulness.

During Edna's next visit to Indonesia, she realized that while it was useful, sometimes necessary, to send workers to Singapore for instruction, it would also be good to have training in Indonesia. As she pursued her travels she tried to take others with her so that they could see what was being done elsewhere in the country.

Finally, as clinics increased and interest grew in various cities, she felt that the time was ripe for an intensive training program. She presented the idea to Clarence Gamble and he agreed that Charles and Bernadine Zukosky, who would be attending the IPPF Conference in Singapore, should go on to Indonesia and lead an intensive three-day course.

The Zukoskys were the long-time friends Edna had first known during her stay in Alabama. Now Charles Zukosky had retired from his position with the bank in Birmingham, and he and his wife were volunteers for the Pathfinder Fund in different parts of the world. Their capabilities and experience brought a new professionalism to the volunteer effort, for Charles Zukosky was able to formulate goals and organize work. Edna was delighted to be associated once again with these bright, genteel, able people.

The three-day training course, carefully arranged after weeks of thought and discussion, was a success. The family planning program in Indonesia seemed to be on its way. But there was one other need: for a paid national executive, someone to keep the clinics running at full capacity, someone to encourage educational programs, someone to unify and inspire the local committees—someone, in short, who could concentrate full time and talent on birth control in Indonesia.

But Edna had encountered the hazards of pride before. She was aware of the eminence of Madam Subandrio's position and the jealous guardianship such a position fostered. While the Zukoskys were in Indonesia, Edna shared her problem with them and after they had completed leadership of the training course they agreed that employment of a director must, indeed, be the next step.

In addition to Madam Subandrio's personal feelings, there was another hazard involving the old bureaucratic red tape that had entangled Edna before. In Singapore, she had told Mrs. Goh Koh Kee that the only way to consolidate the work that had been done in Indonesia was to hire a paid executive who could carry on nationwide. But Mrs. Goh Koh Kee pointed out that the IPPF would not give money to any organization until they asked for membership in the IPPF.

The trouble was that Indonesia was feeling its growing pains acutely, and its exacerbated sense of nationalism had led it to sever connections with even such international groups as the Rotary, the Masons, the YMCA, and the Boy Scouts. Indonesia rejected all outside help (which made Edna' accomplishments even more dazzling), and it had no intention of asking for IPPF membership. Edna explained the situation and stressed the need to Mrs. Goh Koh Kee.

Despite past differences and Edna's apprehensions, Mrs.

Goh replied, "In this instance, since we know the facts and know they need help more than anyone else right now, we will agree to pay the salary of a worker —if you can find one."

Edna could find one. She had had one in mind for some time. But she waited for Madam Subandrio to suggest the name. And finally, pressed by the Zukoskys, Madam Subandrio stated that she would like to ask Mrs. O. Djoewari. This was Edna's choice. A trained woman of ability and energy, Mrs. Djoewari seemed to be just the person to fill her country's need. She accepted the offer to become a paid executive of the family planning work.

Edna had loved Indonesia and its people. She had played with them and worked with them, entertained and given presents, made circuitous journeys, talked, educated, and learned. She had spoken at hospitals, military bases, and the University of Indonesia; at dinner parties, in planes, and on sight-seeing trips. On return trips to America she had worked in Washington to help the Agency for International Development realize that millions for military aid could never ensure safety or stability when not a penny was spent on birth control in the countries that were assisted. In Chicago she had told old friends and colleagues about Indonesia's beauty and its needs. Mrs. James Offield had given her two thousand dollars, and the John Leslies five thousand. She wrote them of the Jeep and other necessities that the Indonesian FPA bought with their money.

She had made a journey to Lucknow, India, where she visited an experiment in adult education, Literacy Village, founded by an American, Mrs. Welthy Monsinger Fisher. One of Edna's reasons for this visit was to learn how puppet shows were incorporated into family planning education. Much of Indonesia's theater centered around the ancient art of puppetry. Indeed, the Zukoskys, who followed Edna in Indonesia, adopted this means of communication in their work across the country.

After expending any energy in Indonesia, a Westerner was left dripping with perspiration. In one of the lengthy letters Edna wrote to Clarence Gamble she mentioned that it was hot and there was no air conditioning available. In his reply, Dr.

Gamble remarked that it was his understanding that people could keep very comfortable in the tropics sitting under a fan.

To which Edna shot back, "And who could do my job sitting under a fan?" Dr. Gamble was delighted by her rejoinder.

As she made ready to step out of the work in Indonesia, Edna assessed its achievements. When she had first come to the country in June 1961, there was only one small family planning clinic in all of Indonesia. When she left there were fifty-six centers in operation. On this foundation, a hundred and sixty-five clinics were built by 1968, when Edna made a final visit to Indonesia. Everywhere there was general acceptance of family planning as an important health measure. Doctors, medical students, nurses, and midwives—all seemed eager to help.

Characteristically, Edna could not rest on her laurels. She evaluated needs for the future as well as past successes. She saw that the dedication and efforts of a few indefatigable workers in the beginning might make them possessive and narrow in the work yet to be done. She suggested that the time would arrive when some of the earliest recruits must turn over the responsibility to new volunteers, while they themselves should continue even more actively in guiding, counseling, and training. "This may be the very hardest job the Indonesia FPA will face—that of relinquishing full charge and still not deserting the ship!" She was telling them to grow, but not to grow in upon themselves.

With all her philosophical counseling, Edna also had some bits of hard-nosed advice. She advised her friends that if they wrote to the Pathfinder Fund asking for money, they had better send at least two or three copies and mail them on different days. "That way, *one* will surely arrive!"

In her farewell speech to Edna, Madam Subandrio observed, "The reason we are so grateful to Mrs. McKinnon and Pathfinder is this: others come to study us and see if we need help. We know we need help. And Pathfinder came, through Mrs. McKinnon, and set up a program, and now we help ourselves."

In June 1970, Mrs. Djoewari wrote a letter to Edna.

I am in Jogjakarta now in the front yard of the Hotel Garuda looking out at the Radja Farma Dispensary with the old Dutch architecture. Now you will remember again the place where we have been in our pioneering work in family planning. . . . While working in Jogja I cannot help thinking of you, so I am writing you this. I hope everything is fine with you and your family. I often wish you would come to Indonesia and see the seed flourish that you have sown.

In a news dispatch from Djakarta on August 16, 1971, President Suharto

called today for an intensified birth control program for Indonesia, saying that her future depends on it. . . . "Particularly in this field of planned parenthood, I also want to call upon you to step up its implementation right from this moment. It is not exaggerated to say that the success or failure of this planned parenthood drive is a challenge to the future of the Indonesia nation."

He said the country, with a population estimated at 120 million, had increased food, mineral, and industrial production, but he warned: "If these increases are not balanced with controlled population increase, then that production output will be, nationally speaking, meaningless. . . ."

Edna's emphasis on the family's happiness and survival had grown to embrace the nation's happiness and survival.

10

Nothing succeeds like excess.

—Oscar Wilde

Each child who comes into the world is at once a possible source of enrichment for all mankind and a threat to the well-being of all others who share his need for food, space, air, water.

—Director of the National Institute
of Child Health and Human Development

It is widely accepted that person-to-person contacts are the most effective means by which knowledge and information about fertility planning become diffused throughout society.

—*Human Fertility and National Development*

In February 1963, on her way to revisit Malaya and Indonesia, Edna arrived in Singapore for a worldwide conference of the International Planned Parenthood Federation. Laden down with handsome handwoven baskets of many sizes and shapes, mats and carvings, and generous quantities of exotic tapa cloth, she greeted her Pathfinder colleagues Clarence and Sarah Gamble, Charles and Bernadine Zukosky, and Margaret Roots, who were already at the Singapore hotel.

Breathless with excitement, she could scarcely finish her greetings—while spontaneously presenting most of her treasures of baskets and trophies to her friends—before she turned to the Gambles. "I have to have a thousand dollars, Clarence. Fiji needs it and I promised it to them. If you don't let them have it, I'll take it out of my own pocket. Fiji is doing something important. And I promised."

Dr. Gamble was elated to meet her request. It represented the sort of pragmatic expediency he admired.

Fiji and Tonga flashed through Edna's years of travel and work like two of the islands' brilliantly plumed parrots winging through dense tropical foliage. Her weeks there were brief, fascinating, hilarious, and successful. They tested all her powers of concentration and accommodation. And they provided her with confirmation of the belief that one person was still capable of making a difference in the course of events.

Edna went to Fiji at the suggestion of a World Health Organization (WHO) doctor for the South Pacific Islands. Although the doctor's church (Roman Catholic) and official organization did not sanction public discussion and advocacy of the use of contraceptives, he had become increasingly aware of the acute situation in Fiji.

In 1961 it was discovered that the birth rate was nearly forty-one per thousand, while the death rate was six per thousand. At this rate of increase, the population would be doubled in little more than twenty years. And while there might be simply space enough for all these people on the more than three hundred Fiji Islands scattered through the southwest Pacific (only some one hundred of them inhabited), there was certainly not food, shelter, or resources adequate to supply the needs of so many. Alarmed, the government admitted that "family planning" ultimately meant planning the nation, too. A commission report on natural resources and population produced a hundred twenty-four recommendations. The first one stated: "Government should provide additional family planning clinics, and contraceptives should be provided free of charge to married persons."

The need for family planning was apparent and admitted. The appropriation for such an effort was approved. Support was ready to be mustered. But know-how at each level of work was lacking. This was what Edna could bring to Fiji.

When she arrived in Suva, the capital city with some forty thousand people, on Viti Levu, the largest of the islands and almost exactly the size of Hawaii, she discovered a blue and green world of ocean and sky, mountains and palm trees, and a tall, dark-skinned, strongly muscled race of people whose upswept beehive hair styles were an unacknowledged forerunner of U.S. fashions a few years later. Their thatched houses of reed and palm, with posts hewn from trees in the nearby hills, suited the balmy temperatures just south of the equator. The easy availability of a variety of luscious fruits, tubers, and vegetables, kept the people healthy looking (the diet had once included "long pig," or humans). But cannibalism—along with several other brutal forms of population control such as war, plague, and human sacrifice—had long since yielded to the twentieth century and the influences inevitable in a British Crown Colony. Gracious in manner, graceful in movement, the Fijians had created what seemed to Edna a healthy, happy social atmosphere.

But the islands were not totally tranquil and untroubled. Among Fijians and Indians alike the birth rate was excessive, the death rate among children high. Encouraged by the British, Indians had come to Fiji originally as indentured laborers. Following World War II their number was found to exceed that of the natives. Immigration had almost ceased as early as 1917, but the customary family of ten or twelve children had multiplied the Indian population by geometric ratios. And the fantastic number of pregnancies took a terrible toll of dead babies and haggard mothers.

The most common cause of ill health during pregnancy was anemia. A three-year hospital survey found four out of ten mothers anemic, with the severest cases naturally occurring among those who had had too quickly repeated pregnancies. Hemorrhage following birth was frequent. Fijian mothers were four times more prone to postpartum hemorrhage than Indian mothers, but for all the races there was a clear relationship between the number of pregnancies and hemorrhage.

The colony's health officer welcomed Edna and introduced her to Betty Knowles, the gynecologist in charge of maternal and child health programs. Dr. Knowles was a young British woman, initially reserved, somewhat shy, and thoroughly delightful. After they had visited various parts of Suva together, looking at the beginning of the family planning work, Dr. Knowles told Edna that the government had scheduled her to go throughout the islands introducing the program.

"Wouldn't it be fun if I could go with you?" Edna exclaimed.

"Would you?" Dr. Knowles asked enthusiastically.

And so the young British doctor and the "retired grandmother"—as the *Fiji Times* described Edna in an interview—traveled together to cities and villages and tiny islands, carrying the word of the new freedom.

Edna discovered that Dr. Knowles, new to public discussion of this intimate subject, needed the bracing confidence and thrust that a battle-scarred veteran like herself could provide. At first the Fijian people, even doctors and nurses in the clinics, were dumbfounded that this strange woman would talk publicly about such matters. But her matter-of-fact attitude soon put them at ease. Then they, like the general public, began to listen and finally accept what she was telling them.

In ways large and small she recognized the need for adaptation. There was, for instance, the matter of the leaflet, "You Can Plan Your Family." This simple story, told mostly in pictures to reach the largest possible audience, was useful for distribution in new countries where planned parenthood was being introduced. But in Fiji the pictures of a rabbit were meaningless. There were no rabbits on the islands. The picture of a mongoose was substituted.

In a little plane that held only three or four passengers, Betty Knowles and Edna island-hopped above the cobalt and azure of the Pacific, laying the foundation for a network of clinics and becoming fast friends in the process. When they arrived back in Suva, Edna said, "Now! You must have a committee of distinguished laymen to support this family planning part of the health program. They can help win approval, educate the public, and make people aware of the location and availability of clinics."

"That," Dr. Knowles replied, "is something I couldn't possibly do: organize such a group."

"I'll help," Edna said.

Dr. Knowles compiled a list of people whose support would strengthen family planning work. The head of the council of social agencies proved to be cooperative and suggested key names. Then Edna invited these people—individuals, couples, and small groups—to come to the Grand Pacific Hotel for luncheon, tea, or dinner, whichever seemed most appropriate, where she explained the purpose of her visit to Fiji and described the aims and methods of family planning on the islands. With few exceptions she was rewarded with their interest and favorable response. When all of these new-found friends were eventually called together for a meeting, Edna decided that this was a good time for her to visit Tonga and let the people in Suva go forward on their own initiative for a little while.

Under the auspices of the head of the Tonga Hospital, Edna arrived after a five hundred-mile flight southeast from Melanesian Fiji to the Polynesian kingdom of Queen Salote and her son, Prince Tungi, who would succeed her to the throne only two years later. The lack of mountains and the lighter skin of the people offered immediate contrast to Fiji, but there was just as definite an atmosphere of dignity and friendliness in this last of the island kingdoms.

A constitutional monarchy under British protection and influence, Tonga was a realm of encircling ocean and coral reefs, coconut palms, bananas and yams, hand-printed tapa cloth pounded from mulberry bark, rhythmic dancing—and children. They swarmed everywhere, shy, curious, smiling. Edna saw in the streets, villages, and countryside a flesh and blood statement of the fact that Tonga was one of the most densely populated island groups in the Pacific; a third of its population of some 65,000 less than ten years old. With the cooperation of the island's medical leaders, Edna set about establishing a program which would function for years to come.

In tropical heat, among strange people and customs, she traveled over Tonga, learning about the system of medical care that reached out into villages and countryside. With the custom of dividing land among the children of each family and with the limited amount of land on the small islands that made up Tonga, space was becoming scarce. Edna worked out a plan to integrate birth control education into the traveling medical service. For the need of Tonga was education: to let people know the necessity and availability of contraceptive help.

Along the way she faced tests of many kinds—some of them social. Knowing that the success of her work depended on effective use of all her contacts, she neglected no opportunity, and overlooked incidental inconveniences.

Luxury hotels were not yet a part of the island's economy, and she found accommodations near the airfield at a place that seemed to be a combination private home and public hotel. Like Topsy, it had just grown, with a porch enclosed to make bedrooms and walls that were mere partitions, failing to reach the ceiling, through which and above which sounds trickled as easily as the water from the improvised shower where Edna pulled a string and was met with a refreshing stream. The Englishwoman who was the establishment's proprietor became fashion adviser when Edna was invited to a cocktail party at the palace.

"Wear the finest that you have," was her admonition.

The most formal dress she owned proved to be sufficient,

and Edna enjoyed a lively time at the party, where she spread the word of family planning to the British high commissioner, as well as to the native leaders present. When she told the commissioner's secretary that she was invited to a luncheon the next day which would be hosted by Prince Tungi, the secretary warned her: "There are a few rules you must follow. A hat and gloves and stockings are mandatory." She surveyed Edna. "Your girdle, too, most likely."

"But I didn't bring a hat or gloves," Edna replied.

"I have dozens. Come by my home and I'll be happy to lend you whatever you need."

The following day Edna set forth in the sweltering temperature, sporting borrowed snow-white gloves and decked out in the borrowed finery of a white mushroom-shaped hat whose pleating exactly matched the knife pleats in her white nylon dress. Underneath, however, she could claim her own girdle and stockings.

When she was ushered into the dining area, she realized that the luncheon was actually a Tonga feast. This meant sitting on the floor on a tapa cloth mat in front of a long table about six inches high—and disposing of legs and feet as inconspicuously and gracefully as possible.

With some twenty-eight guests arrayed on either side, Prince Tungi took his place at the head of the board. After the delicate people of Bali, all of the men on Fiji and Tonga appeared conspicuously tall to Edna. They had an elegant stature, and while many of the women were bulky they were not gross. But even among his large fellow Tongans, Prince Tungi was notable: six feet two inches tall, apparently weighing his reputed three hundred pounds, he was one of the largest men Edna had ever seen. She knew of his reputation for keen and thoughtful questions, his curiosity about the outside world, which indicated an appetite of mind to complement that of body. In Suva, Fiji, it was rumored that once he had visited the hotel and enjoyed the lavish dinner, a full-course production ranging the gamut from hors d'oeuvres, soup, fish, through entree, salad, dessert, and cheeses—and when he had polished off the meal, he ordered another exactly duplicating the first.

The festive board now spread before Edna reflected the

prince's own hospitality as well as that of his people: dominating all else were the eight roast suckling pigs crouching at intervals along the length of the table. These were interspersed with large fowls—turkeys and chickens baked to a tawny brown—and heaping dishes of various vegetables. In front of each guest rested a mammoth yam—some twelve inches long and six inches wide. Half a coconut was filled with an exotic crabmeat mixture. When Edna saw others pick up the shell and drink from it, she followed their example and was pleased by the cold, delicious taste. Fruit juices—innocent of ice but nonetheless cool and welcome—helped satisfy her thirst throughout the meal.

The girdle was Private Enemy Number One. Edna had never been adept at the art of perching on the floor. Now, fortunately, the full skirt of her dress provided refuge for her folded legs and numb feet. But the girdle held her in its vise. She peeled off the white gloves and deposited them in her purse, then made good use of her fingers in lieu of knives and forks. Ladies kneeling on the opposite side of the table sliced off chunks of the succulent pig, turkey, and chicken and handed it across the table on the point of a knife. After a few such morsels, interspersed with fruit and pieces of the yam in front of each guest, hands became greasy and juicy. The tapa cloth napkins were totally nonabsorbent—a little like trying to dry one's fingers on waxed paper—and Edna gave thanks for the Kleenex tucked in her purse.

The girdle was becoming unbearable; her stockings seemed to have been knit out of wool yarn rather than nylon. As the midday heat intensified so did Edna's sweat. Rivulets streamed down her back and face and chest. The large pleated, mushroom-shaped hat tilted forward lower and lower over her forehead. A borrowed white hat was not something to rearrange with greasy fingers. And still the feasting continued.

At last, begirdled, begrimed, and besoaked, peering out from under the hat, feeling as stuffed and basted in her own juices as one of the roast suckling pigs, Edna rose from the floor, paid proper respect to her host, and returned to her small improvised room.

Only a few minutes after she had arrived and begun stripping away her soggy finery, a porter from the palace appeared. He bore an enormous platter of food left over from the feast. She felt at the moment as if she might never wish to see food again. But she accepted the royal generosity with all the graciousness she could muster. As a matter of fact, a little later she enjoyed this leftover food more than its original serving, because she could feast free of the hazards of protocol and the confinements of high fashion.

Her work went well. On a smaller scale she set up a program similar to those she had established in Indonesia and elsewhere, centered in this instance around the hospital's traveling medical services program. Then she returned to Fiji to see what progress was taking place there.

Back in Suva, Edna found that Dr. Betty Knowles and some of those who were working to establish the clinics, publicize their purposes, and form a committee were convinced that a couple named Mr. and Mrs. Robert Munro would be ideal leaders for the committee. But Robert Munro had already refused Betty Knowles. "He won't touch it," the young English woman lamented.

Edna asked if she might approach Mr. Munro. It was just the sort of pioneer chore she felt particularly suited to tackle. In a city in the United States or in Fiji she was the visiting fireman who could say what needed to be said, risk wrath or embarrassment. She could and would take risks of ridicule, rejection, and misunderstanding, which made it possible for her to win her way more often than seemed probable.

Robert Munro, member of a prestigious law firm, enjoyed an imposing reputation. Tall, slender in build, with dark hair and a lawyer's suspicion of Causes, he told her: "I do not underestimate the importance of this work at all. But we cannot organize effectively without some money."

"That's why I'm here. How much would you need?"

"About three hundred pounds, I should think."

"Would one thousand U.S. dollars be enough?" Edna asked.

"How do you have authority to promise that?" he asked. Edna wondered if he would have had the same doubts about a man in her position.

"That's the way Pathfinder Fund works," Edna explained. "The Fund wants to help support the important activity in each country. But we can't possibly know what each place needs until you and others examine your own situation and then tell us." Mr. Munro nodded. "Now here on Fiji," Edna continued, "we don't need to give contraceptives, as we did in Indonesia, because you have money for that. But if you need money for an organization to promote birth control, we'll provide it."

Robert Munro saw the logic of Edna's statements but he still doubted her authority.

"Would it help if I sent a cable to Dr. Gamble and received his promise to send the funds?" she asked.

"Of course," Mr. Munro replied.

Edna returned to her hotel immediately and cabled Clarence Gamble in Milton, Massachusetts. The only difficulty was that Dr. Gamble was not in Milton. He was on his way to Japan. When Edna learned this, she realized it might be days or weeks before she could get in touch with him. By then much of the momentum for the movement in Fiji might be lost. She made a difficult decision and went back to Robert Munro's office.

"We have the word," said Edna.

Munro was greatly pleased.

"Now," Edna burrowed on, "here are some things we must talk over. Would you be willing to become temporary chairman of an enabling committee till we can get something firmly under way?" He agreed. "Then here's a charter, or a pattern of one—"

"That's one thing I can do," Munro assured her. "I'm a lawyer. I'll write the charter."

"Wonderful!" Edna had brought about just what she hoped for—his real involvement in family planning.

At a meeting of perhaps one hundred of Suva's most distinguished people, the health officer of Fiji, Dr. Knowles, and Edna were the initial speakers. After the others had presented medical, family, and national reasons making family planning imperative, Edna presented some of the day-to-day tasks and procedures to be followed. Throughout her work on Fiji, because of the multi-racial situation on the islands—the native

Fijians, rapidly multiplying Indians, and British colonizers—Edna insisted that each committee formed should have an equal number representing these three groups.

"You should form an enabling committee to put your wishes into effect and go forward," Edna concluded her public speech.

Dr. Knowles stood up. "Maybe Mr. Munro would consent to start us off and chair the committee."

"Mr. Munro would be excellent," Edna said.

The audience applauded and when Robert Munro agreed to accept the temporary chairmanship there was great general approval. The Family Planning Association of Fiji was born—and has continued under Robert Munro's presidency until the present. He, as much as anyone with whom she ever worked, confirmed Edna's belief that one dedicated and intelligent person can make a difference in the course of events.

To the work in Fiji, Munro brought the energy of a paid executive director, the prestige of a chairman, the concern of a health worker who saw the problems firsthand, and the communications expertise of an educator and publicist. During the years that followed, every community in Fiji voluntarily accepted family planning. Munro attended international conferences of the IPPF in Chile and elsewhere, while Dr. Knowles took part in conferences and meetings in Singapore.

The result was dramatic. Fiji's decrease in birth rate became one of the most spectacular recorded anywhere in the world. From a rate of forty births per thousand people in 1960, the number fell to twenty-nine per thousand in 1970. The thousand dollars Edna had asked from Clarence Gamble on that day she arrived in Singapore from Fiji bore demonstrable results.

In June 1966, the *Fiji Times* carried an interview with Sir Colville Deverell, secretary general of the IPPF, who was visiting the colony on a worldwide tour of the Family Planning Associations. His comments on the structure of the work made headlines. "The organization of Fiji's family planning campaign is a model of its kind." When Robert Munro sent a copy of the newspaper article to the Pathfinder offices, he wrote, "You can see what Mrs. McKinnon started."

While Edna was in Tonga, she often carried a small, folded fan she had brought from Indonesia. Made of buffalo skin, the pliable leather used in creating shadow play figures, it had attracted considerable admiration among the Tonganese.

When she returned to Indonesia later that spring she bought a dozen of these fans and sent them to the wife of the doctor with whom she had worked. "Please give these to my friends on Tonga who were so kind to me," she wrote. For months afterward she received letters about the little Indonesian fans.

Fans to Tonga, tapa cloth from Fiji! Edna was a clearing-house for gifts. She loved to bestow presents on her friends. In reality, though, wherever she went, the real gift was herself.

"The Tongans and Fijians," she once said, "are about the loveliest people I have ever met."

They reciprocated her appreciation.

11

Hell is other people.

—Jean Paul Sartre,
No Exit

". . . resistance to change in family size may have
been overestimated. The need to find better ways to
overcome apathy remains. It seems important for
the family to realize that under present conditions
more of its children can live to maturity. . . .

"Dr. Carl Taylor tells a delightful story of talking
with a group of village men in a Turkish village. He
went around asking the simple question of how
many brothers and sisters each man had and how
many had lived to maturity. Then he asked about
the individual's own family. After only three or four
men had replied, one of them spoke up and said,
'Don't bother anymore, Doctor, we already know
that today one doesn't have to have as many children
as one had in the past in order to have sons and
daughters in the fields and in the house.' "

—Dr. Leona Baumgartner

IRAN—THAT KINGDOM known in her childhood as Persia, dazzling in its treasures and its harshness, its fabled past and its potential—lodged in Edna's memory as a curious experience of satisfaction and frustration, acceptance and rejection. Here she had special need of her capacity to be a continuing self-starter.

There was never enough time or opportunity to tarry and watch her ideas take root and grow. There was never an interval for her to bask in the satisfaction of seeing her effort—sometimes her battle—justified. From one problem she always moved immediately to another. Leaving one strange but fascinating country with its newfound friends, culture, and landscape, she plunged directly into another—with a quite different history and people. She was forever beginning again. And each new beginning required new hope, fresh awareness, and unflagging faith.

To casual acquaintances, even to close associates and friends, Edna seemed an indestructible source of physical drive, professional know-how, and supreme confidence. But in the private uncertainty and loneliness that sometimes drove her to despair, she faced over and over the gnawing fear of failure.

Her cause of birth control was sometimes unknown and often misunderstood, either deliberately or through naiveté. Her role was often ambiguous, even to herself, and the fact that she was a woman—alone, aggressive when necessary—made her work perhaps more difficult on the official level, but somewhat more effective on a personal basis. For the very experiences of her childhood which had implanted the sense of insecurity and inadequacy against which she struggled and compensated for a lifetime, also provided her with an uncommon and acute sympathy for the people and countries around the world who suffered under similar handicaps.

As she entered each country, then, settling into a comfortable hotel, a small inexpensive pension, a strange private home, or some dreary improvised accommodation, trying to understand and conform to the life around her, she struggled with the doubts and discouragements that harass those dark hours from midnight to dawn. Again and again she put the struggle behind her and went on to discover as much as she could and do as much as was permitted.

In January 1964, on her way to Iran, Edna stopped in India—chiefly at Bombay and New Delhi—and Pakistan, to observe for Dr. Gamble what progress was being made in certain programs he was sponsoring in those countries. She also wished to gain pointers on training courses and educational materials which might be useful in other countries.

Unfortunately, she found little that was encouraging in Pakistan. Its birth rate was as high as India's (some forty-five per thousand) and its infant deaths were higher: approximately one hundred and forty-two compared with one hundred and ten to twenty for India per thousand live births. There seemed to be more projected plans than solid programs under way in both Dacca and Karachi. After listening to one official of the government explain his country's third Five Year Plan, which incorporated twelve thousand family planning workers—men and women in equal proportion—in each of the two wings (East and West Pakistan), with a hundred mobile vans in each wing and an adequate appropriation of funds, Edna discovered that this was all merely a proposal, with not a rupee yet appropriated. Thinking of all the women and families out there aching for relief from the burden of relentless childbearing, Edna chafed under the delays of such official plans without implementation.

She did encounter individuals at various clinics who were carrying out effective work, but lack of cooperation between the government and volunteer organizations crippled the larger effort that was necessary. At a dinner one health educator summed up for Edna a prevalent attitude: Pakistan is hopeless. But Edna could not accept any situation as hopeless. Bleak, she would admit, but there were still those doctors and officials she had met plugging away in their own spheres of training, treatment, or research—if only they could be multiplied a thousand times.

India had become somewhat familiar to Edna during visits and conferences and travels there with Jeannette, who had made several journeys to study Gandhi's philosophy and methods of peace. With its more than four hundred and sixty million people, only twenty-eight percent of them literate, despite its claims to the world's oldest and largest family planning program, Edna could only feel a suffocating desperation when she again entered the human tumult that was India.

In Bombay Edna saw once more the regal Lady Rama Rau and was urged to attend the All-India Family Planning Conference that would be held later in the month. But Edna explained that she was on her way to Iran. She surveyed details of the methods and success of the five family planning branches in Bombay. She soaked up information—from doctors, nurses, administrators, and patients. She worried about the effectiveness and deterioration of foaming and nonfoaming tablets, acceptance of the IUDs which were just beginning to be introduced, and the fact that the Indian Government had not yet approved use of the oral pill. Above all, she suggested and urged, pleaded and nagged for training of family planning workers, such as she found in one astonishing facility, founded and directed by Dr. Shushila Gore, the Family Planning Training and Research Center located in an old hospital on one of the main streets of Bombay. Here again, one person had made a difference by creating a facility that trained effective birth control workers.

But in New Delhi Edna found other doctors and ministers of health who contended that what worked in the large cities was not possible at the village level, and it was here that much of India's breakthrough in family planning must be made. They were planning training courses, sponsored by the government and the Ford Foundation, for village workers. Edna attended all sorts of meetings—from teachers' discussions in suburban schools (where the interest was intense and the lack of information appalling) to a trip in a beautifully equipped van (given by the women of Sweden) far into the outskirts of New Delhi. Two doctors and two social workers (a man and a woman on each team), a drug dispenser, and a driver made up the personnel. In the large courtyard of a Sikh temple they set up five tables and many chairs from the van. People with all sorts of ills came in large numbers. As the doctors treated the ailments, they asked if the patients wanted family planning. If so, they were turned over to the social worker.

Representatives of many funds, researchers for numerous organizations, and other contributors from several countries— all sought to have some impact—and yet the problem of India's population seemed to remain untouched. As Edna listened to all the officials and workers who crowded her days there, she finally concluded, "It all sounds so hopeful. But I realize that no one *anywhere* is doing the adequate training which is badly needed *everywhere*." She could muster only the most qualified hopefulness as she departed for Iran; human horizons seemed unlimited but so, too, did the human capacity for delay and waste.

In Teheran she entered a modern metropolis of some two million people, capital of a country with twenty-three million people scattered over an area larger than France, Italy, Germany, and Great Britain combined. The city reflected much of the contrast between a half-remembered past when such Persian rulers as Cyrus, Darius, and Xerxes bestrode the kingdom and the modern urge toward a realistic future wherein all citizens might have the opportunity to better their own small world.

Iran's birth rate was higher than that of India, Pakistan, or any of the countries in which Edna had yet worked, and she was told that more than half the babies died before they reached school age.

Organized family planning work had begun in Iran in 1958, when the Pathfinder Fund's Edith Gates aroused the interest and cooperation of several highly influential leaders. These included Dr. J. Saleh, the minister of health who had become, by the time Edna arrived, the powerful chancellor of the University of Teheran; Madam Hagar Tarbian, who helped organize a family planning committee and later became one of the first women members of Parliament; and Dr. M. Motameni, director of the Farah Hospital, who had been a prime mover in starting a family planning clinic at the hospital. This small initial group had received its greatest impetus when a brilliant young woman, a member of one of Iran's oldest and most distinguished families, returned home after receiving her degree at the University of Southern California and involved herself in shaping the future of her country.

Miss Sattareh Farman-Farmaian founded the Teheran School of Social Work, became president of the family planning group, and integrated it into the teaching of the school. Students were sent to various medical centers to further the cause of family planning, and the school defrayed much of the expense of birth control work. In 1963, Charles and Bernadine Zukosky made a brief visit to assess the benefits derived from some of the materials which the Pathfinder Fund had been supplying, and Miss Farman-Farmaian encouraged them to invite Edna to come to Iran and help broaden the base and outreach of family planning.

After moving from the expensive hotel where her initial reservation had been made to a small "pansion," as it was spelled in Iran—which cost half as much, included two delicious meals, and gave her a deeper sense of being a part of the city's life and not a transient—Edna invited Miss Farman-Farmaian to dinner.

At that first meeting Edna knew that she had met a distinctive personality. Here was a beautiful woman—dark thick hair framed the even features of her face. Of medium height, wearing stylish clothes with the air of a princess, Miss Farman-Farmaian was also intelligent, forthright, and practical. Her family permeated the whole of Iran. They had been one of the most wealthy and powerful families in the country until the Shah's "white revolution" (so-called because it shed no blood, merely ancient traditions) redistributed among the people who tilled the land some of the vast private landholdings (previously, as many as forty villages might belong to one man). This "white revolution" had also brought, just the year before Edna's arrival, the right for women to vote. Miss Farman-Farmaian met all these changes with vigor and efficiency. She demonstrated superior ability in winning money and support for her school and any project she undertook. She helped Edna arrange a schedule for the first part of her stay in Teheran and seemed eager for all the advice and assistance possible.

Edna went to health centers and hospitals in all parts of the city, and repeatedly visited the two existing family planning clinics. She had more than sixty interviews with a wide range of officials and medical personnel and patients. Every contact underscored her judgment that Iran desperately needed a strong, functioning family planning program, and that it was ready to accept such a program.

At one hospital she found patients whose records showed they had undergone as many as ten, twelve, or fourteen pregnancies. A half-dozen abortions and several infant deaths were not uncommon. The result was an average of two to three living children for each mother. The faces of those women would haunt Edna for years to come.

At another hospital, the young doctor for a large insurance company escorted Edna through a maternity ward. As they stopped by each of the two dozen beds, where the doctor spoke with each patient in Farsi and then interpreted for Edna, she heard additional accounts of waste and grief. No woman there had had fewer than six children. All were now under care because of a bad abortion, either by a clumsy, indifferent doctor or by the desperate use of their own crude home remedies and improvised instruments. Out of eight to fifteen pregnancies, these women, too, averaged only two to three living children—although one woman had nine children in her household. When the young doctor told the women that Edna was there to help them keep from becoming pregnant again, a light flooded all but the most hopeless faces. And Edna would remember that, too.

When she attended meetings of the Teheran family planning association, under its chairman, Miss Farman-Farmaian, Edna assured them that the Pathfinder Fund stood ready to provide generous supplies of any contraceptives suitable for broad distribution—foaming tablets, condoms, and intrauterine devices—especially if the personnel was well trained in how to present family planning in all its aspects. She pointed out that Pathfinder's purpose was not to remain permanently, however, but to initiate a program appropriate to each country's needs, which could then be turned over to that country itself and to other international organizations whose purpose was long-term.

She encouraged them to look into the possibility of distributing the oral pill. She helped develop a system of medical history cards so that the hospitals and clinics could keep accurate records of effective or ineffective methods. As the group assimilated her suggestions and formed plans, Mrs. Tarbiat—now in Parliament, who had preceded Miss Farman-Farmaian as chairman of the family planning work—related a significant anecdote. The year before, much publicity had been generated by an announcement that the Shah would give a prize to the woman who had the largest number of children. On the day the prize was handed out, the winner and her family presented a sight more pitiable than enviable, and as the Shah gave her the award the mother, to the consternation of the whole gathering, fell on her knees and begged His Majesty to please give her something so that she wouldn't have any more children!

The Shah had spoken to Mrs. Tarbiat after the ceremony and said that something should be done for those like this poor mother who had entreated him for help. Mrs. Tarbiat told him of the family planning clinic at Farah Hospital. The Shah expressed approval and suggested that the program should be spread over all of Iran.

Edna agreed. It was time, she believed, for the message of family planning to reach out from the capital across the salt-caked deserts and towering mountains, from the rain-drenched area of the Caspian Sea to the parched sands of the Persian Gulf. Accompanied by Miss B. Mobed, director of the Teheran School of Midwifery, who enjoyed a position of some prestige in her country, Edna set out on a journey to Isfahan and Shiraz, south of Teheran.

These were proud and ancient repositories of Persia's grandeur, Iran's history and culture. "Isfahan is half the world," was an old Persian claim during the seventeenth century when the city could boast almost as large a population and wide an influence as London. Once the capital, its importance as a seat of power had waned, but its glory as a guardian of Persian architecture and art endured. The old summer palace of the Shahs and the fabulous Blue Mosque awed Edna with their rich and intricate designs created by artisans who could wed delicacy to strength. And in the sprawling bazaar she found that liveliness and energy and craftsmanship which remained part of the country's character.

With the indispensable Miss Mobed as her interpreter and adviser, Edna called on the director of provincial health during her first morning in Isfahan. And there, on his desk, lay a letter to Dr. Clarence Gamble in Massachusetts. Having listened to requests for help at the clinics he directed, and having consulted several Mulahs and other Muslim leaders to receive assurances of religious approval for child-spacing programs, the health director was writing to ask Dr. Gamble for help in securing contraceptives. Of course he welcomed Edna and Miss Mobed and helped pave the way for their successful visit.

At tea with influential religious leaders whose sanction was absolutely essential for any successful birth control program, during trips to maternal health centers, schools, and the offices of the Red Lion and Sun (the Iranian Red Cross), and through talks—in both Farsi and English—to women agricultural extension workers, Edna was buoyed up by the eagerness with which every shred of information and help was welcomed. Before she and Miss Mobed left, the decision had been made to establish two clinics in the city with plans to develop two rural services shortly thereafter. Regular distribution of contraceptives would begin as soon as they could be obtained. Edna assured them that the delay would be short.

Much the same held true in Shiraz. Called a city of "roses, nightingales, and heroes," boasting the nearby tombs of Darius and Xerxes, Shiraz also enshrined the burial places of poets as well as warriors. And thirty-five miles northeast stood the impressive ruins of Persepolis. Built in 500 B.C., the remains of its walls and mighty columns stood as mute testimony to the magnificence this capital had once known when kings came here to celebrate the arrival of spring each year. Edna made the pilgrimage to Persepolis. But it was the challenge in Shiraz—where readiness for family planning exceeded all expectations—that really claimed her attention.

Here again, she and Miss Mobed left with the commitment of provincial health officials and doctors to set up two clinics and promote a widespread educational campaign. Edna urged Dr. Gamble to send supplies of leaflets on use of the IUDs as well as books by Margaret Sanger, Dr. John Rock, Dr. Alan Guttmacher, and pamphlets and reprints of all sorts.

In Shiraz, Edna also met an able young American, Dr. Bruce Jessup, about whom she had heard in Pakistan and then in Teheran. Through AID, he was carrying out excellent studies and programs in rural villages. When she met the tall, handsome young man with reddish hair, he expressed amazement and satisfaction at the progress toward family planning being made in the capital, and he agreed to come to the meeting in Shiraz. Then he told Edna that he had recently received a request from AID asking him to return to the United States and head the population division of that agency. He knew very little of the history of the birth control movement. When Edna found that they were to be on the same flight to Teheran on the following Friday, she promised him a crash course in the life and hard times of the birth control cause—from Sadie Sachs and Margaret Sanger to the new oral pill and IUDs which were altering traditional ways of life.

When Dr. Jessup came back to Teheran from the United States, he told Edna that her capsule history had served him well in his Washington interviews. Flying over the deserted spaces and ancient sites of Iran, he had learned about the numerous birth control agencies, their purposes and leaders, and some of the inside politics of each. Without that background much of his Washington experience would have been meaningless. Later, when Dr. Jessup left Shiraz to accept his new post, Edna felt more than ordinary interest in the move and her small part in it.

On her return to Teheran, Edna helped draw up a budget and a sample constitution which she urged the FPA to translate while they organized and registered as an official national organization. Miss Farman-Farmaian was encouraged to attend an IPPF conference to be held in London a little later in the year, and to apply for her association's membership in the Federation.

Edna felt good about her stay in Iran. Family planning had expanded from one clinic to eight in Teheran; the message had been extended to two other provinces, moving it into a national program. Professional interest and wide public enthusiasm had been aroused. Miss Farman-Farmaian, with many demands upon her time, administrative abilities, and influence, had remained receptive and cordial. She had not responded to any of Edna's suggestions that they interest Queen Farah or the Shah's sisters in lending royal support to family planning — but, given the history and pride of the Farman-Farmaian family, perhaps this was understandable. Knowing what a surge of progress royal support could achieve for the program, Edna deplored the intervention of personal considerations or bias, but it was a fact of life wherever she worked. And in other ways Miss Farman-Farmaian had been the real bulwark of the family planning movement in Iran, as well as a friend to Edna.

At Miss Farman-Farmaian's invitation, Edna had visited in her mother's home, and just before Edna was to leave Iran she received an invitation to celebrate the Iranian New Year. Of the twenty-seven legal and religious holidays observed annually throughout the country, "No-Ruz"—a springtime welcoming of the New Year—was one of the most important. The particular occasion Edna shared was a quiet, lovely family party. Later, Miss Farman-Farmaian thanked Edna for all that had been accomplished, and said that she would probably take Edna's advice and attend the London conference. She then asked Edna to return to Iran in the near future. A year and a half later Edna did revisit Teheran—on Thanksgiving Day, 1965.

In the interim, Miss Farman-Farmaian, on her trip to the IPPF Conference in London, had met Dr. Shokooh Ghorbani, a young Iranian doctor who was working for family planning in England while her husband was finishing his studies. With the assistance of the IPPF, Dr. Ghorbani was employed as medical director of the FPA of Iran.

A little later, another doctor was also officially appointed to promote family planning work in the public health clinics. These two important steps indicated the growing national interest in the program. But they did not reveal some of the sources of frustration Edna promptly encountered on her return.

Among these were the group's postponement of action on the constitution Edna had left behind and on the necessary registration with the government, promotion of fewer clinical services than had seemed likely the year before, failure to claim from customs a shipment of oral pills Edna had persuaded a U.S. drug manufacturer to donate to Iran's FPA, and reluctance to seek possible assistance from AID.

An incident, and the reaction it evoked, was merely one example of the altered attitude Edna confronted. Visiting the outpatient services at one of Teheran's clinics, Edna and the doctor accompanying her were surrounded by crowds of destitute people. To Edna they appeared to be the poorest, most forlorn group she had ever seen. One tiny room seemed to be the only space available for all clinic services, which did not include the insertion of the IUDs, about which the young doctor had just been instructed by Dr. Ghorbani. But next to this cubicle Edna discovered a totally empty room containing only a washbowl. When she asked why this space wasn't used, the answer came, "No furniture and no money to buy any."

Edna asked if a family planning clinic could be started if they had a secondhand examining table and some other simple necessities? Yes, and the cost would probably be about a hundred dollars. This, Edna decided, would be her Christmas gift to Iran's FPA. Accompanied by two of the doctors, she went out at once and bought the necessary furnishings. The nurse who was assigned to work with the doctors was pleased as she promised Edna that the clinic would be packed each week. And yet—Miss Farman-Farmaian was displeased when Edna told her of what had been done.

The hostility which surfaced during this episode, and also when Edna was trying to get the oral birth control pills released from customs, seemed to harden as Edna continued to work. Miss Farman-Farmaian had greeted her cordially enough at the start of this second visit; early association with Dr. Ghorbani had been mutually agreeable. Edna found the young doctor able, productive, cooperative, and a hard worker. The doctor's only assistance came from a volunteer worker who handled some of the office duties, and the social workers who helped at each of the family planning centers where they, in turn, trained student social workers. After several weeks of laboring together, Dr. Ghorbani abruptly terminated her calls to Edna. On the telephone she explained, in answer to Edna's calls, that she should be studying for her Iranian medical examinations, having only passed the British exams so far. Edna found herself suddenly alone in her work. There had been no quarrels, no rifts of which she was aware. Doctors, midwives, and nurses, seemed appreciative of her presence. Officials of AID and other agencies whose support she was enlisting were receptive to her ideas. But Miss Farman-Farmaian and her administrative director, Dr. Ghorbani, were now inaccessible.

This was one of the most puzzling and depressing experiences of her career. The only similar circumstances she could recall were those involving leaders, especially in Nepal, who told her that they had received an ultimatum from IPPF not to work with Pathfinder or its representative if they wished to continue to receive that organization's assistance. Had this happened in Iran?

Believing that the country was on the threshold of a real breakthrough in family planning, Edna pursued her work in those areas where she could. After considerable effort she secured an appointment with Dr. J. Saleh, former minister of health who was now chancellor of the University of Teheran. A doctor to the Shah, Dr. Saleh was one of the key people whose approval had to be reiterated at every step if effective family planning training were to be carried on.

When Edna called on Dr. Saleh, she found a number of young medical students and colleagues with him; and to Edna's delight, he listened to her brief remarks, then explained at some length to his associates that he was one of the earliest to approve of family planning in Iran, that it was essential for their country's well-being, and that he was ready to support it fully. Edna felt that was a significant achievement, especially since the doctor's approval had been pledged before this particular influential group.

Another special effort she made involved the need for including family planning in the research being carried on by various agencies. Edna knew the necessity for research, indeed she encouraged it—but she was also driven by daily awareness of the needs for immediate services to women and families whose suffering and problems were not open to postponement. Working through a maze of officialdom, introducing government health officials, AID representatives, personnel of population organizations, and doctors to each other, Edna was able to initiate a research cum service plan which would include some contraceptive assistance at each step of a lengthy (or even brief) research project. She felt that thus two imperatives might be met.

But she could not continue to work in the loneliness to which she had been assigned without explanation. She knew that another trip to Isfahan and Shiraz would be productive. She saw so much to be done—and Miss Farman-Farmaian, with her School of Social Work and numerous posts of leadership could give only limited time to the FPA, while Dr. Ghorbani had more demands on her time than the hours of the day could accommodate.

There was need for a program of education, for a community and field organization to strengthen public support, and for a budget which would encourage local help as well as financial assistance from abroad—although the United Nations, WHO, and AID should still be enlisted for help. These were some of the chores to be done so that that terrible death rate of infants could be lessened, so that the wasted bodies of those women who had known a dozen pregnancies and half as many abortions could be healed, so that the pitiful daily parade of people crying for care and relief from the burden of too many children could be heeded.

But Edna was excluded from meeting those chores. Was she pushing too hard? Or was her opposition really from outside, beyond her control? She became so dejected that when an attack of flu sent her to bed she almost welcomed the physical reflection of her inner sense of defeat. What could be more frustrating than to see the task and the solution—and not be able to bring the two together because of factors she could not even define, much less control?

Such wretched moments as these Edna did not share with her friends or family. Whenever she spoke of Iran in later years she sparkled with memories of the magnificence that was Persepolis and the antiquity that was Isfahan and Shiraz, of the human needs of the friendly people she had known throughout Iran, and of the handsome and brilliant Miss Farman-Farmaian. Indeed, when Edna was back in the United States for a short while in 1966, she received a letter from Miss Farman-Farmaian telling of progress in Teheran and of a trip she had just made through southwest Iran with the head of the department of public health. They wanted Edna to know of their appreciation for her contribution to Iran's growing success in family planning. Without overt acknowledgment, they were utilizing her program of family planning services cum research.

Like so much about Iran, the letter was surprising, pleasing, and puzzling.

From Iran, Edna went on a short sojourn through Jordan, Syria, Lebanon, and then to Turkey with her good friends Bernadine and Charles Zukosky. They arrived in Ankara on the last day of March.

Her natural optimism and unquenchable faith (sometimes doused but never extinguished) were revived by the Holy Land trip and by the clear, spring-like weather of Ankara's five thousand-foot altitude. There was also the exhilaration of being with the Zukoskys. This spring of 1964 they were in the midst of an especially outstanding achievement in Egypt, where they helped create a remarkable family planning program. Now they were returning briefly to Turkey and their basic work of the previous year in impressing upon government officials the need for intensive family planning and contacting doctors about use of the IUDs.

They were pleased to learn that during their absence developments had been generally favorable. Discussion of family planning had been opened sufficiently for a serious survey to be made. The bill to repeal Turkey's law against contraception was due for early passage, a family planning association was in existence—at least on paper—and a government program was being organized as a department of Maternal and Child Health Care.

During their stay in Turkey, Edna and the Zukoskys visited Ankara, Ismir, and Istanbul. Modern Ankara, declared the capital by Ataturk, was an inland city of white villas, government buildings, long boulevards, and many roses, surrounded by low steppes. At ancient Istanbul the Bosporus met the Golden Horn and formed a crossroads of Greek, Christian, and Muslim worlds, three cities in one astride two continents. The contrast between the two cities was as sharp as that between the riches of Santa Sophia, a thousand years older than St. Peter's in Rome, and the daily poverty of the rural people wrestling with the twentieth century. Among their problems was a high birth rate and a terrible infant death rate (one hundred fifty-three per thousand live births). Wars from 1911 to 1922 had inflicted heavy manpower losses on Turkey. In an effort to offset these losses, national policy had encouraged large families. Importation of contraceptives was prohibited. Abortion was illegal. Families with many children received financial rewards. During the 1950s and the 1960s, however, there had been a mounting realization that uncontrolled population growth posed a threat. In 1963, the Population Council, at the request of the Turkish Government, made a study of the population figures and national attitudes toward family planning. With much interest in and approval for family planning, the time for setting to work seemed at hand. Edna and the Zukoskys now added momentum by helping with the permanent formation of an FPA and the establishment of effective hospital and clinic services.

After a month, they felt that they had accomplished all that was possible for them in Turkey at this stage. They had helped establish in the Association the fundamentals of a strong organization; they had promoted clinics in a variety of places. By the end of the decade there would be 491 clinics, mobile units visiting 16 provincial districts, 863 doctors trained for the program, and 5,650 other personnel. Pathfinder had helped open the way for this progress, the Zukoskys had been its pioneers, and no one could appreciate—or support—their success more fully than Edna.

12

In societies where women have little voice in matters pertaining to the family, often along with a lack of communication between husband and wife, it is very difficult for them to adopt contraceptive methods. The problem is further complicated if the family planning communication program is aimed primarily at women, and the emphasis is on dissemination of female methods.

—*Human Fertility and National Development*

Life is short, and provided a woman produces children, what more does a man want?

—Napoleon

IF EDNA'S ROLE as a pathfinder was to initiate and support family planning around the world in its struggles of birth and infancy, her challenge as a Pathfinder employee was to remain flexible—shifting emphases, approaches, and programs to adapt to the culture, mores, needs, and aspirations of individual countries and peoples. There was, for instance, Saudi Arabia.

Success in Saudi Arabia, as in neighboring Kuwait, could be measured by merely breaching the barrier of silence. In this vast land of Islam and oil-rich sands, where the nomadic life of desert Bedouins most brutally burdened its camels and women, education for girls at just the primary level had begun only four years before Edna's arrival and even then required, in some instances, military enforcement because local citizens believed literacy would corrupt girls. In this land a woman lived with her face hidden by a veil and her clothes covered by a full-length abaya, or black cloak. Her life might be spent in isolation from all men except her most immediate relatives. In such a land the mere arrival of a woman discussing family planning seemed revolutionary.

The arrival was not easy. In fact, it was regarded in some quarters—ranging from her daughter's home in Montana to the offices of Aramco, the Arabian American Oil Company—as nothing less than miraculous.

While Edna was still in Iran, she had received a letter from Dr. Gamble advising that Saudi Arabia might be her next effort. Two young doctors from Saudi Arabia attending the Harvard School of Public Health had suggested that it might be useful for Pathfinder to blaze a trail for family planning while

Aramco was in the country with its excellent hospital services. Edna agreed. Dhahran, on the Persian Gulf, was headquarters for Aramco and seemed her logical destination. While there might not be ambitious achievements at this time, a simple beginning could be significant. The problem was to secure a visa. Edna fortunately did not realize that it was supposed to be an overwhelming problem until she had already mastered it. Blithely she went to the Saudi Arabian consulate in Teheran. The large, dark, young Arab official to whom she handed her passport gave one glance at the birth date and looked up in astonishment when he realized this vivacious, smiling blond woman was past seventy.

"You can't go to Saudi Arabia!" he declared.

"Oh? Why not?"

"Well . . . why do you want to go to Saudi Arabia?"

Edna's eyes were wide and bright. "Because I've been traveling—as you can see from my passport—in many parts of the world, and I thought while I was here it would be interesting if I could go to Saudi Arabia."

"Oh no, no. You can't possibly go."

"But I don't understand why," Edna said.

The young man gave her a quizzical look. "Who are you going with?"

"With no one," Edna replied. "I travel alone."

"You can't go alone in Saudi Arabia."

"Why not? Is there a law against it?"

"No law." And in spite of himself the young man smiled. "You aren't very proud of your country," Edna said. "Haven't you read the *Arabian Nights?*"

At this the smile turned to open laughter. "Where did you want to go in Saudi Arabia?"

Suddenly it dawned on Edna that she didn't know anything about this country. "Dhahran—" she remembered Aramco. And she had heard of the big port . . . "Jidda—"

"And the capital?" he assumed.

"Yes."

"Riyadh."

"Oh yes! Riyadh, of course." Actually this was the first time Edna had ever heard the name of the capital.

"Well, you'll have to have a letter from your American embassy."

"Why do I need that? They don't know I'm here."

"It's one of our rules. You must have a letter."

"All right. I'll get a letter." And Edna went to the American embassy.

The young lady to whom she was referred said, "You can't go to Saudi Arabia."

"Why not?" Edna asked—for what seemed the dozenth time.

"Nobody can get a visa."

"Well, the young man in the Saudi Arabian office told me to get a letter from my embassy," Edna said. "Do you mind writing one for me?"

"Oh, I'll write a letter," the woman replied, "but it won't do you any good. You can't go to Saudi Arabia." Those last six words were beginning to sound like the chorus to some bad song.

Now Edna was determined to go to this country if she had to crawl across the border on hands and knees! She phoned for another appointment with the Saudi Arabian official.

The next morning at eleven Edna was at the office. A second, older man now made his appearance. Edna was introduced as "the lady who wants to go to Saudi Arabia alone." Edna handed them her passport and letter. Together her young acquaintance of the previous day and his older, more dignified associate interrogated Edna at length. Where was she born, educated? What was her family situation? They asked if she knew President Kennedy who had been recently assassinated. While they were discussing this terrible event, a clerk came in and deposited some papers on the desk. The younger man handed Edna her passport.

She was taken aback. "Oh, won't you let me go—"

"It's there. Look inside. Your visa is in order."

Edna's thanks were profuse. She shook hands with each of them. Then the young official said, "Will you be coming back to Iran?"

"I think so, eventually. I always like to return to places I've visited."

227

"Would you do me a favor?"

With visions of bringing in a baby camel or carrying out some bizarre task, Edna said, "I'll do anything I can, I'm so grateful for this visa."

"When you come back, will you let me know? I'd like for my wife to meet you."

Surprised and touched, Edna agreed. And carried out her passport—with visa—as triumphantly as a medieval warrior bearing the standard of victory from the jousting field. Her triumph was even greater when, at a dinner party the following night, someone asked which country she would be entering next.

"Saudi Arabia," she replied.

"You can't go to Saudi Arabia."

"What *is* this?" Edna asked. "Everyone says, 'You can't go to Saudi Arabia.'"

And an American official across the table explained, "You can't get a visa. Nobody can get in."

"I can't understand it—" Edna began.

An oil company executive sitting next to Edna volunteered that he had been waiting for five months to receive a visa for someone the company needed to go to Saudi Arabia—and he was still waiting. A man from the American embassy said it could take six or seven months—or never—to get a visa.

"But I'm going," Edna said. And reached down in the evening purse she was carrying to produce the evidence of her success. The gentlemen's astonishment fully satisfied her instinct for drama.

The surprise was shared by the Pathfinder Fund officials who had been working in Massachusetts through Aramco and the U.S. Government to ease her effort in securing a visa. In fact, they had become so pessimistic about her chances for an early trip to Saudi Arabia that arrangements had already been made for the trip to the Holy Land and the stay in Turkey with the Zukoskys. So Edna asked to have the date for her visit pushed forward to April 1964.

Hazards still lay in store before she arrived in Dhahran. In Istanbul Edna went to the Pan American Airlines ticket office to buy passage to Saudi Arabia, via Lebanon, where she wished to spend a few days in Beirut. When the girl at the desk told her only one airline was permitted to fly into Saudi Arabia—the Saudi Arabian Airlines—Edna said this was agreeable with her. Arrangements were made for Edna to leave Beirut on Saturday and fly down to Dhahran.

Actually the clerk in Teheran had been mistaken. There was another commercial service, Mideast Airlines, with a flight twice a week to Saudi Arabia. When the late Friday flight of Mideast Airlines was unable to land in Lebanon, it flew on into a choking sandstorm and plunged into the Persian Gulf early Saturday morning. Everyone who knew of Edna's plans—her daughter, Dorothy, far away in Missoula, and the Aramco people, closer by—assumed that she was on that plane.

Dorothy was doubly frantic because she could not find out anything about the plane crash. News broadcasts spoke of a plane from Lebanon to Saudi Arabia down in the Persian Gulf. Part of its wing was visible above water. All the people aboard apparently were killed. Dorothy telephoned the State Department to get a list of names—to no avail. She telephoned the offices of Aramco.

"Is your mother with Aramco?"

"No, but—"

"If she isn't with Aramco, I'm sorry but we can't give you any information."

As the list of passengers was gradually released to the public, one name was almost identical with Zukosky. This clinched Dorothy's apprehension. She knew that her mother and the Zukoskys had been together in Turkey. Undoubtedly they had decided to go on to Saudi Arabia together. She had visions of fish swimming around Edna's lifeless body strapped in an airplane seat.

She called Mideast Airlines long distance and was assured that there were only two flights a week into Saudi Arabia. No one thought to mention the small Saudi Arabian airline.

The weekend ticked by. There was no word from Edna, from anyone. A Western Union operator in New York, through whom Dorothy had tried to cable Dhahran, gave her little reassurance. "They're probably delivering your message by three-legged camel out into the desert."

Actually, Edna's flight had been delayed four hours on Saturday morning because of the sandstorm. When she arrived in Dhahran and one of the airport officials saw her passport he said, "Mrs. McKinnon! We thought you were dead!"

Dorothy was both incredulous and overjoyed when she learned, at last, of her mother's narrow escape. Edna's reaction to both Dorothy's and the airport official's attitude was one of amazement: had they really thought she crashed in the Persian Gulf?

The people of Aramco were stricken at the death of several of their colleagues in the plane accident. Because of the pall cast by this tragedy and the relaxation of schedule due to observance of a long religious holiday, "The Eid"—a sort of Thanksgiving—Edna's visit began with discouraging slowness. She was comfortable at the Aramco Guest House but found it impossible to see several of the men whose names had been suggested by the young Harvard students. However, as she became more and more aware of the precarious situation of Saudi Arabian women—only beginning to emerge from the harsh restrictions of laws and traditions laid down thirteen centuries before for a sternly puritanical desert people—Edna came to the conclusion that it was best for her to push no program, no action, and no organization at that time. If, through her presence and conversation, she could merely introduce the idea of family planning and make it acceptable, if she could break through silence, suspicion, and tradition and leave a glimpse of the benefit which could flow from family planning—that would be sufficient achievement for that time and place.

Under the guidance of Dr. Hazel Blair, director of the maternal and child health program of Aramco, who had been in Saudi Arabia for eight and a half years, Edna finally met several leading doctors and health educators who could introduce family planning work in an acceptable way to their own people. At meetings and luncheons in the small city of Dhahran that was the center of the Aramco government, if not of the Saudi Arabian Government, she learned that health education was just beginning in this country, that the idea of girls attending school was still not fully accepted, and that even the concept of a club for women was only a few months old. Some men or their families (and women were peculiarly the creatures of the family, susceptible to all of the extended family's advice and notions) did not yet permit "their" women to leave home at all—even to visit other women in the neighborhood.

There were exceptions, and through conversations with some of the wise and experienced Arabs and foreigners Edna began to understand the subtleties and nuances of the country. She became convinced that she should not visit Riyadh, the royal capital, because of its extreme conservatism, especially relating to women.

Jidda, on the Red Sea, gateway to Mecca, was another matter. The country's largest seaport, it had also been more open to the twentieth century and to westernization than the other cities. Only the year before, the equivalent of a Woman's Welfare Society had been launched there, including in recent months a maternal and child health service in its program.

Before she left Dhahran, Edna had one particularly touching experience. A Palestinian refugee who had married a Saudi Arabian and worked in health education accompanied Edna to a community in the country some thirty miles beyond Dhahran. The mud-walled villages and houses out in the desert sands seemed unspeakably lonely and isolated. One small hut had been cleaned up and set aside for this meeting. The occasion was a women's gathering to discuss sanitation and health, but the word used was "hafla," meaning "party," a sort of club. They would see a movie, have cokes and cookies—and talk!

Edna and her hostess arrived a little early. The women came quietly, diffidently, each brought by a man in her family, each in her long veil and black abaya. One who arrived early brought her three-year-old girl—and when she threw back her abaya revealed an extremely low-cut evening gown trimmed in white lace! The public health film and cokes (provided by Aramco) were for her and her friends a great social event. As they waited, Edna suggested that the social worker give this guest a copy of the family planning booklet to look through. "See what she thinks of it." The social worker did so, and after she and the woman had talked with considerable animation for a few minutes she translated for Edna. "Our friend thinks this booklet is interesting. But she is on the pill, and so am I."

Apparently even the isolation of the harem, the women's sequestered dwelling place, had been penetrated more than casual observers realized. With the interest in IUDs shown by the distinguished gynecologist who was director of clinics, Edna began to see a future for family planning.

She arrived in Jidda at the end of the time of pilgrimage to Mecca. The pilgrim trade during the centuries, coupled with oil money after World War II, had made Jidda a prosperous commercial city—a combination of the sun-baked old and the shiny present. Through the wife of the American ambassador, a perceptive woman, Edna learned of some of the people she should meet in Jidda. She also learned that here she could not run around making appointments for herself and keeping engagements. She must let Mrs. Hart, or others in a position to do so, advise various leaders of Edna's presence—and they would contact Edna and call upon her.

The response was gratifying. A number of influential doctors came to call at Edna's hotel. They discussed methods, even arranged for a visit to a maternity hospital, and indicated varying degrees of interest in accepting Pathfinder's offer to send supplies for any family planning services they would arrange.

Wives of leading businessmen invited Edna to their homes. None of the women came into the hotel but sent their cars to bring Edna to them. She was advised of the interest in women's improved status, quietly demonstrated by Princess Iffat, only wife of Prince Faisal, who would soon become King Faisal, succeeding his half-brother and father to the throne. The princess's influence had established the first school for women and she had founded the Women's Welfare League in Jidda.

One of Edna's most enlightening moments came when she suggested that Princess Iffat's physician might arrrange an introduction so that Edna could tell her about family planning. The physician said he couldn't do that because he'd never really met the princess.

"Oh, I'm sorry," Edna apologized. "I thought you were her doctor."

"I am," the distinguished gentleman replied. "I have delivered her nine babies. But I don't talk with the princess."

All of the women Edna met agreed that it was essential to have Princess Iffat's approval before they could really make progress in family planning. Under Mrs. Hart's direction of what to say and how delivery should be made, Edna wrote her own message to Princess Iffat. A friend of the princess reported that she was very interested in family planning and wished to find out from her husband if there was any law against it. Then she hoped to see Edna. The following day news came that the princess was ill. Her flu developed into pneumonia.

Their meeting did not take place until two years later, when Edna returned to Saudi Arabia in 1966. During the intervening time, Pathfinder, as was customary, had sent pamphlets and educational material and some contraceptive supplies to at least two clinics and medical centers, but progress had been discouragingly slow.

By this time, Princess Iffat had become Queen Iffat and lived in the capital city of Riyadh. From a small village surrounded by date groves and desert only two decades earlier had grown this city of 170,000 people and modern new government office buildings, tree-lined avenues with oleander and bougainvillaea, hospitals, schools, and traffic—with the mile-square complex of Naseryah Palace at its heart.

Anyone meeting the royal family had to be covered and this presented a problem in a hot climate. But Mrs. Suad Juffali, the Women's Welfare Center board member who had arranged for Edna's audience, assured her that the Italian silk suit Edna chose, blue and green with long sleeves and a decorous neckline, was totally satisfactory. The weather turned cool, as well, which made a pleasant day.

At the palace Edna was escorted into a huge drawing room, heavy with mammoth divans and overstuffed chairs which seemed to serve as the chief decoration as well as furniture. As she waited, Edna remembered that she had been told that Queen Iffat was Greek, brought by her mother to Saudi Arabia to be one of King Saud's many wives. Prince Faisal had been sent to bring her to the King but found her so charming he fell in love with her and wanted to marry her himself. King Saud, who already had a number of wives, agreed. Iffat's mother would agree only if Faisal promised to make her his only wife. He promised—and for the first time, Saudi Arabia had a ruler with only one wife.

The Emira, as she was called, was preceded into the room by her secretary-interpreter. Of medium height, wearing a loose, starkly simple long-sleeved gown of light moss-green with one band of embroidery full-length from throat to hem, the Queen proved to be a calm, attentive, gracious woman. Her dark hair was drawn back loosely from her calm and very kind face. As soon as they began to talk, Edna could see that Queen Iffat understood much of what Edna was saying without the interpreter. The atmosphere was very informal, with the Emira listening to all of Edna's explanations of family planning, Pathfinder's work, and hopes for Saudi Arabia. She asked questions. At one point she told Edna that having had nine children of her own and all the servants she needed, she could not imagine how difficult—how impossible—it must be for most of the women in her country, especially the Bedouins out in the harsh deserts.

Her sympathy and interest finally produced a promise to discuss family planning with the king's physician. She could not speak of it to her husband; she could make no official statement. But her approval, Edna knew, would become common knowledge and by the next day Edna would begin to see the results of Emira Iffat's consent.

When their conversation—or, as Edna considered it, monologue—was finished, a waiter ushered in several other guests, ladies who were friends of the Queen. Then he passed tiny china coffee cups and with a great flourish poured black coffee which Edna immediately discovered was strongly flavored with cardamom. This was not her favorite flavor. But she could certainly do away with one cupful. When the waiter reappeared presently, Edna handed her empty cup toward him—and promptly had it refilled from the slender little brass coffee server. Edna was not so sure about this second cup, but the Emira was smiling at her and explaining that in Saudi Arabia if you want more coffee you extend your cup, if you are finished you rock the cup back and forth between thumb and middle finger. On the waiter's next passage, Edna rocked the cup wildly.

After the coffee, tea and cakes were served. Edna was impressed with the simplicity of the whole occasion, in a palace that was hardly more than a rather elaborate home. (Faisal was living in contrast to his extravagant half-brother whose reign had been characterized by a tremendous palace, numerous wives, and sumptuous self-indulgence.)

The next morning Edna received a telephone call from the King's physician. He expressed personal approval of family planning and explained that he could not issue any public statement on the subject although he had arranged an appointment for Edna with the under secretary of health. This appointment itself revealed the changes altering the country's social life during the brief two-year period since Edna's last visit. Women were emerging from their chrysalises, and she could be received in offices and hospitals and clinics where previously her presence would have been considered indiscreet.

The following day the under secretary of health sent his car for Edna and when they met she was pleased to learn that he had recently returned from training as a dentist in Philadelphia and in Indiana. He would work to interest colleagues in Jidda in family planning, he would help integrate family planning into maternal child health dispensaries, and he urged Edna to visit as many health centers and talk with as many doctors as possible.

With the car and driver he furnished, Edna visited these institutions in all parts of Riyadh. The interest of the majority of doctors astonished her. Even in this conservative capital, women were beginning to ask for the new freedom.

Back in Jidda, Edna spoke to a gathering sponsored by Mrs. Juffali: members of the Women's Welfare Center, doctors, ambassadors' wives, wives of Aramco officials. She told them of the approval given by Queen Iffat and the under secretary of health. She promised them that if there was difficulty in obtaining regular services by public health doctors at the Welfare Center's maternal child health center, Pathfinder Fund, if asked, would pay for a doctor's services. An atmosphere of hope and positive action was created. It summarized for Edna all that she had been able to do in Saudi Arabia: breach a few barriers, open a few windows, break a long silence. It was a very little—and a great deal.

In neighboring Kuwait, Edna encountered a wholly unique situation.

To begin with, the tiny emirate—about two-thirds the size of the state of Maryland—with a population estimated at less than half a million, was what might be termed a welfare country. Due to the riches of oil reserves under its broiling desert sands, Kuwait had catapulted from a nomadic, pastoral Bedouin past into the streamlined twentieth century.

Situated at the head of the Persian Gulf, between Iran and Saudi Arabia, it could boast one of the highest per capita incomes in the world, no personal income taxes, free compulsory education for all its youth, free health care, and triumph over its ancient adversary—the climate: through the world's largest plant for distilling fresh water from salt water, the eternal drought resulting from one to six inches of annual rainfall had been quenched; and through almost total air conditioning in its capital city (also named Kuwait), the suffocating heat, which could climb to 120 degrees F. in summer, had been subdued.

When Edna arrived in Kuwait, her taxi from the airport into the city—looming like a glass and concrete mirage set in the immense expanse of desert—cost five dollars. At the hotel she was given an adequate but not lavish room and shower at the cost of twenty-two dollars per day. Everything in Kuwait is expensive, she was told. Everything must be imported. People here can afford the universally high prices.

Through the head of the American Mission Hospital, Edna met the deputy minister of health, a cultured, gentle, and slightly embarrassed Kuwaiti who was unaccustomed to discussing such delicate subjects with a woman. But when he invited her to visit the government's family planning center, it was Edna's turn to be surprised. The real surprise, however, came

236

when she arrived at the center and discovered that in Kuwait family planning meant overcoming sterility problems, not birth control.

With an estimated hundred thousand Kuwaitis and more than three hundred thousand foreigners, any real birth control effort would more likely be expected among those from other countries. Edna did learn that in addition to the fertility service there was an active program of sex education for marriage, and in the gynecological department of the maternity hospital contraceptive services were given when requested.

Edna's visits to four hospitals and several schools, interviews with more than a dozen doctors and numerous officials and teachers impressed her with the splendid facilities available for universal education and health care. The people were cordial and receptive but reinforced her ultimate verdict that family planning in Kuwait was premature.

If it were only to meet the Khans, her journey to Kuwait would have been worthwhile, however. M.Q. and Nayeema Khan were both doctors, born in Pakistan, who had worked in Tanzania at one time and met a Pathfinder Fund representative who later sent Edna their address. They had been in Kuwait for some five years and had established a private eighteen-bed lying-in clinic and hospital. Their living quarters, on the top floor, were spacious, even luxurious, and hospitable to the constant stream of guests that seemed to flow through the large living room and guest rooms. The Khan family consisted of four children (two adopted), two elderly grandparents, two poodles, two parrots, and two canaries. Since much of the public health service was administered by foreigners (some six hundred foreign doctors compared with around thirty Kuwaiti doctors) who were occasionally considered slack in their government-paid work, the Khans' private service flourished.

When they called at Edna's hotel, they immediately insisted that she should come and be their guest for the rest of her stay. In a large beautiful bedroom with private bath and balcony, she remained through the period of Ramadan.

During Ramadan, each day's fast was broken shortly after five in the afternoon, and then there was a pleasant time of eating and socializing. Fresh fruit was brought to Edna's room each morning, and often there were roses which had been brought to Dr. Khan by one of her patients. At the end of Ramadan, marked by the arrival of the moon at a certain place in the heavens, the two youngest boys in the household appeared at Edna's door. Dressed in exquisite little Muslim suits, jackets trimmed with beads, they brought her gifts: a necklace of Persian amber, a ring made of baroque pearls, and a gold bracelet. Edna was charmed and touched—and forthwith distressed. How would she return their courtesy? She searched through her luggage. A new silver mesh evening bag she had bought in Singapore would be right for Mrs. Khan. But what about the children? Tucked in one corner of her bag were several small carvings of animals that she had found on one of her sojourns. Would the Khan children like these? Indeed they would—and did. The Eid, a time of feasting which followed the fast of Ramadan, was the climax of Edna's stay in Kuwait.

But one other experience remained in her memory. In many ways it was a symbol of the whole country. Mrs. Khan, an obstetrician and gynecologist, invited Edna to go on a house call with her one day. The patient was the young widow of a sheik who had died a short while before. As they went into a side entrance of the home, Edna could see that this was an area isolated, set apart. Inside, the woman lay on a sort of divan, surrounded and supported by many cushions. For months she could have no communication at all with any man—and little exchange with anyone else. She would stay indoors, imprisoned as surely as if iron chains bound her. As she and the doctor left, Edna glanced back at the quiet, dark-eyed girl on the luxurious divan in the small cell-like room with only one window and one door.

Some day women—if not this woman—would leave the stifling room and emerge into the wide open world. Family planning might be "premature" in Kuwait, but as the wealthy little country gained a genuine maturity it, like so many other parts of the world, would realize the need to grant women total freedom and make family planning a first priority.

13

He who hides an ailment, hides its remedy.

—Ethiopian folk saying

One element that underlines all our difficulties in devising meaningful and effective nonpopulation programs is plain ignorance.

Babies are not mass produced in government owned factories where the volume of output coming off the production lines could be made easily responsive to the wishes of a planning board —at any rate not yet. Babies, instead, are homemade goods: the products of multitudes of individual couples, manufactured and delivered by millions of individual women.

—Paul Demeny, director of the East-
West Population Institute

The newness and urgency of this type of program call for leadership having high status, visibility, and nearness to the seat of governmental power.

—Moye W. Freymann, director of the University
of North Carolina Population Center

ALL OF THE ACQUIRED PATIENCE and natural resource-fulness cultivated by Edna through the years was summoned into practice during her work in Africa. Except for brief excursions to Kenya and Uganda for consultation and evaluation, her main effort was in Ethiopia and in the West Coast countries of Nigeria, Liberia, and Sierra Leone.

Her initiation rite involved time—and was a foretaste of situations and exasperations awaiting anyone in Africa who wished to follow Western ideas of "keeping time," "saving time," or, in fact, even knowing what time it was. For, in some of these countries south of the Sahara and just north of the equator, time was measured in many different ways. And whatever the measure there never seemed any stress or pressure. There were times when this absence of precision and tension could reduce an American visitor to a state of bewilderment. There was, for example, Edna's introduction to the continent. Simply scheduling an arrival began to seem impossible.

Edna was to fly from Jidda, on the Saudi Arabian coast, across the Red Sea to Asmara, in the northern corner of Ethiopia. But at what hour? There were five times from which residents of Jidda might choose to arrange schedules: sun time, Greenwich time, airplane time, hotel time, and official Jidda time. Visiting Jidda, Edna had learned to set each appointment with an understanding of which time was involved—and to synchronize her watch accordingly. (Each simple engagement took on an atmosphere of intrigue and importance out of proportion to its purpose.) But in making her plane reservation there had been some confusion about the hour of departure. As a result she was awakened in the small hours of the morning and arrived at the airport at about 4:00 A.M. As she checked her bags she discovered that there was no one—service official or fellow customer—who spoke a word of English.

Many times Edna had been asked by friends in the United States how she traveled and worked with people in such an assortment of countries without any knowledge of their languages. The chief answer to this, of course, was that she was usually working with the leaders in each country, many of whom had received at least part of their education in English-speaking schools, and that she relied on these friends to interpret when she ventured into the countryside and marketplace. In her family planning, she had to approach each country through its leaders, for the general public would not have accepted the birth control message directly from her. At this airport, for one of the only times in her life, Edna felt completely cut off from communication with those around her.

Over a loudspeaker an announcer was keeping up a flow of information, in Arabic. Edna sat waiting for the word "Asmara," which she could certainly comprehend. She was burdened like one of the desert camels: a coat and raincoat on her arm; a shoulder bag full of books to read during anticipated waits and delays; a portable typewriter which felt less portable every minute; a pocketbook which was first cousin to a suitcase; a small attaché case full of reports, papers, and pamphlets on family planning. Altogether they made a heavy burden.

The terminal was crowded. Everywhere people were sitting, lying, sleeping, eating, and talking. At last Edna spied a very tall man with a Muslim cap on his head, who looked as if he might be an Egyptian. She approached him. "Do you speak English?"

He shook his head. "French," he replied.

Edna asked, "You go to *Asmara?*"

"Asmara! Yes—" And he thrust forward a hand for her to shake.

"I—" Edna pointed to herself, "go with you—" pointing to her new friend.

He beamed, bowed, and strode over to rejoin his group. They sat chatting while Edna watched them with an eagle eye, for she had decided to follow them in hopes that she would arrive at the right plane.

Suddenly the group arose. Edna arose. She gathered the typewriter and attaché case and coat and raincoat and books and pocketbook and dashed after them. Since they were all men they walked with long strides which Edna found it difficult to follow.

They went through a door. Edna struggled through only to find that they had disappeared. She saw a desk and rushed toward it, and in her haste missed two small steps. She sprawled on the floor. Her typewriter slid across the room, her pocketbook flew in one direction and her attaché case in another. When Edna looked up she saw a number of men standing, watching her. No one moved to retrieve her from this embarrassing plight.

"Damn it!" she suddenly exploded. "Can't anyone help me?"

No one moved. She struggled to her feet, gathered her scattered inventory, and approached the desk. Then she spied a dining room just beyond—and her party eating breakfast there. A Frenchman coming from the dining room, who had witnessed her fall and scramble from a distance, offered her sympathy and explained in French, which she could barely comprehend, that in Saudi Arabia women were just beasts of burden. No one would have thought of helping her.

She settled in for another wait. Under her watchful gaze, the men finished eating. She also listened, but still there was no announcement including the magic word "Asmara." After a while the men finished eating and headed for the departure area. Edna followed them to the gate and handed the keeper her ticket. It was punched. She pointed to the word "Asmara" on it and the official nodded. For the first time she felt some degree of certainty that there might be such a destination as Asmara and that she might reach it. Indeed, the flight to that Ethiopian city was shorter than her wait for departure—and much less trying.

Edna's work in Africa began and ended in Ethiopia. Interspersed between these visits were periods in Nigeria, Liberia, and Sierra Leone. In each of these she tried to adapt her basic approach—of inspiration and organization—to the needs and people as she found them.

The Pathfinder Fund had sent the first family planning worker to West Africa in the 1950s. The decision had been made at that time that the former English colonies would offer more chance of success than the French colonies, which would not have a tradition favorable to family planning. Edith Gates had inaugurated some family planning services in Nigeria, Liberia, and Sierra Leone, but these were small and largely unknown. Several years had elapsed since anyone had brought any outside organizational impetus to family planning, and in some ways Edna's approach had to be that of pioneering—at least clearing undergrowth from paths blazed half a decade before.

In Nigeria, Edna found a tropical country of cacao, palm oil, peanuts, grain sorghum, and mahogany, about the size of Texas and Oklahoma combined. Some forty million people splintered into two hundred and fifty tribes of varying languages, religions, politics, and customs. Between the three largest—the Moslem Hausas in the north, the Yorubas in the west, and the more advanced Ibos in the east—there were ancient conflicts. History had left Nigeria a sad legacy as the central country in the ugly slave trade. Its rivers, once arteries feeding the traffic in human flesh which flourished along the continent's west coast, were now busy with shipment of palm oil and other modern necessities. Heat wrapped every object and activity in a humid blanket that fostered inertia and disease; this was the country once known as "the white man's grave."

As Edna arrived in the sticky heat and turmoil of its capital city, Lagos, she determined to pay as little heed as possible to the weather in this mélange of bicycles and market baskets, seaport traffic and trade drawn from inland, flimsy stores and spacious residences of a long-time European colony. This city of about a quarter-million people seemed to be engaged in a shotgun wedding of past and present.

Dr. O. Adeniyi-Jones, director of public health for Lagos, had conducted a weekly family planning clinic at the municipal health center ever since Edith Gates' visits, but early in 1964 he decided the time was ripe for broader education and services supported by a well-organized public group. Edna went in July in answer to his request. She plunged into work immediately, speaking and interviewing. She reached a broad cross section of public and private citizens. Response was so favorable that following a talk to the National Council of Women's Societies the decision was made for a mass public meeting. From that meeting came the Family Planning Council of Nigeria, sponsored by the National Council of Women's Societies.

Again, however, there was need for that "one person" who could make the difference between indifferent and real success. So far, Dr. Adeniyi-Jones, busy with official burdens in addition to his professional concerns, had provided the family planning leadership for Nigeria. Now someone was needed to give full-time attention to nurturing and enlarging what he had begun. A nurse-midwife, Mrs. Ayo Ilumoka, was the answer.

Mrs. Ilumoka had grown up in Lagos, received training in Great Britain, and a certificate from the IPPF for family planning study in London. She and her husband, who was with the Nigerian Electric Corporation, had lived in Ibadan, northwest of Lagos, when Edith Gates was in Nigeria, but subsequently they had returned to Lagos, where interest in family planning was stirring. When Edna appeared, Mrs. Ilumoka gave her unstinting help, arranging numerous introductions and interviews, accompanying her to meetings arranged by others, driving her throughout the city and countryside with skill and pleasure.

The Ilumoka family became Edna's close friends. With her penchant for children, Edna embraced the four little girls, ranging from three to nine years old, in an immediate alliance. One day she invited them, just by themselves, for a tea party with her at the Ikoyi Hotel. On the stone benches of the terrace, at a table shaded by a bright umbrella, they shared refreshments, opened the little gifts Edna had wrapped, and played with the party favors she had ordered. The children did not speak English and Edna did not speak their dialect, but there was a language each understood which lay beyond mere words: the language of tone and inflection, of gesture and glance. The bright responsive faces of the four beautifully behaved children communicated all the essentials.

Before the close of Edna's first visit to Nigeria, Mrs. Ilumoka was engaged to assist at clinics and spread understanding of family planning work. Her salary was assured by the Pathfinder Fund. Edna felt that this arrangement, and the formal addition of family planning to an outpatient clinic of the maternity hospital, were sound achievements of her first effort in this country.

Later in 1964, in November, Edna returned to Lagos. Interest in family planning had not waned. When Mrs. Ilumoka met Edna at the airport, she reported that a Mrs. Ruth Rasmussen, representing the Danish FPA and interviewing for the IPPF, was also in the country, staying at Edna's hotel.

When Edna came into the dining room for breakfast the next morning she had no difficulty spotting her attractive Scandinavian colleague. Edna introduced herself. They visited and arranged to lunch together. Lunch lasted until four o'clock in the afternoon and by that time they had become friends and coworkers. Mrs. Rasmussen, a nurse-midwife representing her country in some of the underdeveloped countries whose recent rush to develop natural resources had often not been matched by an equal commitment to human resources, expressed much hope for cooperation with Edna in such a big task. Until Edna left in February 1965, she found this a beneficial friendship.

With the help of funds from the Unitarian-Universalist Service Committee of the United States, the family planning clinics began to grow stronger and more numerous. Leaflets, programs, and films were distributed for public information. Bylaws and a budget were drawn up for IPPF satisfaction and a series of training courses informing nurses and midwives about family planning methods was initiated. It was ironic that nurse-midwives, trained at home and abroad at much expense to the government, started their work and often became pregnant soon thereafter—with six months maternity leave. Babies tended to follow in rapid succession, as did the long periods of absence, until it became evident that education about family planning needed to begin with the nurse-midwives themselves.

Although all types of contraceptives were available at most of the clinics, the Pathfinder Fund found generally that the oral pill and diaphragm were too expensive. The pill still lent itself to mistakes, too. One of the trained nurses in Lagos spoke vehemently to Edna against the pill because she had taken it—and become pregnant. "Now tell me," Edna finally pinned her down, "did you take it every single day without fail?"

"Every single day—except for the few when I had a cold and I didn't take the pill then because I didn't want to mix the two medications."

The IUD was the Fund's basic contraceptive at this time. But at one point Edna sent Dr. Gamble an appeal for help. Dr. G. A. Williams, assistant to Dr. Adeniyi-Jones, was reporting complaints from women in whom he had inserted the spiral IUDs. They said that their husbands could feel the beads attached to the small thread in the vagina by which the spiral could be removed from the uterus. "I think they are letting the tails of thread stick out too far," Edna explained. "Could you send more explicit instructions?"

In addition to Lagos, Edna went several times to Nigeria's largest city, Ibadan. With more than a half-million people, it boasted of being the largest all-African city built for and by Africans. Its university—glass and steel contrasting with a crowded maze of mud and plaster houses, colorful markets, and wandering goats and sheep—made Ibadan a major educational center. Attitudes here were more conservative than in Lagos, and Edna soon decided that time and a major arousing of opinion would be necessary before family planning could be included in the city's health services. She encouraged unofficial efforts, however.

A family planning committee had been part of the Marriage Guidance Council, and now Edna pushed it to offer a service as well. When space was requested in a city maternity clinic it was granted. Sources of salaries for the doctors and nurses needed to serve in the clinic were hard to find, however. Political crises had diminished all health services. Activity in birth control was largely volunteer—in abeyance until a more hopeful, peaceful period arrived.

By the time Edna left Nigeria, there were four birth control clinics open in Lagos, strong public approval of family planning, and discussion of how the message might be extended to other parts of the country and ways by which contraceptives could be shipped tax free to a church organization in the capital. Edna felt that the work in Nigeria had been one of Pathfinder's achievements.

The greatest single asset was the able and hard-working Mrs. Ilumoka, who brought both initiative and imagination to her task. She was also willing to follow through on small details. In family planning, as in most difficult, permanent work, it was sometimes easy to find those who made a fast and impressive start and then flagged in their effort; it was also easy to find some who could drudge away at a task but never give it spark or new dimensions. What was needed, of course, was a blend of the two.

But Edna warned the Nigerian group that even Mrs. Ilumoka could not carry all the work load required; she needed paid assistants. Edna also advised them to reach out into other towns as soon as possible. Through Ruth Rasmussen Edna had learned that the Danish Government wished to send a team of three women doctors to train medical personnel in Nigeria in the use of IUDs and a midwife to help in the education of nurses, but this help would have to be invited by the Nigerians themselves. Edna urged them to extend the invitation.

Finally, she described the total program envisioned as their goal extending across much of the country, including mobile distribution units, promoting visual aids in many languages, including men in all of the family planning effort. She felt that Nigeria could well become a model for other African countries in effective family planning.

Certainly some of those other countries needed models. Liberia and Sierra Leone, located on the big western bulge of Africa, were two of these.

When Edna arrived in Liberia's capital of Monrovia, in July 1964, and again in March 1965, its main houses, favoring white columns and broad verandas, reminded her of cities she had known years before in the Deep South of the United States. Monrovia presented a relaxed atmosphere with its population of only some ninety thousand people, many palm trees and brightly colored flowers, humid temperatures, and the most elusive situation Edna had ever confronted.

A small FPA had existed for a half-dozen years but its intermittent meetings had grown more and more desultory, and actual clinical services had not been offered in recent memory. One reason for this situation lay in the national policy to increase the population. A government attitude encouraging growth reinforced traditional beliefs in the asset of many children. Mrs. May Keller, matron of the government maternity center and president of the FPA, who almost singlehandedly had kept the idea of family planning alive, answered the popular slogan "Operation Production" with the reply, "This means *quality* production, not mere quantity of sick, undernourished people. We must decrease our alarming infant death rate if we are to have a bigger and stronger population."

Ever since its birth in the early nineteenth century, Liberia had struggled to grow—both in size and in health. And its relationship with the United States had always been a curiously ambivalent one, balancing independence against dependence. The two major factors in Liberia's existence were the American Colonization Society and the Firestone Rubber Company.

Sponsored by such luminaries as Henry Clay, Daniel Webster, Francis Scott Key, and President James Monroe, the American Colonization Society was organized to send Negroes from America to Africa if they wished to return to their native land. In 1822 the first permanent settlement was made on Cape Montserrado.

The beleaguered group survived sickness, discouragement, and the hostility of native chieftains who did not welcome any likelihood of interference with their trade in slaves. By 1847, however, with four thousand American Negroes who had become Liberians, the band of scattered colonies was able to declare its unity and freedom. The capital city, named after President Monroe, became the residence of the first President, and the name of the country reflected its official motto: "The Love of Liberty Brought Us Here." Following the Emancipation Proclamation, more freedmen arrived from the United States.

Freedom was not enough for survival. Economic instability

threatened the nation for decades. Then, in 1926, the Firestone Rubber Company ended a long and intensive search for the ideal place to grow its basic crop. Liberia's climate and soil were perfect for the growth of rubber trees, and its government situation was adaptable to the company's needs. A million acres of land was leased to Firestone. A five million dollar loan was arranged for the Liberian Government.

From the moment Edna landed at the capital's airport— near a Firestone rubber plantation and plant some fifty miles from Monrovia—she was keenly aware of the presence and influence of this company. Many of her activities were guided by its personnel. The nursing director of the company, Mrs. Mervell Bracewell, invited Edna to speak to her graduating class of nurses, mostly men. To Edna's surprise and delight they were keenly interested in family planning. (The most vocal nurse had six children and said the whole idea of birth control was news to him!) Here Edna learned of the so-called "belly camp," to which pregnant women were brought two or three weeks before delivery. She suggested that this would be an ideal place for educational work—and she made plans for Pathfinder to send a supply of leaflets for "belly camp" distribution. Edna also encouraged Mrs. Bracewell's participation in a national family planning program. That participation lasted through many years and involved active leadership in the revived FPA of Liberia.

Dr. Pearl Romeo, an American woman born in the Dominican Republic, who had been working in Liberia for several years, accompanied Edna on many visits to the medical facilities and hospitals of the Firestone plantations. Edna interested and encouraged doctors, nurses, and administrators, and after seeing only a few of the malnourished children and needy adults at the clinics, Edna could realize what family planning might mean.

In Dr. Romeo Edna found personification of the best and the unpredictability of the whole country. This bright, trained young black woman was incredibly charming and erratic. The only intervals when Edna could be absolutely sure of her presence and attention were during their long drives together out into the countryside to villages of mud, thatch, and children. Then Pearl Romeo's dedication and her interest in securing IUDs was even more apparent than during her busy days in the city. Because one of Mrs. Romeo's characteristics was disdain for punctuality and appointments, Edna found herself waiting at odd times and places for intervals ranging from two minutes to two hours, and most often the latter. When Mrs. Romeo finally arrived, there were no contrite apologies or lengthy explanations—just a picking-up of the action.

Such minor irritations became—at another level—frustration. When Edna decided that one way to help energize the FPA would be to sponsor a large public gathering, there was no way to reach that public by telephone. Soon after her arrival Edna discovered that the telephone in her room would reach only people in the hotel. Several years earlier, there had been a national decision to bury all telephone wires. The telephone poles and lines had been dismantled forthwith. Burial of the wires proved more difficult and expensive than expected, however, and work was delayed. The system remained in a disheveled state, and beyond use.

When a committee met to make arrangements, Edna could not suggest a telephone roundup of key leaders. Therefore she proposed that written invitations be mailed to prospective participants. Her friends shook their heads. "That would do no good. The invitations might not arrive for two or three weeks."

Undaunted, Edna tried another tack. "Then let's hire some young men to be messengers. I'll pay them to deliver our invitations on their bicycles."

"But they'd only get out of sight and throw away the invitations if they decided not to carry them."

Edna felt as if she were working with quicksilver!

Gradually, however, word of the public meetings was circulated by a variety of not wholly satisfactory means, with a satisfactory enough result. Response was favorable.

When Mrs. Keller, who had no car, told her friend, President Tubman, of Edna's visit and work, the President provided a car for their use, despite official encouragement and promotion of larger families. On trips into the country Edna and Mrs. Keller visited five hospitals at Nimba, two at Bomi Hills, and several sites in the outskirts of Monrovia. Each trip underscored the fact that Liberia had one of the highest infant death rates in the world and needed family planning. As her message of happier families and healthier communities began to be circulated, new supporters—medical and public—gathered to the FPA.

At one hospital, when Edna was talking to the staff, a Liberian nurse came up afterward and told Edna that family planning for Liberia had been on her mind for a long time—in fact, ever since she had first heard about the subject in Louisville, Kentucky. And her friends in Louisville had been Jean and Charles Tachau. Edna assured the nurse that the world of family planning was indeed small.

In Liberia Edna also became acquainted with a personable young Englishman, Ludovic Kennedy. He was a lively television personality who had his own BBC program, and from this trip he would glean material for a book, *Very Lovely People.* His Very Lovely People were Americans working in foreign countries at many different undertakings. Edna spent their introductory conversation answering his specific questions with very precise answers about her work—producing samples of contraceptives from the handbag she always carried. From that moment she became his favorite VLP.

Kennedy accompanied Edna on a trip to the Firestone company hospital, where she spoke to the nurses and others on various family planning methods, citing drawbacks and advantages of each method. Her candor, enthusiasm, and genuine interest in others—including himself—charmed Ludovic Kennedy. Years later, on the David Frost television show in the United States, Kennedy would mention Edna McKinnon as the most memorable of all those VLPs he had met around the world.

Edna left Liberia with the mixed feelings she had experienced several times previously. There was so much to be done, and although she knew she had revitalized the work in family planning she was not sure who would continue it, or how. She was hopeful that the nucleus of leaders she had brought together would go ahead—as, indeed, they did, dramatically increasing the number of people served at the government hospital clinic each year.

Among the suggestions she left, in writing, was advice to ask the Pathfinder Fund for money to hire a part-time clerk. The explicitness of her instructions revealed her experience in this odd and unpredictable country. "It is important to send the name and proper address of the treasurer to whom this money should be sent."

Adjoining Liberia on the north was the small and beautiful country of Sierra Leone, similar in climate, in rampant illiteracy (about ninety percent), and in need of family planning, with a high rate of birth and infant mortality. It, too, seemed to Edna nebulous, touched with a quality of never-never land. In February 1965, between her visits to Nigeria and Liberia, Edna spent a month reactivating the FPA in Freetown.

Here, again, government fears of "population control" and public encouragement of large families led to reactions ranging from hesitancy over family planning to open hostility. But the intrepid little committee inspired by Pathfinder's Edith Gates and Ruth Martin had survived. Edna was troubled to learn that the clinic it offered was open only one day a week, late in the afternoon, and received so little publicity that it was one of the best kept secrets in Sierra Leone.

The president of the FPA, Dr. Majorie Nicol, wife of the president of the Fourah Bay College, was a beautiful woman whose interest in working at the hard daily problems of the presidency had gradually lapsed. The secretary was Mrs. A. M. Adams, who had been decorated by Queen Elizabeth for her work with orphans in Sierra Leone. And one of the most active lay workers in the clinic was an English lady, Helen Woodcock. These three were rejuvenated by Edna's ideas, and during the whirlwind schedule of her stay in Sierra Leone numerous obstacles, real and imagined, were overcome. They resembled those Edna had faced in previous work.

The national minister of health, for instance, was approached for the first time about family planning—and gave it approval and support. His chief medical officer, in turn—a man considered to be strongly opposed to the work—listened to Edna's explanation and suggested that she give this same presentation over radio and television. She wrote a script, received his approval, and appeared on the air telling the people of Sierra Leone about family planning.

It was the old story which had become so familiar to Edna: leaders reputed to be unshakeable in their hostility became supporters when provided with facts, experiences, and a clear statement of family planning's purpose. Other leaders in this small African nation were won to unexpected approval. Among these were the chief gynecologist at the hospital and the secretary of the United Council of Churches. And perhaps most improbable of all, was the American ambassador, a bachelor and a Roman Catholic, who had a luncheon for Edna and asked that she tell the other guests how family planning was progressing in Freetown. Of course, the fact that he was originally from Montana had not hurt Edna's cause.

In addition to the usual heavy schedule of speeches there were the accidental encounters that always "happened" along Edna's way. One instance occurred the day she left the radio station after she had made her broadcast at the doctor's invitation.

At the station no taxis were available and when a young man offered Edna a ride, she accepted gladly. He asked about her visit in Freetown and she told him of her work. He seemed fascinated and asked to see her literature. When it developed that he was a commercial artist, Edna invited him to return to her hotel. He came the next day with several large posters. As they surveyed the posters in the lobby a friend of the artist came by. "You can't do anything like that in Sierra Leone," he said. "We want all the people we can have." Edna asked if he were married, and he said yes.

"How many children?" she inquired.

"Two."

"And how long have you been married?"

"Two and a half years."

"And you mean for your wife to go on having a baby each year?"

"Oh no. We can hardly look after those we have now."

"But you don't believe in family planning?"

"Is *that* what you mean by family planning?" he asked. "I

thought you meant government population control." And added, "Could I come and talk with you tomorrow?" When he came, Edna discovered that he was a young minister of interior affairs. She had won a useful ally to her cause.

In addition to the capital, Edna visited the city of Bo, inland and southeast of Freetown. Her stay was brief but she was reassured that the medical director of the local hospital and his wife, who was also the chief nurse, would start a program in Bo as soon as one was established and flourishing in Freetown.

She worked hard in Freetown. At the women's meetings it seemed impossible to get down to essentials. Finally, desperately, she invited four key people to lunch—and passed out multiple copies of a program, bylaws, and budget, which she asked them to read at once and respond to.

Three months later, after stopovers in three other countries, when Edna arrived in London for talks with Sir Colville Deverel at the IPPF headquarters, Sierra Leone had already sent in an application for membership. She and an IPPF staff member called upon the British Overseas Development Division to secure some financial help for West Africa, especially Sierra Leone.

Sierra Leone had been an odd, troubling, friendly land. It needed education in family planning methods for doctors, nurses, and midwives; training for its staff; and mobilized public support—all those essentials she had learned to recognize and rally in other countries. She hoped that she had rallied them in these West African countries, too—to preserve lives from waste and misery through family planning.

Princess Seble Desta—granddaughter of His Imperial Majesty Emperor Haile Selassie I, Lion of Judah—was the talisman, charm, open sesame for Edna's family planning in Ethiopia. In many ways Ethiopia became the epitome of her long experience on three continents and at home.

Here she verified her hard-won lifetime knowledge of the importance of enlisting a city's or a country's most influential and respected citizens for family planning leadership; of refusing to accept others' misconceptions as to who would or would not support family planning; of recognizing differences in pace and rhythm of life and adapting herself to slower tempos where necessary and adjusting them to her purposes where possible; and, above all, of bringing genuine attentiveness and respect to everyone, so that there was never any suggestion of the galloping, know-it-all American do-gooder, but only the reality of an informed, steadfast friend.

From the moment of her arrival, in May 1964, through subsequent visits in 1965 and 1966, Ethiopia gave Edna surprises—some pleasant, some disquieting.

Edna discovered the country's second largest city, Asmara, in the northern neck, distinguished by a strong Italian flavor; and sleepy ancient Aksum with its towering granite shaft of mysterious origin; the majestic antiquities of Gondar—once the country's capital; the incredible churches of Lalibala, carved out of solid rock eight centuries earlier; the walled city of Harar built by Arabs in the seventh century; and the capital of Addis Ababa, "new flower," with its half-million people, wide streets, and modern buildings, crowned by the famous Africa Hall convention center, as she also discovered a fine climate of clear air and sparkling sunlight and a pleasant friendly people.

Gradually she understood that a series of circumstances had combined to create this curiously fortress-like country, isolated and set apart in many ways. Geographically, it was a high plateau of rugged mountains, plunging gorges, and winding rivers, surrounded by scorching plains and desert. Religiously it was a Christian citadel, dating back to the Egyptian Coptic Church, surrounded by militant Islam. Commercially and culturally it was a country of undeveloped resources, unbuilt roads, and undereducated people (ninety-five percent illiterate) surrounded by twentieth-century pressures for change.

Thinly scattered across the large country, most of the twenty-two million Ethiopians were herdsmen and farmers, divided into some one hundred tribes speaking more than thirty languages, with chiseled classic features resembling their ancient Hamitic forbears from the Mediterranean more often than their native Negroid ancestors. Proud (their Emperor Haile Selassie a proclaimed descendant of King Solomon and the Queen of Sheba) and primitive (sexual customs of certain tribes left some of the women mutilated for life), they suffered harsh lifelong health conditions. Life expectancy was less than thirty-five years. The sparseness of population was not due to a low birth rate but to a high infant mortality rate. In fact, the birth rate was forty-three percent higher than that found in European and North American nations. At least one survey found that the death rate for infants, especially in the first month of life, was five times greater in Ethiopia than in highly developed countries.

Thus, as Edna would explain time after time to government officials, doctors, and the people themselves, her mission of family planning was to reclaim control over birth (and death) from the random tolls of disease, malnutrition, and neglect, and place control over birth (and life) in the parents' hands.

It was just this message that Edna took to her first meeting with Princess Seble Desta. By the time the introduction was arranged, Edna had received almost totally negative reactions to the mere possibility of starting family planning work in Ethiopia. Repeatedly she heard the litany: population pressures, from the standpoint of geography, were not as great here as in most countries where she had worked; the government was un-interested in family planning; the country was primitive, with women held in low esteem; communications were almost nonexistent; and roads were poor and many villages virtually isolated. It was apparent that any beginning of her work would have to be made in Addis Ababa. And so in May 1964, with only one letter of introduction, she settled in there to lay siege to the capital.

At first, with a few exceptions, the Americans with the AID program were more pessimistic about family planning than were the Ethiopians. Even the chief medical adviser, who had gained considerable renown for his work at the School of Public Health in Gondar, was alternately cool and gruff when Edna first visited him. But she had been told that he was the one person who could introduce her to Ethiopia's minister of health, therefore she went back to talk to him a second time. Meanwhile, she had learned through hearsay that one reason for the doctor's hostility was his experience with a relative who talked family planning so incessantly that he had become thoroughly fed up with the subject. Once again, she realized how easily small personal foibles and circumstances could block or destroy such an intimate cause as family planning. As soon as Edna received the doctor's assurance that he would deliver any letter she wrote to the health minister, she turned to leave. Suddenly she stopped. "Doctor," she said, "I don't want to go any farther with this idea of family planning in this country unless *you* believe it is a good idea. What do you personally think?"

Startled, the doctor fumbled a moment. Then he replied. "The way you're going about it is right. I suppose we have to make a start sometime. Yes, I'm behind it."

It was Pat Korry, however, wife of the U.S. ambassador, who gave Edna's work its initial breakthrough. Mrs. Korry was a Roman Catholic, but she understood the necessity for family planning in Ethiopia. She arranged for Edna to receive an invitation from Emebet Seble Desta.

The princess was a grave, unaffected young woman of medium size with thick dark hair that hung loosely around her serious, attentive face. Her husband was the president of Haile Selassie I University. She herself represented a breakthrough of women into public life, for she was an active volunteer in the Ethiopian Women's Welfare Association, in the Haile Selassie I Foundation, in the Red Cross, and in other programs. Charming and straightforward, she retained an aura of personal formality which made it appropriate for everyone to stand until she was seated, and an atmosphere of simplicity which made it seemly for everyone to relax as she opened the conversation. During this and later meetings, Edna appreciated the princess's quiet dignity and sense of duty; if she rarely smiled, it seemed a result of shyness rather than aloofness.

In addition, there was an awareness of responsibility in this young woman that soon became evident. Eventually Edna would learn that Seble Desta had been encouraged by her grandfather, the Emperor, to realize that she and his other grandchildren had inherited unusual opportunities, which should be used for the good of their people. As she and Edna talked, she listened intently to Edna's every word. Edna explained as briefly and sincerely as she knew how all that family planning could mean to Ethiopia.

"What does the minister of health say about this?" the princess asked.

"I haven't talked with him yet," Edna said. She could not admit that she had heard of the minister's implacable opposition to family planning.

"We must have him with us," Seble Desta said.

Edna dared hardly believe her ears. "We." "Us." The words signified all and more than Edna had hoped for.

Two days later the telephone rang. "This is Seble Desta. I have an appointment arranged for you with the minister of health, His Excellency Ato Abeba Retta. And I hope you will present your work to him just as you did to me."

When Edna was shown in to the minister's office she was told she would have five minutes. She made her points as forcefully as possible: family planning was a preventive health measure (contraception was legal in Ethiopia and could prevent much of the abortion which was denounced by both government and church), the initial program could be a pilot study to test public acceptance or rejection of family planning, the government did not need to state any "policy" on family planning, and this beginning work would be carried out without any cost to the government. Then she thanked him and stood up to leave.

"Come back. Do sit down, please. We have much to talk about."

And Edna and Abeba Retta talked for almost an hour. Finally, he inquired: "And who do you plan to have on your committee?"

"I wouldn't presume—"

"But you've been getting around, meeting people—who would you like to have on a committee?"

"Well, of course, if I had my choice, I'd wish Princess Seble Desta to be chairman."

"You're right. And when you ask the princess, you tell her that if she'll serve as chairman, I'll be on her board."

When the princess accepted, Edna was ecstatic. With the princess and the minister and his deputy minister all committed to the cause and providing guidance and support, Edna proceeded full steam ahead. As in other countries, there were meetings with doctors, nurses, and midwives, as well as visits to health centers and training schools. Among many people, especially in rural areas, there was so much misinformation about birth control and so little understanding of the basic idea—much less methods—that Edna agreed that they were not ready for any help except the most fundamental education.

She wrote Dr. Gamble asking for books and pamphlets. Some of the doctors had not seen an IUD until Edna brought forth her sample, but most of them immediately asked to have some sent. Because of the high duty on imports, the contraceptives to be supplied by Pathfinder had to be sent as gifts or through a central medical supply agency. When Seble Desta called her committee to meet, it was agreed that three hospitals in Addis Ababa should offer regular family planning services. Anyone too poor to pay would receive free help.

After traveling to other cities and villages, Edna decided that this was the main step which could be taken at the moment. She made radio talks, attended the inevitable round of meetings, and at the hospitals saw some of the forlorn and desperate women who needed help.

The path was not always smooth. Between Edna's first visit in 1964 and her second in 1965, the work lagged. She had seen this happen before, however, and she told the members of the princess's Family Guidance Committee, when they met to decide whether or not they wanted to pursue family planning, that a full-time person must be employed to pull all the work together and meet daily demands of organization and information.

When Edna learned that the AID agency was ready to finance a family planning program if asked by the Imperial Ethiopian Government, she and Dr. Brooks Ryder—the agency's director of development and evaluation—worked out a series of programs and budgets. Due to red tape snarls in the functioning of the bureaucracy—Ato Abeba Reta was out of the country when the signature of the ministry of health was essential on a form—the time limit on some of the special funds for family planning expired. But Edna found in Brooks Ryder one of those persons who reinforce belief in individual influence. An attractive American whose head was shaved like Yul Bryner's with much the same distinguished effect, Ryder became a close friend of Edna's, and he and his wife were very helpful to her. Later they would work in Indonesia and expand programs she had initiated there.

In Ethiopia, Ryder helped interview candidates for the office of organizing secretary of the Family Guidance Committee, and finally he and Edna recommended Sophia Zacharias. With her employment as a full-time staff member and the location of the Family Guidance Association in the Haile Selassie I Foundation Building, a sense of permanence seemed to be emerging.

Sophia was effective but she had difficulty understanding Edna's time schedule. She, like most of the other Ethiopians, was amazed to have something discussed in a meeting and the very next day have Edna produce a plan or statement dealing with that subject.

"But Mrs. McKinnon, we can't work that fast." It became a familiar warning from Sophia to Edna.

One incident perhaps more than any other illustrated the relaxed attitude of Ethiopians toward any schedule. After a home office for family planning had been located at the Foundation, and after a year's financing had been assured by Pathfinder, it became necessary to locate a place where a clinic could be opened. The search proved unsuccessful until Edna one day noticed a small building on the grounds of St. Paul's Hospital, to the left of the front gate. "What is that?" she asked.

"The X-ray hospital," she was told, "but it is not used right now."

"Could we have it for our clinic?"

"It's very run down—"

Edna went to look. The situation of the little structure in relation to the hospital was ideal. So were the general facilities: a large central room, running water for a small toilet and lavatory, an extra room where visitors could wait, and another which could be used for consultation. There was one fairly unnerving drawback. In the middle of the main room stood a mammoth old-fashioned X-ray machine. The firmness with which it was attached to the ceiling and floor suggested a long life expectancy.

Edna turned to her Ethiopian colleague. "Will this machine actually come out?"

"Oh yes. It has been promised."

"How long would it take?"

"Three, maybe four days. It has been promised."

After consultation with the proper authorities, wheels were set in motion to re-create the X-ray lab into a birth control clinic. But Ethiopia's bureaucratic mills ground exceedingly slowly. Two weeks were allotted for removing the giant machine, restoring the toilet to running order, and finishing a general soap and water scrubbing. When Edna returned at the end of two weeks, she found the little building reposing in undisturbed tranquillity. Her obvious disappointment came as a great surprise to her associates. They tried to reassure her that work would be under way forthwith.

Edna, having experienced by this time several broken dinner engagements—without any subsequent explanation—was increasingly skeptical of such promises. In a few days she telephoned. "Is the room ready?"

"Not just yet."

"Has the X-ray machine been uprooted?"

"No—but soon."

As long as that bulging presence remained clamped to floor and ceiling, Edna knew no other renovation could begin. She instituted Operation Nag. Much as she disliked the process, she knew no other way to achieve her goal in this instance. Each day she telephoned. "Is the machine gone?"

"You're pushing too fast for us, Mrs. McKinnon."

After a while, they grew weary of answering the phone and she grew weary of asking—but at last they reported, "The machine has been removed."

Then the plaster was repaired. Water ran in the pipes and out of the faucets once more. Paint refreshed the walls. Edna had contacted some of her faithful allies back in the U.S. and received five hundred dollars from the John Leslies of Evanston, with which she helped restore the clinic. Furniture was donated by the Haile Selassie I Foundation and medical necessities were supplied by UNICEF.

The clinic represented a truly cooperative achievement. Edna's persistence became a matter of pride rather than irritation when a tea marking the clinic's opening was attended by the Princess Seble Desta, many embassy and hospital officials, and other members of Addis Ababa's medical and international community. The real initiation, the one most eagerly anticipated by Edna, came the day that the first proud, shy, long-suffering Ethiopian woman presented herself in the waiting room and asked for help in planning her family.

Throughout her work in Ethiopia, Edna realized again and again the necessity for making clear the fact that in this country it was not population control for which she worked but improved health for mothers and children. The former was viewed with suspicion, even alarm, while the latter was welcomed.

When Walker Williams, a remarkable young black official of the AID mission, accompanied Edna to Gondar and the Public Health Training College there, she realized that the time was not ripe to try to include family planning in its curriculum. During later years, however, she saw the fruits of her effort at education, from college level down to villages, several of which she visited with Walker Williams. Williams and Brooks Ryder were two American officials working abroad whom Edna would remember with the highest regard.

During her 1965 visit to Ethiopia, Edna was joined by her old friends and associates the Zukoskys. Charles and Bernadine had achieved remarkable goals in Egypt, but when they arrived in Addis Ababa they had other grave matters to discuss. Clarence Gamble was ill with leukemia. He could not follow through on requests as rapidly as necessary for those who were working far afield. While the office staff in Milton was capable, no one but Dr. Gamble himself had authority for final decisions.

Edna, too, had been concerned about this situation. In fact, on her way to Ethiopia she had stopped in Lagos for an extended stay with Dr. Gamble's son, Dick, and his wife, Fran, and their children. Dick Gamble had wedded philanthropic goals to business in establishing several enterprises in the Nigerian capital, where he and his family now lived. Neither he nor his two brothers—Walter, a doctor, and Robert, a minister—nor his two sisters, Judy and Sally, had ever known much about their father's work or the Pathfinder Fund. Consequently they had remained only marginally interested. Edna had become a warmly welcomed guest in their home and friend to all of them—from Dr. Gamble himself to the youngest toddler grandchild (especially when she arrived on one grandchild's birthday and, caught unprepared, had to improvise a gift from her luggage. The little round tape measure which pulled out and then rewound itself at pressure from a little button proved to be the most popular gift of the many the child received). Now she hoped to render this family a great favor.

During earnest hours of conversation she tried to convey to Dick and Fran Gamble some of the extent and import of Dr. Gamble's work. She suggested that if he and the other children had any desire to carry on the Pathfinder effort begun by Clarence Gamble they should begin to make plans for an orderly transition. Someone, preferably a doctor, should be found as soon as possible so that he could become thoroughly acquainted with Pathfinder and its mentor. In addition, a group of Gamble's distinguished coworkers in family planning should be asked to serve as a supportive board or council for this new director.

When Dick Gamble wrote a tentative explanation and inquiry to his sister Judy in Washington, she replied that she favored Edna's proposals. The other brothers and sisters agreed.

When the Zukoskys came to Ethiopia, then, there were two major undertakings awaiting them. The first was, of course, the family planning work in this immediate country. The second was nothing less than the future of the Pathfinder Fund itself and its work in many countries.

With Edna, in a small rented Cessna, the Zukoskys became acquainted with some of the beauty and harshness, backwardness and potential of Africa's second largest country. At a luncheon given by Edna at her hotel in Addis Ababa, they met Her Royal Highness Princess Seble Desta and her husband, Ambassador Edward Korry's wife, AID's Brooks Ryder, the head of the Haile Selassie I Foundation, and several other persons whose cooperation Edna had been nurturing. The Zukoskys marveled at the path she had opened in this country which had been considered so hostile to any suggestion of family planning.

For three days, however, they put aside Ethiopia and worked at formulating some practical plans for Pathfinder's future. Everything was predicated on the question: did Clarence Gamble's family want to continue his work in family planning? As she thought about this, Edna could visualize all those struggling programs in far-flung villages and cities in many parts of the world, which might flourish or wither according to this decision. After long hard hours of formulating specific goals and procedures, Charles Zuksoky organized their thoughts into a lucid presentation which was sent on to the Gambles.

In April, following a meeting of the family, Edna heard from Dr. Gamble. He told her that he had just experienced one of the happiest days of his life: his children had voted unanimously to carry on his work. Now they wanted a statement about the Pathfinder Fund to give to prospective advisory council members and a prospective executive director. They also wanted a financial statement from Clarence for the past five years so that they would have some guideline for preparation of a budget. None of them had any inkling about how much he had invested in Pathfinder each year. This latter requirement irked Clarence Gamble, who had always been remarkably secretive about anything involving finances.

But he wanted Edna to come to Massachusetts and help write the brochure about Pathfinder. Edna intensified her effort at creating a solid foundation for Ethiopia's Family Guidance Association. She outlined the steps they must take to become part of the IPPF and receive their continuing support. She helped broaden the base of public support by securing a wider representation on their advisory committee. She secured reaffirmation of approval from His Excellency Ato Abeba Reta, the nation's minister of health. She helped secure a full-time paid executive director for the Association, who was also to be trained in family planning. Cooperation with the AID mission was established. And the day before Edna left Ethiopia, she and Brooks Ryder presented a discussion to the Association outlining alternate steps which might be taken in the immediate future.

On June 2 she left for the U.S.—with a few detours along the way. In Greece, her first stop, she met her dear friends from Chicago days, Olga and David Baxt, and enjoyed with them a two-week holiday. Then there was a brief stop in Rome and Genoa, to assess the family planning success of a remarkable couple, the De Marchis, whose work would make an impact on their entire country. From Geneva, Switzerland, where she interviewed Douglas Deane, who would eventually join the Pathfinder work, Edna went on to London and a meeting with IPPF officials.

Back in the United States, she worked from early July until late November with Clarence and Sarah Gamble and assorted others recording the Pathfinder story. It was tedious labor; Dr. Gamble was not an easy man with whom to collaborate. Edna was one of the few persons who would oppose him, who dared argue with him. He tolerated, perhaps respected, her opposition, in part because they were alike in certain ways (quick, impatient, eager, and hard-driving) and because he knew she cared deeply and completely about their work. So they discussed and argued and wrote and rewrote, Dr. Gamble growing a little less strong each day. Edna was part of the family as they summered in Maine and returned to the spacious white frame home in Milton for the winter.

Early in 1966, Edna arrived in Ethiopia for her last extended stay. Except for a brief trip to Kenya and Uganda in May to observe family planning there and request aid for West Africa, she spent three months intensifying and extending the programs begun earlier in Ethiopia. Doctors' and nurses' training in family planning was encouraged, interested physicians and clinics multiplied, and arrangements were improved for receiving imports of duty-free contraceptives.

In June, in Addis Ababa, Edna received a message that her

brother, Wellington, was dead. Wellington Rankin, who had become a Montana legend as multimillionaire lawyer and rancher, who had altered the course of Edna's life when he insisted she become a public speaker and study law and help their sister, Jeannette, in campaigns for Congress; Wellington, whom she adored, feared, hated, and worshiped, could no longer deplore her work and plunge her into despair, or delight her with the surprise of some lavish gift.

She remembered a dream that had recurred several times during her life. Wellington was fastened in a fort, searching for help, calling to be free. She could see him and hear him and she struggled to reach him and break through the stockade— but she never quite made it. Like a slow-motion movie of frontier days and heroic suspense, her dream would unfold—and vanish.

Edna returned immediately to Montana.

There, in July, she received word of the death of Dr. Gamble. Clarence Gamble, who had been a gadfly to the whole cause of birth control, who had altered the course of Edna's life when he released her onto the highways and byways to find the public and the leadership for family planning, whom she had respected, resented, scolded, and emulated, would no longer be cajoling or commanding her to go to some incredible place and achieve some impossible task in the cause that was more than life to him. She recalled numerous hilarious and embarrassing instances when he had pinched pennies. She thought of the controversies which seemed to surround him like the ceaseless gales swirling around a Himalayan pinnacle. And she knew that he had saved dimes so that he could give away millions; often he had stirred personal dissatisfaction against himself so that he could foster larger satisfactions of health and happiness among families everywhere.

In September, news came of Margaret Sanger's death. Margaret Sanger had become a symbol around the world, had altered the course of Edna's life when she invited her to take part in the struggle for freedom of birth control. Edna admired and criticized, followed and revered her. She would no longer stir Edna and the multitudes with her passion and charm, the memories of her persecutions and her triumphs.

Odd, Edna thought, as she brought her labors for birth control, her journeys for Pathfinder, and her intimate work with people all around the world to a close: three of the great personalities shaping her career and work all disappeared within the space of four months.

She had one more journey to make for Pathfinder. In 1968, at the request of a new executive director and the Gamble family, she returned to Indonesia, Nigeria, and Ethiopia to offer evaluations and specific suggestions on their family planning work. Indonesia and Ethiopia represented two of her most successful ventures, and she found herself strangely thrilled and moved to find that the work was strongly rooted, growing.

With considerable pride in her Indonesian colleagues she pointed out to a friend that while it had taken fifty years— from World War I to 1966—for the United States to publicly recognize the need for birth control, it had taken Indonesia only seven years—from 1961 to 1968—to go from nothing at all to national approval.

But, as always, good was not enough for Edna; it must lead to better; and better was a stepping-stone to best. In each country, as she greeted old friends and was welcomed—sometimes tearfully—by them and as she found new faces, she gave them both praise and criticism, reward for the past and goals for the future.

One example might stand for many: on the visit, her last, to Ethiopia, Edna renewed one friendship, formed another, and opened new areas into which she urged family planning to reach.

One of the great problems of Ethiopia was the prevalence of leprosy—with its terrible physical disfigurement and social stigma. No reliable figures were available on the actual number of cases in the country, but estimates ranged anywhere from three hundred thousand to half a million. The need for family planning work at the tubercular hospital and the leprosarium was acute. No one could adopt the offspring of a leper and babies born to anyone in the leprosy hospital compound were placed in an orphanage where they would probably spend the rest of their lives.

The Public Health Ministry which should have provided birth control care had been afflicted with personality conflicts and jealousies which prevented the necessary official approval of such a program. Edna knew that prodding would have to come from higher authority—but there weren't many higher!

Edna asked her friend, Ato Abeba Kebede, head of the Haile Selassie I Foundation, if he could arrange a meeting with Seble Desta's mother, Princess Tenangeworq. Edna was invited to the palace—and she took full advantage of the opportunity, both to renew her friendship with Seble Desta, who was also present, and to ask the older princess for assistance with a thorny problem.

Princess Tenangeworq was a matronly woman, somewhat heavier and prettier than her daughter, simply dressed and gracious. She listened seriously as Edna poured forth her pleas for the princess to appeal to her father, His Imperial Majesty the Emperor, on behalf of securing family planning clinics at the tuberculosis and leprosy hospitals. She listened—and made no promises. Her face became really animated only once. Did Edna, she asked, travel around to many places? Edna said that she did. And did she travel alone? Edna said yes. The princess thought Edna showed great courage to go about the world alone doing the work she did.

Edna never learned whether Princess Tenangeworq was able to speak to her father on the subject Edna had urged. If not, Edna understood, because the questions she had asked, and the way she had spoken of courage, let Edna realize how even a princess could not be free in a country where women were held in low regard.

Her effort at stopping the waste and pain did not seem altogether futile, however, when she read the AID Report on Population Program Assistance two years later, in 1970.

> Since 1966 Ethiopia has had a Family Guidance Association, a voluntary organization operating as part of the Haile Selassie I Welfare Foundation. Its establishment was stimulated by visits of Pathfinder Fund representatives beginning in 1964.

Included on the Association's executive committee are representatives of the Ministries of Education, Community Development, and Public Health; the Addis Ababa Municipal Government; and the University School of Social Work. . . .

Altogether, about 6,000 clinic visits are handled monthly in 55 hospitals and family planning clinics in Ethiopia.

14

We struggled against the machismo Jeannette encountered, "I'm a man because I can kill"; and the one I encountered, "I'm a man because I can sire twenty children."

—Edna

To me, it is disturbing that so many people think of the population problem only as numbers of people versus available food. This seems to equate man with animal, and food with fodder. The question, as I see it, has, in fact, three dimensions. It is numbers of people versus material resources —but also cultural resources. This third dimension of the population problem is society's ability to satisfy man's mental, emotional, and spiritual needs and aspirations, what every man needs in addition to bare necessities and creature comforts, to lead a life of satisfaction and purpose, to achieve in life more than mere existence.

—John D. Rockefeller III,
International Conference on
Family Planning Programs, 1965

The TELEPHONE RINGS.

"Edna McKinnon here!" Her voice is clear, decisive, at once questioning and welcoming.

Who are you? Ethiopian student touring the U.S., next-door neighbor at the Hacienda in California's picturesque Carmel valley, grandson stopping by for a visit, old Chicago friend planning a holiday, doctor from Indonesia? Whoever you are—young or old, glamorous or unknown, male or female, Hindu, Christian Scientist, Presbyterian, or pantheist, successful or searching, black, white, pink, yellow, brown—welcome! During a full lifetime, Edna went out to the world. Now it comes to her. And many who cannot come remember.

What do they remember about Edna?

Small, pert Belle Fliegelman Winstine, surrounded by books and Montana memorabilia in her trim white house nestled under a giant Norway spruce on one of Helena's main streets, says:

"I was Jeannette Rankin's secretary when she went to Washington, the first woman in Congress. And one of the moments I remember most clearly out of all that exciting time was when Edna first walked into her sister's campaign office here in Helena. She was the most elegant person I'd ever seen. Such a fine bearing! She appeared to me all golden, shedding warmth and light."

"During those days when Edna was getting around all over the country with foam powder and faith her main stock in trade, she visited Mary and Jack Bickel—he was the actor Frederic March's brother, you know. Mary and Jack adored Edna, and they had this posh party for her and before it was over she was telling everyone about birth control." A California friend smiles at the memory of that unique evening.

"Jack finally persuaded her to bring out the pelvic model she carried with her to use in demonstrating to doctors the fitting of the diaphragm. Before she had finished everyone was limp with laughter, and Edna had given one of the Oscar performances of her life. But no one left Mary and Jack's party uninformed about birth control."

"The chairman of our Planned Parenthood Association board in Chicago used to say, 'If the whole earth were buried by an earthquake, after a few minutes there would be a little stirring underneath the rubble, a few stones would roll aside, some earth would crumble, and suddenly there would be Edna, rising up from the wreckage, announcing, "All right, everyone. Let's get to work. There's more to be done than you think—and everyone can do something." ' " The retired businessman—tall, distinguished, now gray-haired—nods his approval of this woman with whom he worked for a common cause during pioneer years of setback and triumph. "In Chicago, I know now, Edna was never paid her worth. First, because she was a woman. Second, because she never asked for it. She demanded everything in the way of commitment and effort for planned parenthood—but not money for herself."

A Tennessee admirer from the 1930s, who knew Edna both as a professional catalyst and as a personal friend, recollects, with a smile: "Edna often said, 'I haven't any patience with the "travel-light" people. I believe in being prepared for anything. I always take an evening dress and a bathing suit.'

"She always took a sample of one of the IUDs in her purse, too. She liked the coil best. And no matter where she was—at a luncheon or on a plane—she'd bring it out for display if anyone exhibited the slightest interest. Edna never believed that ignorance is bliss."

"I only knew her through the work with Clarence Gamble," one of the highly competent, traditional Bostonians at the Pathfinder Fund observes. "Edna was fearless. She'd go anywhere, meet anyone, venture anything—and always beautifully dressed, in command of the situation. She wasn't my style, however. I can't imagine a woman alone going to all those places—on that sort of work! Of course, she was from Montana. And I've always lived here in Boston."

"People in Nigeria still ask about Edna," a young businessman with interests in that country states admiringly. "Wherever she went, she made a vivid impression. She's deeply and sincerely interested in others, and they know this—perhaps none more readily than the very ones she chose to win to family planning: the reticent leaders of other races, the sensitive people of underdeveloped regions and underdeveloped countries, and the proud and the prolific who needed—and need—to know about family planning but who are reluctant to ask."

"I worked with Edna during much of my lifetime. She was never able to see the worst in people. Maybe her faith, her optimism, her belief in the light, gave her a one-sided view, but she was acquainted with darkness, too. She suffered. I know that. But she refused to wallow in self-pity. She was impatient with passive sympathy. She wouldn't cry with you but she'd work with you. Work with the big splashy efforts and with the utterly boring 'creeping details' as she called them. Whenever I think of her, which is often, two words come to mind: faith; enthusiasm."

It is the simple tribute of a friend whose own losses, most recently of her husband, have sharpened her appreciation of Edna's fortitude, her "grace under pressure."

And what does Edna remember as the essence of all her years of pioneering and struggling?

"Every single child born on this earth should be wanted and cherished. Birth control and peace are the answers we must give to death control by war and pollution."

"One person—in any cause or place—can make a difference in his part of the world."

"It's a struggle to be a woman and become yourself and work in dignity and receive respect."

"Everywhere I went I looked for the children first. In the Asian and African countries it was often amazing how seldom you heard a child cry. There weren't many outward signs of discipline but there seemed a sense of harmony. Sometimes when I'd be in a village or waiting in a car or bus in some city, children would gather—wide-eyed but not frightened—and I'd say to them, with appropriate gestures, 'I — love — you. You — love — me.' After a few minutes they'd begin to repeat it after me. And people with whom I was traveling, or along the streets, would be amazed to hear these children, who didn't know a word of English, chanting: 'I — love — you. You — love—me.' That's what my work was all about, really."

The telephone rings.
"Edna McKinnon here!" A pause. "Of course I remember. That was in Nepal, at Christmas—"